DRAMATIC DICKENS

Dramatic Dickens

Edited by
Carol Hanbery MacKay

Professor of English
University of Texas at Austin

MACMILLAN
PRESS

First published 1989

Published by
THE MACMILLAN PRESS LTD
Houndmills, Basingstoke, Hampshire RG21 2XS
and London
Companies and representatives
throughout the world

Filmsetting by Vantage Photosetting & Co Ltd,
Eastleigh and London

Printed in China

British Library Cataloguing in Publication Data
Dramatic Dickens. — (Macmillan studies in
Victorian literature).
1.   Fiction in English. Dickens, Charles,
1812–1870 — Critical studies
I.   MacKay, Carol Hanbery, 1944
823'.8
ISBN 0–333–43416–1

Contents

Preface and Acknowledgements

Dramatic Dickens emerges from the arena of the 'The Dickens Theatre' – a conference held at the University of Texas at Austin early in 1986. Designed to celebrate Dickens's affinities with the theatre, this conference brought together scholars and performers from the United States, Canada, and the United Kingdom. Its call for papers elicited far more qualified proposals than conference space could allow – thus testifying to the vitality and timeliness of its subject. In fact, although this volume could not reproduce all the essays presented at the conference, a number of those not represented here have already been published or accepted for publication elsewhere (many have also been in further demand at other scholarly gatherings), and several of the participants are currently engaged in related full-length studies that should provide a fine accompaniment to this volume. Because this collection of revised and expanded essays has been informed by the full conference agenda, it seems appropriate at this stage to describe that agenda in some detail.

In many ways, 'The Dickens Theatre' was inspired by and modelled on the conferences conducted by the Dickens Project – an annual consortium sponsored by the member institutions of the University of California system. Centred at the University of California at Santa Cruz, 'The Dickens Universe' has been meeting for ten-day periods each August since 1981 to present a conference on Charles Dickens. The programme combines formal lectures, small discussion groups, workshops, and various media events – in effect interweaving an adult education course, a graduate seminar, and a scholarly forum. Murray Baumgarten, founding Director of the Dickens Project, and John O. Jordan, its current Director, have both worked hard to make this consortium a model community of collegiality. Thanks to their efforts, a number of other universities have joined the consortium (the University of Texas became a participant in 1983), and the project continues to function as a national resource on the teaching of Dickens. As organizer and Chair of 'The Dickens Theatre', I was particularly grateful to have the Texas conference 'framed' by two relevant conferences conducted by the Dickens Project – the preceding 1985 'Cinematic Affinities: Dickens, Fiction, and Film', and the following 1986 'Dickens, Shakespeare, and the Theatre'.

In addition to the three-day conference scheduled for 31 January to

2 February 1986, 'The Dickens Theatre' co-sponsored a series of pre-conference activities which helped to prepare the community for the themes and issues to be addressed by the conference participants. Paul Gray and Lynn Miller of the Speech Communication Department produced a delightful 'Victorian Reading Hour', which featured perform-ances adapted from *The Uncommercial Traveller, Dombey and Son, Barchester Towers, Middlemarch,* and *Dracula.* Thanks to Marcia Parsons, Media Librarian, the videotape of the Royal Shakespeare production of *Nicholas Nickleby* was made available for serial review as well as a single marathon screening. Finally, Cinema-Texas, under the direction of Mark Alvey, undertook a week-long festival of Dickens films, including *Pickwick Papers* (1954), *Oliver Twist* (1947), *David Copperfield* (1935), *A Tale of Two Cities* (1935), and *Great Expectations* (1946). Preceding the last showing, I presented my own paper, 'A Novel's Journey into Film: The Case of *Great Expectations*'.

Holding the conference at the University of Texas enabled participants to work with various collections at the Harry Ransom Humanities Research Center – notably the VanderPoel Dickens Collection, the Robert Lee Wolff Nineteenth-Century Fiction Library, the Gernsheim Photography Collection, and the Hoblitzelle Theatre Arts Library. To bring these holdings more immediately to the public eye, an exhibition entitled 'Dickens Revisited' was mounted in the Leeds Gallery of the Peter T. Flawn Academic Center by Sally Leach, Assistant to the Director of the HRHRC. In addition, the Theatre Arts Library, under the direction of William Crain and Raymond Daum, drew from its repository to create a display of items celebrating stage and screen productions of Dickens's works. I am indebted especially to John Chalmers, Librarian of the HRHRC, for his splendid pre-conference seminar on the history and description of the library holdings, as well as for his 'keepsake' facsimile of the 1857 opening-night programme of *The Frozen Deep* printed on the HRHRC's 1858 Columbian Press; and to Roy Flukinger, Curator of the Photography Collection, for his fine lecture and slide-show entitled 'The Victorian Image in Photography'. And to Decherd Turner, Director of the HRHRC, I am immensely grateful for his goodwill and generosity in co-sponsoring these events and hosting the first evening's reception.

The conference itself was officially set in motion by a telegram from Cedric Charles Dickens – great-grandson of Charles Dickens – who wished us good luck and signed off with 'GOD BLESS YOU EVERYONE'. Besides the special events, featured lectures, and pre- and post-conference presentations, the papers were organized into six panels, which brought into focus the chief issues and concerns we believed should be addressed:

Theatricality and Performance; Archetypes and the Presentation of the Self; Dickens as Playwright, Actor, Director, and Producer; The Uses of the Past; Adaptation and Collaboration; and The Lure of the Theatre. This combined range and scope allowed us all to recognize that 'The Dickens Theatre' had created a forum for the kind of inter-disciplinary study that could break new ground in the fields of both English literature and the dramatic arts.

Central to a number of our debates and discussions was the question of Dickens's direct contributions to the Victorian stage, and I was pleased to produce *The Frozen Deep*, which provided us with a showcase for judging Dickens's various dramatic talents. SOMA Theatre's revival of the play marked the first fully-realized production of the drama since it was originally performed in 1857, initially as a private theatrical at Tavistock House and later that year as a benefit for the widow and family of Douglas Jerrold. Dickens and Wilkie Collins sketched out the plot in Paris the year before, and Collins drafted it – but Dickens significantly revised it to enhance the role of Richard Wardour, whom he would eventually portray. By all accounts, Dickens's performance caused quite a sensation. Collins reports that he played the part 'with a truth, vigour, and pathos never to be forgotten by those who were fortunate enough to witness it'. The play appealed to the mid-Victorian fascination with contemporary Arctic exploration and permitted Dickens to explore the theme of moral goodness under stress. Two years later Dickens would give us Sydney Carton, acknowledging his debt to the character of Richard Wardour in the preface to *A Tale of Two Cities*.

Under the direction of Edwin Eigner, the topic of Dickens as playwright, actor, director, and producer was confronted by a panel consisting of Alan McKendree, director of *The Frozen Deep*; Clay Goodwin, the actor portraying Richard Wardour; Robert Louis Brannan, editor of the original prompt-book for Cornell University Press (1966); and Gordon Peacock, head of directing at the University of Texas. Working closely with the manuscript at the Pierpont Morgan Library, Brannan was the first scholar to realize that the play truly represented the co-authorship of Collins and Dickens, and he discussed with us in more detail the personal crisis in Dickens's life that helped to feed the play's emotional intensity. Emotional responses vary with time and convention, however, and McKendree, Goodwin, and Peacock all spoke of the challenge of playing serious melodrama on the stage today. In fact, in its nine-performance run the play encountered its most challenging audience on the night the conference participants filled the auditorium, for this audience could often interpret high-seriousness as high-camp.

Adapted Dickens appeared on the various stages of 'The Dickens Theatre' as well. Illustrating some of the many theories discussed about Dickens in performance, Philip Collins presented one of his inimitable readings from Dickens's works. Renowned for his editing and enactment of Dickens's public readings, Collins drew from the twenty-one readings he has edited to evoke not only Dickens's characters and texts but Dickens's own practice of turning his public recitations into dramatic performances. For our added pleasure, Elliot Gilbert assumed full costume to conduct his performance-reading from *Bleak House*. And finally, at our farewell banquet, 'The Dickens Players' performed 'Dickens on Stage' – 'Being a Medley of Romantic, Sentimental, and Farcical Interludes with Musical Accompaniment'. Sponsored by the Dickens Project, this highly versatile group consists of Robert Fenwick, Simon Kelly, Gene Lewis, and Kate Rickman. They kindly agreed to remain after the conference to perform their Dickensian songs and sketches for secondary-school groups in the area. All in all, this range of adapter-performers proved once again that Dickens is best served when we can combine scholarly knowledge and the art of presenting his works to living, breathing audiences.

After the conference had officially concluded, we still co-sponsored a post-conference programme on 'Dickens and Opera'. Prepared and arranged by Walter DuCloux and William Girard of the University of Texas Music Department, this session featured the following papers: 'The French Revolution in Different Voices', by Cynthia Patton (Indiana University); 'Dickens, Glück, and Gounod: Opera and the Novelist', by Robert Bledsoe (University of Texas at El Paso); and 'Dickens and Ballad Opera', by John Dizikes (University of California at Santa Cruz). Selected songs from a variety of Victorian and contemporary compositions related to Dickens were then performed by Kathy Elbourne, David Stevens, William Girard, Robert Bledsoe, and Rose Taylor. Lastly, Robert Fenwick and Gene Lewis performed from selected operettas and music-hall sketches. A tape of this complete session has been re-recorded and is available for broadcasting purposes.

To round out the picture of 'The Dickens Theatre', I would now like to thank the participants not otherwise acknowledged in this volume. They include the following presenters: Paul Schlicke (Aberdeen University), 'Mr Dickens at Home on the Stage'; Peggy Stamon (University of California at San Diego), 'Proscenic Imagining: Conceptions of Stage Placement in Dickens's Fiction'; Toby Anne Bird (Nassau Community College), 'Dickens's Use of the Comic Pairing of Tricksters and Gulls'; Cherie Rae Dunham (National Association of Professional Storytellers), 'Turn Back the Hands of Time'; Alexander Welsh (University of California at Los

Angeles), 'Shakespeare's Contribution to Dickens's Social Theory'; Karen Reifel (University of Texas at Austin), 'On the Border of the City: Substantiating History in *Barnaby Rudge*'; Linda K. Hughes (Washburn University) and Michael Lund (Longwood College), 'The Police in Different Voices: The Oral Tradition in Dickens and His Contemporaries'; Joel Brattin (Southern Missouri State University), 'From Drama into Fiction: *The Lamplighter* and "The Lamplighter's Story"'; George Worth (Kansas University), '*Great Expectations:* A Drama in Three Stages (1861)'; Patrice Caldwell (Eastern New Mexico University), 'The Female Hero in Collins's Dramatized Version of *The Woman in White*'; Jerome Bump (University of Texas at Austin), 'Creativity and Collaboration: Dickens and Collins'; and John Hall (City University of New York), '"Stagey and Melodramatic . . . like Boucicault's Plays": Trollope on Dickens'. In addition, I would also like to thank those scholars who served as moderator/respondents – John Frazee, Albert Hutter, George Ford, John O. Jordan, and Michal Ginsburg; as introducers – Robert Patten, Fred Kaplan, John P. Farrell, John Brokow, Murray Baumgarten, and Robert McLean; and as resource consultants – H. Philip Bolton, author of *Dickens Dramatized* (1987), and Robert Bledsoe, representing the National Endowment for the Humanities. Finally, I would like to direct the reader to the selected bibliography at the end of the volume; it reflects the core research and criticism on the subject of Dickens and the theatre that underlay the planning of this conference.

Special thanks for support and encouragement also go to various members of the University of Texas administration. I am particularly grateful to William Sutherland, Chair of the English Department; Robert D. King, Dean of the College of Liberal Arts; William S. Livingston, Vice-President and Dean of the Graduate School; Peter T. Flawn, former President; and William Cunningham, President. Over the past seven years, and especially during the period of this conference's preparation, they have helped me develop the kind of liaison and administrative skills that made it possible for me to conduct such a wide-ranging conference. I am also indebted to the University Research Institute for its 1985 Summer Award, which launched my next book-length project, 'Thwarted Drama: Victorian Novelists and the Lure of the Theatre', in timely fashion. And lastly, I want to extend my profound gratitude to C. L. and Henriette Cline. Their Centennial Visiting Professorship in the Humanities provided the major sponsorship for 'The Dickens Theatre', and without their substantial assistance a conference of this magnitude would not have been possible.

To my conference co-ordinators – Nancy Warrington, Lissa Anderson,

Kay Avery, Susann Thompson, and Denise Berglund – I extend my special thanks; they met with me weekly during the months preceding the conference, helping me to anticipate the many details that called for our close attention. I am also pleased to acknowledge Beverly McKendree and Jean Mandeville, who planned and mounted a superb reception following the 31 January performance of *The Frozen Deep*. I am grateful, too, to Laura Williams, Language Arts Co-ordinator of the Eanes School District, who arranged for the extended visit of 'The Dickens Players'. I wish to thank as well Chapman & Hall for permission to reproduce portions of *The Diaries of William Charles Macready: 1833–1851*, edited by William Toynbee (London: 1912). And to three of the graduate students who have accompanied me to 'The Dickens Universe' conferences – Vera Dellwardt, Anne Wallace, and Cheri Larsen – I want to convey my gratitude for the extra time and effort they contributed by extending Texas hospitality to our visiting scholars.

I am, of course, very grateful to the contributors to this volume of essays for their care and concern in expanding and revising their conference papers for publication. Mary Margaret Magee, who also served as Assistant Chair for the conference and Assistant Producer for the play, aided me materially in selecting and editing the essays. I am grateful, too, to Frances Arnold for her skilful direction as literature editor, Siân Prentice for her judicious copy-editing, and Heather Moore for her solicitude in compiling the index. And Kirk Hampton once again demonstrated his constructive support and critical acumen during the long period of planning and producing both 'The Dickens Theatre' and *Dramatic Dickens*.

C. H. M.

List of the Contributors

Nina Auerbach is Morton Kornreich Term Professor of English at the University of Pennsylvania. She is the author of *Communities of Women, Woman and the Demon: The Life of a Victorian Myth, Romantic Imprisonment,* and *Ellen Terry, Player in Her Time.*

Regina Barreca is Assistant Professor of English at the University of Connecticut at Storrs. She has introduced and edited a collection of essays for *Women's Studies,* which will be republished as *Last Laughs: Perspectives on Women and Comedy,* and she is currently preparing another volume of essays, *Sex and Death in Victorian Literature,* for Macmillan.

Michael R. Booth, Chair of the Department of Theatre at the University of Victoria, has published *English Melodrama, English Plays of the Nineteenth Century* (in five volumes), and *Victorian Spectacular Theatre.* He is the author of a new study of the Victorian Theatre.

Jean Ferguson Carr, an independent scholar centred in Pittsburgh, is the textual editor for two volumes of *The Collected Works of R. W. Emerson* and has written essays on Dickens, literary pedagogy, and nineteenth-century women writers. She is currently working on a book to be entitled *Contested Territory: Gender, Canon, and Authority in 19th-Century America.*

Robert A. Colby is Professor Emeritus of the Graduate School of Library and Information Studies, Queens College of the City University of New York. Relevant recent publications include *Thackeray's Canvass of Humanity,* '"Scenes of All Sorts . . .": *Vanity Fair* on Stage and Screen', and 'Oliver's Progeny: Some Unfortunate Foundlings'.

Judith L. Fisher, Assistant Professor of English at Trinity University in San Antonio, has published several articles on W. M. Thackeray and is currently annotating Thackeray's art criticism as well as working on a critical study of his aesthetics. She has also co-edited and contributed to a forthcoming collection of essays on nineteenth-century drama.

John J. Glavin, Associate Professor of English at Georgetown University and playwright, has published a new performing text of Oscar Wilde's

The Importance of Being Earnest as well as essays on Trollope, Hopkins, and Milton. He has essays forthcoming on the fiction of Muriel Spark and on the problem of the playwright's authority.

Michael Goldberg, Professor of English at the University of British Columbia, has published numerous articles and chapters on nineteenth-century subjects in a range of scholarly journals. The author of *Carlyle and Dickens*, he has co-edited a critical edition of *Carlyle's Latter-Day Pamphlets* and is currently preparing *On Heroes and Hero-Worship* for the Carlyle Edition.

James R. Kincaid is Aerol Arnold Professor of English at the University of Southern California. The author of books on Tennyson, Dickens, and Anthony Trollope and of numerous editions and essays, he is currently completing a book-length study of Victorian paedophilia.

Coral Lansbury, Professor of English, Adjunct Professor of History, and Dean of the Graduate School at Rutgers, Camden, is the author of six books on Victorian literature and social history, including two studies of Elizabeth Gaskell and *The Old Brown Dog: Women, Workers, and Vivisection in Edwardian England*. She is the author of four novels and is at present working on a study of English pantomime.

Carolyn Buckley LaRocque, who teaches English at Trinity College in Washington, DC, is completing her doctoral work at the Catholic University of America. Her dissertation is an inter-textual reading of the works of anthropologist Victor Turner and comparatist René Girard with selected works of the European historical novel.

Carol Hanbery MacKay, Associate Professor of English at the University of Texas at Austin, is the author of *Soliloquy in Nineteenth-Century Fiction* as well as numerous articles on Victorian literature. Besides recently publishing a two-volume edition of Anne Thackeray Ritchie's introductions to Thackeray's canon, she is preparing a study of Victorian novelists as thwarted dramatists.

Mary Margaret Magee earned her PhD in 1987 from the University of Texas at Austin with a dissertation entitled 'A Dialectic of Submission and Revolt: *Jane Eyre* and the Forms of Women's Autobiography'. She is currently teaching courses in English literature and language at the Dalian Institute of Technology, China.

James Redmond is Director of the Department of Drama, Westfield College, University of London. An active director and producer, he is also the editor of *Themes in Drama*, published annually by Cambridge University Press.

Mary Saunders, Associate Professor of English at Hampden-Sydney College in Virginia, has published articles on various topics in Victorian literature. Her contribution to this volume grew out of work begun in the 1984 National Endowment for the Humanities seminar on Dickens directed by George Ford and is part of a longer study in progress.

1

'Before the Curtain': Entrances to the Dickens Theatre

Carol Hanbery MacKay

I

The subject of Charles Dickens and the Victorian theatre raises a series of issues that have never been satisfactorily explained. Why didn't the Victorian period produce a major dramatist? Why didn't Dickens, the major novelist of the age, create great plays? Was there an essential quality of the era that was inexpressible in the form of significant drama? At the same time, why was the theatre so important as a focal point in Dickens's fiction, and why was it such a crucial element in his creative and personal life? The essays collected here attempt to answer these and related questions by examining the dramatic impulses underlying Dickens's conception of himself and his art and by exploring how those impulses were transformed into the world of his fiction.

Dickens was clearly obsessed by the theatre. Early and late, he trod the stageboards – first as an actor and then as an author performing his own readings. Largely overlooked by extant scholarship, he was a moderately successful playwright as well. His early burletta *The Strange Gentleman* (derived from his *Sketches by Boz*) is a slight comedy about mistaken identities, but it prefigures some of his more complex use of doubling in the later fiction. Moreover, Dickens collaborated with novelist-playwright Wilkie Collins on several novellas and plays, and most notably he revised Collins's script of *The Frozen Deep* into a play with a starring role for himself.[1]

But it is not my intention nor that of my fellow contributors to *Dramatic Dickens* to suggest that either by nineteenth- or twentieth-century standards Dickens could be adjudged a greater dramatist than novelist. Instead, we are interested in exploring the lure of the theatre for Dickens as a means of better understanding what constitutes his narrative art – in an attempt to place it in relation to the Victorian melodramatic stage tradition and the evolution of a poetics of fiction. For example, we are confronted with the dynamic play of 'voices' in Dickens's 'mono-polylogues' – his self-adapted public readings – which can be compared with the public and private reading practice that the author shared with other nineteenth-century literary figures, such as Robert Browning, Alfred Tennyson, and Mark Twain.[2] Stage and film adaptations of Dickens further combine to give us the texts we need in order to penetrate the puzzle of Victorian drama and its predominantly melodramatic orientation.

Dickens's interest in the theatre has been well-documented, although to date only piecemeal critical attention has been paid to the many adaptations of his works,[3] and there has been little sustained study of the interrelations between his fiction and his drama. Over twenty years ago, Ada Nisbet observed that 'the ground remains untilled for a proper study of the complex fusions in Dickens of the dramatic and the melodramatic, the genuinely tragic or comic and the merely theatrical', and in 1978 Philip Collins was still commenting on Dickens's relative failure in the art of playwriting, 'surprising as it is in the classic English novelist with the greatest instinctive knowledge and love of the theatre'.[4] One key to the puzzle of Dickens's melodramatic impulses surely lies in his adaptations of his own work, which point to what he considered theatrical but what was ultimately more 'dramatic' in a narrative context. In addition, Dickens's fiction also contains representations of the theatrical world – in both its letter and spirit – which should help in understanding what appealed to him about drama and in gaining more insight into the differences between fiction and drama. In *Nicholas Nickleby*, for instance, we can witness how the introduction of actors and actresses causes the 'real' world of the novel to dissolve into an array of disconnected, if amusing, perceptions of stage business.[5]

The popularity of Dickens's fiction as reading text – both private and public – and as impetus to stage and screen attests to an on-going dramatic appeal that both partakes of and transcends the nineteenth-century melodramatic imagination. Our task as contributors to *Dramatic Dickens* has been to focus on the widespread appeal of Dickens for an immense variety of readers, critics, and audience members.

II

All of the contributors to this volume of essays – and most readers and students of Dickens as well – perceive and respond to a special Dickensian *energy.* We could simply call it the Dickens vitality. As the essays herein amply demonstrate, this energy largely proceeds from the interaction of Dickens's opposing views of the self. And this introductory essay, besides providing a framework for the other essays in the collection, will follow several speculative directions suggested by the inherent oppositions that fuel the Dickens vitality – a vitality that could also be considered dramatic in the fullest sense of the word.[6]

From the outset, James R. Kincaid establishes the common link among the essays in the concept of opposed definitions of the self. In 'Performance, Roles and the Nature of the Self in Dickens', Kincaid shows how Dickens displays a basic opposition between two types of characters – the earnest 'real' characters who set goals; and the chaotic 'pseudo' characters who disrupt the action. Jean Ferguson Carr confirms this perception by recognizing that theatrical metaphors in Dickens also represent the opposed forces of confessional 'players' versus 'non-selves', who delight in artifice and concealment. And recalling that pantomime comedies represent chaotic freedom, Coral Lansbury's 'Pecksniff and Pratfalls' demonstrates that it is Dickens's high-spirited vulgarity that has made his novels so popular.[7] Both Lansbury and Kincaid see Pecksniff as an *impresario* – the role that Carr ascribes to Dickens himself. Many of Dickens's characters are really non-selves, stand-ins for the impresario in Dickens himself, and the critics in this volume are much more interested in analysing these primitive, mythical pseudo-characters than the psychologically intact 'confessional' ones. Even in structural terms, as Carolyn Buckley LaRocque indicates, Dickens draws on mythical types to convey David Copperfield's ritual passage to manhood – an uneasy development that results in the kind of contradictory complexity that Badri Raina has recently explored in *Dickens and the Dialectic of Growth*.[8]

The topic of Dickens and women presents another problematic arena, and both Mary Saunders and Nina Auerbach provide a perspective from which to consider this set of conflicting views. Saunders demonstrates how Dickens's 'floor scenes' assert, on the one hand, the melodramatic chaos of women fainting and, on the other, the stolid, solid world of the men. In his later novels, however, Dickens came to employ such scenes *expressionistically*, thereby using them to create a vivid psychology of women's internal turmoil. Furthermore, Saunders either hints at or establishes a complicity between Dickens and the reader, since we participate in seeing these scenes as staged. Once again, the concept of opposed forces emerges: one Apollonian, representing rigid order, and subdued emotions; the other Dionysian, chaotic, emotional, melodramatic, spontaneous, unscripted, and deceptive. Auerbach, too,

uncovers this basic opposition in 'Dickens and Acting Women'. In his life
and in his fiction, Dickens reveals the ineluctable order of the world as
opposed to that of fervid boy-women, whose nature defies patterns.[9] As
Auerbach studies the imposition of Dickens's *Weltanschauung* on his
personal life, her essay demonstrates how well textual information can be
profitably used to analyse the living person — and vice versa.

Recognizing the essential opposition in Dickens also permits us to see
how he depicts and illuminates social and ethical concerns. For example,
in 'Melodrama and the Working Class', Michael R. Booth argues that,
contrary to our usual expectations, nineteenth-century melodramas often
convey the realities of urban life, revealing a conceptual opposition
between melodramatic fantasy and the 'dark metropolitanism' of actual
existence. Concomitantly, Regina Barreca's analysis of one of the earliest
adaptations of *Oliver Twist* points to a particular application of this
insight. Although the consensus about stage versions of Dickens's novels
portrays them as removing his humour and originality — leaving 'crude,
sensational' melodramas — Barreca demonstrates how the 1838 adaptation starkly highlights the chaotic 'dark underworld' of his fiction. Even
a much more modern and particularized approach to theatrical transformation reveals the same basic undercurrent. By adapting *Little Dorrit* as an
extension of 'Poor Theatre', John J. Glavin illustrates how the staging of
Dickens's novels in the manner of Jerzy Grotowski acknowledges the
chaos within Dickens; in this case, we observe the chaos being translated
directly to the stage.[10] Part of the perennial power of the Dickens vitality
lies in its ability to expand into other spheres of experience.

As Dickens's fundamental opposition projects itself onto the Victorian
social scene, his texts provide a commentary on the upheaval of a
changing world-view. We can profitably study that change by tracing the
impact of psychology on dramatic form, and once again Dickens provides
us with cases in point. James Redmond epitomizes the essential conflict
between Dickens and the melodramatists of his day by setting character-
orientated plays against the plot-orientated ones. Redmond's analysis
elucidates how psychological probing and realism operate within a
context that takes into account the constant threat of chaos, while
melodramatic idealism, despite its artificiality, implies order and psychological safety.[11] Given the Victorian propensity (and perhaps our own as
well) to seek order and safety, popular adaptations of Dickens have
usually emphasized his melodramatic elements, as Robert A. Colby's
essay ably demonstrates. In contrast, Colby observes, Dickens's more
psychologically-complex contemporary, William Makepeace Thackeray,
has not suffered the fate of having so many of his works adapted to the

stage, but those that have been dramatized have been severely diluted.

However, Dickens remains pivotal to our understanding of the growth of psychological realism in modern literature. For example, although Judith L. Fisher concludes with the irony that 'sensation scenes work against the development of a truly psychological novel or drama, because they assert the power of an Order not susceptible to the human will', examining such scenes in Dickens's fiction helps us to recognize his role in the transition from the Victorian to the modern theatre. Fisher contrasts the tragic tones that colour Dickens's use of sensation scenes with the more comic touches that characterize those of Dion Boucicault. Her analysis shows how Dickens's sensation scenes invoke mental images from the subconscious: his sensationalism surprises us, while that of lesser authors, in fiction or drama, seems entirely predictable. Finally, by studying the 'complex, shifting web of influence and interaction' among Henrik Ibsen, August Strindberg, and George Bernard Shaw, Michael Goldberg demonstrates how they pick up and celebrate the dark, chaotic power of Dickensian image-making.[12] Strindberg in particular reveals an awareness of Dickens's perception of the 'thinged' life of objects — and conversely, the dehumanising of his 'real' people.

Looking back through this collection of essays, Mary Margaret Magee's postscript brings to the fore the characters who defy the 'linearity' of the orderly, straightforward, knowable Victorian world. The interest of many twentieth-century critics lies indeed in the irrepressible lure of ambiguous chaos, embodied in Dickens in his disruptive 'pseudo-characters'. Magee herself celebrates the other critics' taking pleasure in a 'revel in timelessness', thereby underscoring how we might in general read these essays as a high-spirited romp through the fields of Dickens. Connecting the impresario with the narrator's directorial role, Magee makes her examination more problematic by analysing two texts in which the narrator is relating his own story — *David Copperfield* and *Great Expectations*. She astutely establishes the tension at end-points between stasis and release, finding in the tableaux vivants a triumphant artistic fusion of Dickens's two opposing impulses.

The contributors to this volume have focused on many different aspects of the dramatic Dickens, but they all exhibit for our purview the chaos, illusion, and pretence of Dickens's Victorian world. Dickens posits both a sense of the serious ineluctability of life and a carefree manipulation of the concrete, physical world. Presenting both viewpoints lets him shed light on chaos, illusion, and pretence while celebrating them. And the interplay between their opposing forces makes vital Dickens's enterprise — as well as our own in reading and writing about him.

III

None the less, we are still faced with the puzzling fact that much of the Dickensian energy is lost when he writes directly for the stage or when his fiction is adapted for dramatic purposes. Perhaps we can postulate another tension between opposing forces that fuels the creative fires of the novel but contrarily burns up dramatic energy when it is transferred to the stage. Basic to Dickens's fictional *modus operandi* is a sense of constriction and containment; at the same time, however, the narrative mode stretches its own boundaries, expanding its imaginative scope beyond the apparent limitations of the physical stage. In the English-language literary tradition, it seems to take the rich, full range of an Elizabethan word-master or the truncated, elliptical manner of a modernist playwright to create for the stage the same levels of reality that a Dickensian novel manages to produce.[13] By considering Dickens's use of solitary and polyphonic voices, we can better understand the movement between constriction and expansion in his fiction – as well as speculate about the implied limitations posed by both melodrama and the adaptation process.

Constriction in Dickens operates most obviously in the arena of his image-making and name-giving. Take, for example, the case of *Great Expectations*, where Pip's opening words of self-naming present us with a compression of his real name: 'My father's family name being Pirrip, and my Christian name Philip, my infant tongue could make of both names nothing longer or more explicit than Pip. So, I called myself Pip, and came to be called Pip' (ch. 1). Observe how that compression creates an illusion which is solidified: it becomes a virtual reality, drawing attention to itself and creating a focal point for many of the intersecting plot lines. This illusion is more powerful in the context of the novel than it can be on the stage, however. The counteracting indefinability of the name – as it is conceived and reiterated within Pip's mind – is gone when he appears before us as an externalized character, acted out on a physical stage. What does not survive is the *irrepressibility* of the Dickens vitality – something that the living man and his fictional world alone embodied.

Whereas constriction is a containing process, Dickens was also constantly striving to break out of the boundaries he encountered in life and art. His canon records how he developed a narrative form which could contain his energy while not suppressing it. Moreover, his dramatic readings seemed to handle this tension as well, for the actor in Dickens allowed him to orchestrate and perform the energy of many voices. Intriguing for our purposes is Dickens's reading of 'Sikes and Nancy', for it defies any kind of life/art distinction we might try to read into it. Even more than the novel from which it was adapted, this reading drew upon the Dickensian life-giving energy, and eventually its repeated perform-ance – verging on the obsessional – ran the risk of not only tastelessness but life itself. Ultimately, it drained Dickens's life energies, bringing about his demise more decidedly than any other assigned cause.

Polyphony does not exist solely on the platform or stage, of course. As Mikhail Bakhtin has argued, the roots of the modern novel lie in the *polyphonic novel* – itself a hybrid – which orchestrates the many languages (or *heteroglossia*) of different voices. In fact, Bakhtin analyses a series of excerpts from *Little Dorrit* in order to make his telling point that 'varied *play with the boundaries of speech types*, languages and belief systems is one of the most fundamental aspects of comic style'.[14] But for Dickens, the inspiration and impetus to polyphony probably did originate on the platform – in the person of Charles Mathews. Paul Schlicke (among others) cites Mathews's 'At Home' multi-roled performances as a primary influence on Dickens as an actor, novelist, and public reader, and the 'monopolylogue' (the term was coined by Mathews) unites the three functions that Dickens sought to combine in his lifetime.[15] No wonder Dickens was fascinated by acting women, who could assume radically different guises on the conservative Victorian stage. Nor, too, should we be surprised at the success of the recent Royal Shakespeare production of *Nicholas Nickleby*, for its application of chamber theatre techniques allowed the impresario voice to coexist on the stage with or within other characters.[16] Still, we should not forget that first and foremost we have always been able to see and hear in the novels themselves the polyphonic play of Charles Dickens.

Turning to Dickens's fictional monologues or soliloquies, we might expect to find a contrast to his polyphonic impetus, but instead we uncover further confirmation of it. In my own study, *Soliloquy in Nineteenth-Century Fiction*, I delineate Dickens's highly selective use of the soliloquy form in comparison with its much more frequent appearance in the novels of Charlotte and Emily Brontë, Thackeray, and George Eliot, in particular.[17] Dickens reserved the soliloquy for strategic placement, as in the case of Sydney Carton's final 'unspoken' words, or for monumental purposes, as we discover in John Harmon's extensive review of his various identities and future alternatives. Both of the examples just cited seem to recommend that we judge them in isolation – they stand out from the body of the texts in which they appear, and they support the ready assumption that the soliloquist is a solitary figure who can speak only to himself. Yet fictional soliloquies gain their impact precisely because they stand in dramatic juxtaposition to the narrative voice that surrounds them, a voice that in effect frames them within its 'dialogic imagination'. Furthermore, the examples of both Carton and Harmon testify to a mixture of styles or voices within the soliloquies themselves, each soliloquist dramatizing internal conflict to transcend the boundaries that encase him.

Given such inherent dramatic elements in Dickens's fiction, his own fascination with the theatre, and the immense popularity his work achieved, his novels have always seemed prime candidates for adaptation. But the translations to stage or screen lose the Dickens vitality, preserving at best only the chaotic side of the novels' underlying tension. Strangely enough, it is the unreality of a musical like *Oliver!* that replicates the novel's chaos better than orderly attempts to reproduce carefully the full plot and family of characters. What this example and the case of the Grotowski adaptation point to is the same realization that the best film-makers have achieved: no slavish imitation of another artist's work can truly succeed – only recapturing the spirit of the original in a different form or a new medium works. Elsewhere I have analysed in more detail David Lean's 1946 classic film of *Great Expectations*. Lean's willingness to rewrite the novel's ending – an ending that Dickens himself rewrote several times – allowed him to tap both the author's fantasies and the 1940s formula of the happy ending.[18] Such a rendition strikes me as much more effective than stage versions of this novel that try to recreate Dickens's polyphonic playfulness in caricaturish comic acting; the result can only be painfully parodic.

Not only nineteenth-century stage adapters of Dickens but twentieth-century ones as well have tended to rely on the cruder extremes of melodrama to charge their efforts to reclaim the Inimitable's original vision.[19] Contemporary hacks were of course working in the genre of the time when they unthinkingly fell into this mode, but they and more recent adapters were also picking up on Dickens's own propensity to utilize melodramatic conventions. And the basic melodramatic opposition between good and evil should have played into the hands of any dramatist – including Dickens himself – seeking to enliven an already familiar plot. But what both groups of adapters have repeatedly failed to grasp is that Dickens did not employ melodrama as the sole 'dramatic' element in his fiction; he drew freely on the rich variety of popular entertainments that had always inspired him, causing him to mix and juxtapose a panoply of voices – to create the dynamic interplay that constituted his fictional realm.

Notes

1. The 1986 production of *The Frozen Deep* at the University of Texas at Austin employed the script as revised by Dickens for its 1857 performances; the role of Richard Wardour looks ahead to the 1859 depiction of Sydney Carton in *A Tale of Two Cities*. See Robert Louis Brannan (ed.), *Under the Management of Mr Charles Dickens: His Production of 'The Frozen Deep'* (Ithaca: Cornell University Press, 1966). For a study of another collaboration by this pair, see Jerome Bump, 'Parody and the Dickens-Collins Collaboration in "No Thoroughfare"', *The Library Chronicle of the University of Texas at Austin*, vol. 37 (1986) pp. 39–54.

2. Philip Collins has provided the definitive text of the public readings in his edition of *Charles Dickens: The Public Readings* (Oxford: Clarendon Press, 1975). See also his *Reading Aloud: A Victorian Métier* (Lincoln: Tennyson Research Centre, 1972), and Alan Gribben's '"A Splendor of Stars and Suns": Twain as a Reader of Browning's Poems', *Browning Institute Studies*, vol. 6 (1978) pp. 87–103.

3. However, H. Philip Bolton has recently prepared a comprehensive listing of these adaptations upon which others may base more critical assessments. See his *Dickens Dramatized* (London: Mansell, 1987).

4. Ada Nisbet, 'Charles Dickens', in Lionel Stevenson (ed.), *Victorian Fiction: A Guide to Research* (Cambridge, Mass.: Harvard University Press, 1966) p. 104, and Philip Collins, 'Charles Dickens', in George H. Ford (ed.), *Victorian Fiction: A Second Guide to Research* (New York: Modern Language Association, 1978) p. 109.

5. See the scene between Nicholas and Miss Snevellicci when they employ a complex range of acting techniques as a humorous but hollow means of interacting (*Nicholas Nickleby*, ch. 24).

6. Steven Connor has recently demonstrated the flexibility of the Dickensian canon for reading (and complicating) a series of binary oppositions: violence/calm, motion/stasis, interior/exterior, openness/closure, nature/culture, order/chaos, presence/difference, and self/system. See his *Charles Dickens* (Oxford: Basil Blackwell, 1985).

7. For a detailed exploration of this topic, see Edwin Eigner's forthcoming *The Dickens Pantomime* (Berkeley: University of California Press).

8. Badri Raina, *Dickens and the Dialectic of Growth* (London and Madison: University of Wisconsin Press, 1986). Toby Anne Bird (Nassau Community College) also explored the use of archetypes in the paper she delivered to 'The Dickens Theatre' – 'Dickens's Use of the Comic Pairing of Tricksters and Gulls'.

9. Cheri Larsen (Biola University) has examined some of the ramifications of this topic in 'Oliver Twist as Heroine', a paper delivered to 'Dickens and Others', University of California at Santa Barbara, 22 Feb. 1986.

10. John J. Glavin also applied Jerzy Grotowski's theory and techniques to write and direct a production of *Our Mutual Friend* for the Dickens Universe conference at the University of California at Santa Cruz, 8 Aug. 1986.

11. Reversing our expectations, Patrice Caldwell (Eastern New Mexico University) reads Wilkie Collins's dramatic adaptation of his own *The Woman in*

White as intensifying the psychological conflict that we find in the novel. The paper that she delivered to 'The Dickens Theatre' was entitled 'The Female Hero in Collins's Dramatized Version of *The Woman in White*'.

12.   In effect, Mary Saunders's discussion of 'expressionism' and Michael R. Booth's presentation of 'dark metropolitanism' anticipate this argument.

13.   George Bernard Shaw provided his own bridge between the Elizabethan and modernist stages by creating characters who fudge the boundaries between characters and narrators.

14.   Mikhail M. Bakhtin, in Michael Holquist (ed.) and Caryl Emerson and Michael Holquist (trs), *The Dialogic Imagination: Four Essays* (Austin and London: University of Texas Press, 1981) especially pp. 301–08.

15.   Paul Schlicke, *Dickens and Popular Entertainment* (London: George Allen & Unwin, 1985) pp. 234–41.

16.   *Bleak House*, with its alternating dual narration, provides a more complex challenge, of course, but the recent BBC adaptation of the novel shows that challenge poorly met. Rather than revealing discrepancies, the impersonal narrator's expansive vision becomes mere obscurity, while Esther's constriction is reduced to neutral domesticity – all her self-reflexivity is cancelled out as she assumes the role of the conventionally modest heroine.

17.   Carol Hanbery MacKay, *Soliloquy in Nineteenth-Century Fiction: Consciousness Creating Itself* (London: Macmillan; and Totowa, NJ: Barnes & Noble, 1987). I examine Sydney Carton's solitary 'speeches' in more detail in 'The Rhetoric of Soliloquy in *The French Revolution* and *A Tale of Two Cities*', *Dickens Studies Annual: Essays in Victorian Fiction*, vol. 12 (1983) pp. 197–207.

18.   See MacKay, 'A Novel's Journey into Film: The Case of *Great Expectations*', *Literature/Film Quarterly*, vol. 13 (1985) pp. 126–33. Both the screenplay (used as the shooting script) and the post-production script are housed in the UCLA Film Archives.

19.   Readers interested in exploring the principles of melodrama further are advised to consult Peter Brooks, *The Melodramatic Imagination: Balzac, Henry James, Melodrama, and the Mode of Excess* (New Haven, Conn., and London: Yale University Press, 1976).

2

Performance, Roles, and the Nature of the Self in Dickens

James R. Kincaid

And let those that play your clowns speak no more than is set down for them, for there be of them that will themselves laugh to set on some quantity of barren spectators to laugh too, though in the meantime some necessary question of the play be then to be considered. That's villainous and shows most pitiful ambition in the fool that uses it.

(Hamlet, III. ii. 36 – 42.)

It is a general rule in Dickens that a character's readiness to cite authorities stands in inverse proportion to his reliability. One thinks of Mr Pecksniff, Mr Podsnap, Mrs General, or, in the colloquial line, Mrs Nickleby. Something like the same rule applies, I think, to academic essays, especially to their beginnings. Aren't we all suspicious of papers that start straight off with references to the *Oxford English Dictionary*, for instance? One naturally assumes that the writer is more than a little shaky on the nineteenth century and that he is hiding out in the thirteenth, figuring he is less likely to be caught there. Well, according to the *OED*, the word *performance* has a cluster of meanings, beginning at the beginning and continuing until now, a cluster that divides roughly into two contradictory suggestions: one is to complete an imposed task, perform one's duty; the other is to add what is missing, to ornament, to compose, to cause, to act or play, or to play upon.

Dickens is the major Victorian employer of both groups: the steadfast and the irresponsible; he even uses both types to do his narrating for him. On one hand, characters like Mr Brownlow, Nell Trent, Esther Summerson, Amy Dorrit, and a host of others perform their duties with an earnestness and single-mindedness we can and perhaps should emulate. I am not, however, concerned here with rectitude or well-made plots but with the intricacies and delights of the circus-like theatrical in Dickens. I want, then, to touch on those figures who dance about the earnest folk, who

11

add, as the *OED* says, what is missing, ornament it, play with it, create themselves what they take to be missing, often out of nothing. This second group of performers needs no core for action, no plan, no causality; they use whatever comes to hand as the basis for an impromptu skit, full-scale drama, or opera. They gleefully ignore Hamlet's picky directorial edicts, having no regard whatever for the 'necessary question' presumably at hand. They make us lose sight of the necessary questions the plot is posing, raising other questions entirely, often subversive ones, nearly always delightful ones. The earnest performers have plans and proceed as best they can along straight lines; they struggle to constitute what we think of as a plot; the playful performers float free, improvising whatever composition they find to their fancy; they write anti-plots. The first group listens to Hamlet, subordinates itself to the script, plods straight out of Chicago to Wayne Booth anthems; the second group subordinates itself to nothing, grabs the microphone itself, and laughs to set us laughing. The result is a rich, self-reflexive series of novels – or puddings which threaten to burst and shower us with the raisins, nuts, and sweetmeats.

Not only is this second group of performers subversive of linear development, of plot; they force us to wonder what 'character' is, what assumptions about selfhood they are disrupting. The closer we look at this group, the more it seems that there is no 'they' there. Not in the usual sense. If we ask, 'Who is the true Dick Swiveller, Wilkins Micawber, Abel Magwitch, Noddy Boffin?', we find ourselves so helplessly bobbing about in deep waters that we begin to see that we have cast off in the wrong boat, formulated the question in a way that will frustrate a good answer. What does it mean to posit a real being, an identity behind the performance? Dickens, I will argue, presents violently contradictory, fiercely battling notions of what constitutes the self.

We generally assume not only that performances are authorized by pre-set scripts (a deterministic notion Hamlet liked but Dickens did not) but that performances are temporary interruptions in the solidity of being of both the performers and the audience. Samuel Johnson's is only the most lucid insistence that performances are aberrations, not even temporary relinquishments of our basic sensible personalities. 'We are always in our senses', he claims, unthreatened in our illusions of separable being. Just so, roles or role-playing suggests almost inevitably to us a departure from a real self that the role is disguising. My thesis is that Dickens questions these notions of selfhood as an isolated and solid entity, that the lines between performers and performances, roles and role-players are often blurred. How are we to know the dancer from the dance, the past Flora Finching from the present article, from the performances she gives, the roles she plays – more radically, how are we to distinguish her from Mr F's aunt?

Of course we need no one to come from the dead to tell us that the Victorians generally became more than a little uneasy with simple notions of an essentialised self. Presentations of a multiple self or of a hidden, unknown self are common; in Arnold, for instance: 'And each lives half a hundred different lives' ('The Scholar Gypsy', l. 169); 'And long we try in vain to speak and act/ Our hidden self, and what we say and do,/ Is eloquent, is well – but 'tis not true!' ('The Buried Life', ll. 64–66). These poignant laments, and others like them in virtually every major poet, are, arguably, a bargaining manœuvre, a liberal humanist dodge or compromise. They protect, after all, an essentialised self, even if it is splintered or mysterious. A little sweet sadness, in the end, is not much of a price to pay for a securely fortified selfhood.

The security force is not all that reliable, however, judging from the apparent need to deny repeatedly and emphatically more dangerous questions about essentialised being. Arnold is notorious for poems that glimpse and then quickly look away from an absorption or dissolution of self: men who 'dreamed two human hearts might blend' are simply unable to recognize 'their loneliness', unable in their loony ecstasy to detect 'the unplumbed, salt, estranging sea' that is divinely ordained to separate us all ('Isolation: To Marguerite', ll. 38–42; 'To Marguerite – Continued', l. 24). The longing to merge – 'Oh might our marges meet again' ('To Marguerite – Continued', l. 18) – can be expressed so movingly, one might say, only because such merging is bound never to occur. Is there a sigh of relief, a welcoming of separation, here, and in Browning's 'Two in the Campagna',[1] in the general movement of Rossetti's *The House of Life* and Meredith's *Modern Love*, and in the equivocal ending of Tennyson's *The Princess*, where the Prince's vision of marriage as 'The single pure and perfect animal,/ The two-celled heart beating, with one full stroke,/ Life' (VII. ll. 288–90) is shadowed by the decidedly *un*-two-celled action of the narrative, the obvious reluctance of the Princess to accept all this, and the scepticism of the characters in the frame poem? Dickens, I am suggesting, is far more radical, takes many more risks in hinting at dissolution or absorption, a selfhood that is not contained or definable but relational, that may reach out or collapse into nothingness.

All of this is, first, implied by the versatility of his performers and the delight they and their author take in that sheer play. I will deal later with more direct images of unrestrained being in Dickens, but we should note, even with these clowns, that such unrestrained performances raise

questions not only about linear plots but about the solidity of those
trying to play a straight and clear part in them. Many of Dickens's
performers would make Hamlet seek other employment, but probably
none deserves Danish royal censure more than Mr Pecksniff. Mr
Pecksniff, 'architect, artist, and man', is given a part to play in the plot, of
course; but whatever this thing called 'Mr Pecksniff' is, it is too
amorphous to fit into a plot slot. True, he nods amiably in that direction
now and then. The plot calls for him to be a cadging hypocrite, and he
does sometimes find interest in those possibilities – but never for long. He
is too busy constructing a raucous, open-ended farce and has limited
interest in morality plays. One might, rather tiresomely in my view, argue
that Pecksniff's stagings are all self-centred calculations; but it seems to
me also possible to see Pecksniff, like Dickens, as the great impresario,
managing the script, the stage directions, the costumes, the scenery, and,
of course – again like Dickens – adopting the leading roles, whatever they
might be.

Take, for instance, the opening dramatic scene in *Martin Chuzzlewit*
(ch. 2),[2] where he and his two daughters stage, for their own benefit and
without an audience, a mock resurrection scene. Pecksniff has been
attacked by a vindictive doorknob and lies senseless on the floor. He rests
there patiently, waiting for his cue, rousing himself when his daughters
speak, brought to life not by their actions but by their words: 'He comes
to himself!', 'He speaks again'. There follows a lively celebration scene,
starring Miss Charity as Sensible Goodness, Miss Mercy as Kittenish
Innocence, and Mr Pecksniff as Paternal Virtue. The props are important:
tea, buttered toast, ham, and, with Charity's cue – 'eggs'. 'And eggs,' says
Mr Pecksniff, 'even they have their moral.' According to this voice,
morality is meant to minister to comfort: 'If we indulge in harmless fluids,
we get the dropsy; if in exciting liquids, we get drunk. What a soothing
reflection that is.' It turns out that the soothing, oozing warmth is made
possible by the plural 'we', by which Mr Pecksniff means 'mankind in
general; the human race considered as a body, and not as individuals'.
Escaping the trap of the 'individual', the Pecksniffian amalgam (called, for
convenience, 'Mr Pecksniff') can feed, and drink, and experience delight
even in moralisms: 'There is nothing personal in morality, my love'. One
can doubtless read this playlet as an illustration of deep-seated hypocrisy
or as a rehearsal scene for serious hypocrisy to come – but what
uninteresting readings these are! Performances like these run under their
own steam; they are not attempting to get anywhere in particular. Rather,
they cast a dim light on the whole idea of getting anywhere in particular.

Take another: Mrs Jarley and her waxworks. The performance consists not just of the versatile waxworks — where Grimaldi the clown can just as well be Mr Murray the grammarian, depending on the tastes of the audience and Mrs Jarley's whim — but of Mrs Jarley herself, using the waxworks simply as occasions for her own performances: for eloquent soliloquies in defence of the works' classical status, soliloquies worthy of Lady Macbeth. Mrs Jarley creates best when she has an audience; but there are those, like Sairey Gamp, who can create mono-dramas, parodies in advance of Tennyson's *Maud*. Sairey goes on about 'wales of grief' and the virtues of 'cowcumbers and vinegar' when she is by herself as well as when she has a listener. Of course, she never really is alone, since, being a master at dialogue, she has an articulate companion, Mrs Harris. Often explained as a pathetic antidote to Sairey's essential loneliness or as a blatant instrument of self-advertisement, Mrs Harris seems to me a means of creating the sort of drama Sairey loves: the realistic drama of detail, Ibsenesque in its particularity. One thinks of such passages as this one:

> Don't I know as that dear woman is expecting of me at this minnit, Mr. Westlock, and is a-lookin' out of window down the street, with little Tommy Harris in her arms, as calls me his own Gammy, and truly calls, for bless the mottled little legs of that there precious child (like Canterbury Brawn his own dear father says, which so they are) his own I have been, ever since I found him, Mr. Westlock, with his small red worsted shoe a-gurglin' in his throat, where he had put it in his play, a chick, wile they was leavin' of him on the floor a-lookin' for it through the ouse and him a-choakin' sweetly in the parlour! Oh, Betsey Prig, what wickedness you've showed this night, but never shall you darken Sairey's doors agen, you twining serpiant! (ch. 49)

If this were all a matter of self-interest, why does she take such pleasure in talking with Young Bailey, who, at the time, is not a likely candidate for profit, for a laying-out and certainly not for a lying-in. Then, there are the Micawbers, among the most versatile in using any opportunity for performance: a debt-collector roaring in the street below is the occasion for *Antony and Cleopatra*; a party for the ending of *The Marriage of Figaro*.

Dickens's own subversive delight in non-scripted performance is evident everywhere, not only in these wild, non-individual characters but in raucous structural disruption. Chapter 13 of *Martin Chuzzlewit* provides a good illustration. At the end of chapter 12, also the completion of the fourth monthly number, Martin, dismissed from Mr Pecksniff's moral and architectural tutelage, suddenly announces, 'I'll go to America!' The business of chapter 13, then, we might suppose, would be to get him there. Quickly, too, if we are to believe what we have been told so often it must be true: that Dickens's decision to ship Martin to Yankeedoodledom was a desperate move to rouse a sadly lethargic market and boost sales.[3] But chapter 13 seems to be in no hurry at all to get Martin overseas; it barely gets him from Wiltshire to London, not a long haul, and squeezes in the little business it does manage to conduct – uniting Martin and Mark Tapley – only at the end. The time is spent instead in leisure activities: wildly expansive comic dialogues or duets between Martin and William (Bill) Simmons, Montague Tigg and a pawnbroker ('David', Tigg calls him), Tigg and Martin. Dickens has time to provide his narrator with some long and splendid sarcasms on 'nature' and its connection to bestiality, the psychological flimflam of hopefulness, and moralists in general. Clearly, the author has a good time, as does even Mark Tapley, who is less concerned with the plot than with letting us know, in dozens of broad hints, that his perverse search for the greatest misery possible has inevitably led him to smell out the miserably selfish Martin.

Roughly speaking, a third of the long chapter 13 is devoted to Martin-Simmons, a third to the pawnshop Abbot and Costello routines, and a third to Mark. The presumably desperate Dickens somehow seems very relaxed, confidently playful, with all the time in the world. Note the introduction of the man who turns out to be Bill Simmons:

> He was a red-faced burly young fellow; smart in his way, and with a good-humoured countenance. As he advanced towards the fire he touched his shining forehead with the forefinger of his stiff leather glove, by way of salutation; and said (rather unnecessarily) that it was an uncommon wet day.
>
> 'Very wet,' said Martin.
>
> 'I don't know as ever I see a wetter.'[4]
>
> 'I never felt one,' said Martin.

What on earth is going on here? Nothing, we might say. We might say further that nothing-going-on is precisely the point. The narrator even tells us that these remarks are made 'rather unnecessarily'. The clear signal to us is to relax and enjoy ourselves. 'Here we go!' Dickens says, 'I've got these two together and am ready to see what comes of it. You just warm yourself by the fire, get a glass of something agreeable, and look on. I won't disappoint you.'

And of course he does not, providing us in Simmons a coach-driver of remarkable fluidity and versatility. Aspiring to greater things in the coach-driving line, William ('better known' – like some yokel politician

['Vote for Richard (Dick) Kettle for Coroner'] – 'as Bill') turns the chance to make a few extra shillings into a chance for improvising performance, creating in Martin not a gull but an audience for his one-man Astley's show. He is full of entertaining stories about himself, about horses, and about Lummy Ned of the Light Salisbury and his remarkable ability to outface death: ' "Dead!" replied the other, with a contemptuous emphasis. "Not he. You won't catch Ned a-dying easy. No, no. He knows better than that." ' When narrative inventiveness temporarily fails him, he pulls a bugle from a handy pocket and plays a great many tunes, or the first part of them anyway.

What is accomplished here? In the face of the sheer joy offered by Bill Simmons, such a question seems worthy of Malvolio. We who, like Dickens, thrive on cakes and ale will not think to ask. Almost always in Dickens, when a character in one place needs to get to another, and there is a coach to take him, we can count on a high old time of it. Forget about what is getting accomplished. The plot be damned!

Martin does, of course, get to London, a phrase's worth of work that takes seven full pages of horsing around. Once there, we are still not forced into dreary toil. No! We are provided with Tigg and David the pawnbroker going through a familiar routine they both love:

'The old address?'

'Not at all,' said Mr. Tigg; 'I have removed my town establishment from thirty-eight Mayfair, to number fifteen-hundred-and-forty-two Park Lane.'

'Come, I'm not going to put down that, you know,' said the shopman with a grin.

'You may put down what you please, my friend,' quoth Mr. Tigg. 'The fact is still the same. The apartments for the under-butler and the fifth footman being of a most confounded low and vulgar kind at thirty-eight, Mayfair, I have been compelled, in my regard for the feelings which do them so much honour, to take on lease for seven, fourteen, or twenty-one years, renewable at the option of the tenant, the elegant and commodious family mansion, number fifteen-hundred-and-forty-two Park Lane. Make it two-and-six, and come and see me!'

The shopman was so highly entertained by this piece of humour, that Mr. Tigg himself could not repress some little show of exultation.

Martin does not quite get the point or have the wherewithal to enter into this game. Never mind. Tigg can keep things going by using the young dullard as a straight man:

'Here! Please to give me the most you can for this,' said Martin, handing the watch to the shopman, 'I want money sorely.'

'He wants money sorely!' cried Mr. Tigg with excessive sympathy. 'David, will you have the goodness to do your very utmost for my friend, who wants money sorely. You will deal with my friend as if he were myself. A gold hunting-watch, David, engine-turned, capped and jewelled in four holes, escape movement, horizontal lever, and warranted to perform correctly, upon my personal reputation, who have observed it narrowly for many years, under the most trying circumstances.' Here he winked at Martin, that he might understand this recommendation would have an immense effect upon the shopman: 'What do you say, David, to my friend? Be very particular to deserve my custom and recommendation, David.'

Like Simmons, Tigg is after money. Like Dickens too, we presume. But none of them seems very interested in it; none is going to sacrifice the game, the delight for something as mundane as a little tin – or a little plot.

To focus this habit of disruption and to move more explicitly towards the issue of non-individualized, relational being, I would like to shift from the broad issue of 'performance' to the somewhat more controllable one of 'role' or 'role-players'. These role-players, on the face of it, would seem to have considerably less creative freedom than those conducting performances. According to the *OED* – here we go again! – a *roll* (role) is a prescribed list of names, predetermined by some rule; or a part one has to play, undertake, or assume. Note the pre-emptory *has to*; but note also the wonderful ambiguity in 'assume'. *Assume* can suggest simply taking over a part *or* actually creating it, assuming it to be whatever one chooses. Perhaps it is time to admit that Dickens certainly does give ample space to the *has to* part of roles, that he often insists on essential selfhood. Bill Sikes, one senses, can hardly shift at will to the role of the kindly grandfather. He is incurably bad, as is Rigaud; even the sweet-hearted landlady of the 'Break of Day' Inn says so. Similarly, Herbert Pocket, Tommy Traddles, and the like are incurably good. These people simply *are*, come what may. They resemble Browning's Mr Sludge, The Medium: 'Myself am whole and sole reality/ Inside a raree-show' (ll. 909–10). This hammering at essences on Dickens's part may seem a bit hysterical, a kind of reassuring manœuvre that provides him with a few steady poles. In any event, these essences are not to be found with other flying players, who swing round these fixed maypoles. Those who play fast and loose with the 'assume' part of the 'role' definition are most startling, most likely to offend our own assumptions.

For our part, we come to the novels equipped to detect a real essence behind that role, a true face behind the mask. But in Dickens we are forced to wonder. To start with a simple case, that of Mr Bumble: what lives behind the mask of the Beadle costume, the cocked hat and stick, that malicious, unfeeling impostor? A quaking jelly of emasculation, apparently, as we see when he marries. But what about the scene where he looks down at the tiny Oliver he is holding by the hand and hears the child sob out that he is 'So lonely, sir! So very lonely'? Mr Bumble is moved, gets a lump in his throat, and pretends to cough to cover impending tears (ch. 4). What then *is* he: a decent, tender man, forced to play the roles of thunderous Beadle and henpecked husband; one of the latter two people forced to play the other two roles; all three; or none of them? Same with Fagin: is he simply an artful exploiter? Is his maternal solicitude and affectionate terminology malicious, paederastic, or genuinely loving? What about the scene where he bends over the sleeping Oliver to wake him for some thieving exploit, is touched by the innocent beauty of the sleeping child, and says, 'Not now', turning softly away (ch. 19)? Which is he? And what of characters who are apparently indistinguishable from their roles? Who *is* Mr Wopsle, apart from the violent part of Collins's 'Ode on the Passions' throwing his blood-stained sword down in thunder or apart from his well-groomed version of the indecisive Prince of Denmark? And Dick Swiveller. He awakens from his unreal role-playing by means of a cathartic illness and discovers in the loyalty and love of the Marchioness a new being for himself. Right? But is not that new being just about as indefinable as the old one – playful and Micawberesque? He and the Marchioness are still plotless players, passing their happy days with cribbage; and the Marchioness is still whatever she was or was not, the Marchioness, a name being given to her by Dick to make it all seem 'more real and pleasant'. Dick still calls the shots and issues proclamations on what is *real*. How are we to decide whether Dick has changed? The more difficult question is how we are to decide what this Dick Swiveller was or is.

Some characters seem to play multiple roles, then, and others may or may not shift within those roles. Some are pure mysteries entirely. Is Bailey the elfish young spirit who skips about Todgers's Commercial Boarding House or the worldly man-about-town who convinces Poll Sweedlepipe to shave him? We might deal with this problem by saying that Poll is a tender-hearted fool, easily gulled. Sairey Gamp, however, who certainly is neither tender-hearted nor a fool, is more at home with an amorphous Bailey, seeing him either as a child – 'What an impertinent young sparrow it is! I wouldn't be that creetur's mother not for fifty pound!' (ch. 29) – or as a world-weary adult – 'There's nothin' he don't know; that's my opinion. . . . All the wickedness of the world is Print to him' (ch. 26) — as the occasion demands. Where is the real Bailey? And what of Alfred Jingle, the chameleon socialite, cricket-player, lover, strolling actor, vagabond, scoundrel, repentant sinner? Has he, in the end, revealed his true self, his essence? Mr Perker, wise in the ways of the world, is sceptical about permanent reform for such a formless thing as Jingle. Mr Pickwick thinks he has reinforced the true article; but, then, Mr Pickwick is a particularly naïve reader. He has, like us, been asking questions like: where is the real Jingle? Where is the real Bailey? Where is the real Sairey, the real Wopsle, the real Micawber? Perhaps the question itself is misplaced.

These are the questions, interestingly, that the narrator of *David Copperfield* asks. He has, as it happens, a devil of a time locating his own essence, his own real self behind the roles he plays. At the same time, he wants to formulate his own story with himself as hero. The difficulty with the 'himself as hero' formulation lurks not in the 'hero' part but in the 'self' part. As a consequence, he becomes somewhat hysterical in insisting that he and everyone else has a self that is solid, self-contained, and determinate. On landing securely at Dover,[5] all padded and protected at Aunt Betsey's, David proclaims over and over that he is 'new', signalling his need to read and explain his own being as clearly-defined, self-made, totally dissociated from that of the little boy in love with his mother, mistreated by Murdstone and Creakle, humiliated in the blacking warehouse. He reads others in the same individualized way and thus is baffled to the end by Steerforth, who carries with him a disastrous family and class burden, and by Uriah Heep, whose lower-class rebelliousness can find no place in David's atomized, essentialist scheme of human personality. He understands very little about the narrative he writes, therefore, largely because he does not want to understand. He can formulate an Horatio Alger story, but I suspect few besides David have read *David Copperfield* in this way. One reason for his divorce from his own story is that the novel, unlike David, does *not* leave unquestioned the notion of the individualized self.

Our own notions of essential being, of character as marked off and distinct, more than likely match David's; but Dickens's are much more complex. One need only try to locate the essential Micawber, for instance, to see that other ideas of being, ideas antagonistic to essentialism, are running as a counter-current in this novel. The Micawbers are not only endlessly versatile role-players; they are unthinkable except as a unit. They exist in relation, in incorporation; not isolation. They do not grow or change, because they are outside time and change — and plot. They cannot be understood in the linear, developmental terms appropriate to individuals. They are the 'we' of one another. Mrs Micawber's vow never to desert Mr Micawber is a grand and happy redundancy. How could she? Without him, where would she be? More exactly, what would she be?

The move towards alternate, boundaryless conceptions of being is played out throughout the Dickens canon. Even in that most radical of individualist forms, the *Bildungsroman* and its exemplar *Oliver Twist*, we can see Oliver growing towards a being that exists only in relation to that of the boys around Fagin, and to Fagin himself. Fagin's merry pickpocketing pantomimes, co-starring the Dodger and Charley Bates, make Oliver laugh 'till the tears ran down his face' (ch. 9). Later, Fagin's 'droll and curious' stories about exciting robberies make Oliver laugh heartily 'in spite of all his better feelings' (ch. 18). Oliver's ability to be absorbed in purely communal laughter, in spite of his dratted individualized conscience, marks his affinity for incorporation, an affinity that makes us uneasy, I suggest, not so much because he is drawn towards crime as because he is drawn towards a joy that does not differentiate separate selves. As it happens, his 'better feelings' and the brute force of the legal mob gain ascendancy, and he exchanges the healthy, helpless tears of laughter for the real tears of the lugubrious and sickly Brownlow-Maylie fortress. He wins an individuality, but I wonder if his victory makes any reader cheer.

A more complex series of images of merging and dissociation is developed in *Great Expectations*. The early part of the novel presents Pip with a set of possibilities for establishing his being, all involving a mingling and all more or less uninviting: his parents 'dead and buried', the shivering and outcast convict, the loving but apparently impotent Joe. Out of this, it is not surprising that the child settles on the child-father Joe, loves him, as he says, 'perhaps for no better reason in those early days than because the dear fellow let me love him' (ch. 6). The phrasing, from our point of view unsentimental almost to the point of harshness, is, from another, brilliantly suggestive of reciprocity. It is not that he loves Joe and Joe loves him; it is more that he knocks at Joe's heart and Joe lets him in: ' "And bring the poor little child. God bless the poor little child," I said to your sister, "there's room for *him* at the forge!" ' (ch. 7). There's room for the child in Joe. Joe and Pip are not, at this stage, separable beings.

We can see this from, among other things, the letter Pip writes to Joe:

MI DEER JO I OPE U R KRWITE WELL I OPE I SHAL SON B HABELL 4 2 TEEDGE U JO AN THEN WE SHORL B SO GLODD AN WEN I M PRENGTD 2 U JO WOT LARX AN BLEVE ME INF XN PIP. (ch. 7)

This, one might say, is Dickens's answer to the letters of Lord Chesterfield
he so despised, despised precisely because of their unremitting hammering — very unlike Joe's selfless hammering — at self. What one notices
about Pip's epistolary exercise is that it might, reversing the 'PRENGTD'
part, have been written by Joe — at a later stage of his formal education.
The letter contains Joe's awkward, sweet genteelisms — 'I OPE U R
KRWITE WELL'; 'BLEVE ME INF XN' — his concern with 'TEEDGING', and
his openness of heart — 'WOT LARX'. This last phrase blends the two
together into one throughout the novel. Perhaps we never witness any
larks; perhaps they are never realized in the plot. But they exist all the
same, exist even more powerfully because they are in the form of a
promise that defies fulfilment, a sign that need point to no other place,
that is realized in itself.

This last difficult and profound non-causality is the secret of Joe's
wisdom and lies at the core of his teaching in the great pedagogical scene
that follows the presentation of Pip's letter. Teacher and pupil do not so
much change places as unite. Joe's manner throughout his *apologia pro vita
sua*, his explanation of his faith and life, his childhood, love for Pip's sister,
and feelings towards Pip, are sternly tutorial: 'Joe looked firmly at me';
'Don't you see?'; 'Don't you know?'; 'You're a-listening, and understanding, Pip?'. As it happens, Pip decidedly does not understand — not in the
usual sense. He especially does not understand how Joe can love and
admire Mrs Joe or how he can regard his brutal, good-for-nothing father
with respect and affection: 'Whatsume'er the failings on his part,
Remember reader he were that good in his hart'. Joe does not flinch from
the violence and universal unfairness of life; he would not disagree with
Kafka that all are victims and sure to suffer torture. But for Joe it is
innocence and goodness of heart, not guilt, that is never to be doubted.
Pip does not seem to get it, to understand Joe's dissociation of action from
being, his melting of all into a sad, indestructible goodness. But, in a way
that defies our usual Lockean idea of individual growth and understanding, Pip is suckled and nourished by Joe's Christian paradox. He makes
himself part of Joe's wisdom: 'We were equals afterwards, as we had been
before; but, afterwards at quiet times when I sat looking at Joe and
thinking about him, I had a new sensation of feeling conscious that I was
looking up to Joe in my heart.' (ch. 7) Equals and non-equals, pupil and
teacher, they are interchangeable, of one heart.

Pip, of course, tries to defy this learning and his heart for some time. At
the end, however, he leaves behind the sorry, clambering, successful
gentleman whose disguise he has tried to wear and gives himself to Joe's
teaching. In terms of the narrative, he forms himself as, in, and for the

convict Magwitch. As Magwitch 'softens', so does Pip, until the speech of both modulates to a simple and quiet dignity that no longer separates but marks their connecting:

> 'And what's best of all', he said, 'you've been more comfortable alonger me, since I was under a dark cloud, than when the sun shone. That's best of all.'
> He lay on his back, breathing with great difficulty. Do what he would, and love me though he did, the light left his face ever and again, and a film came over the placid look at the white ceiling.
> 'Are you in much pain to-day?'
> 'I don't complain of none, dear boy.'
> 'You never do complain.'
> He had spoken his last words. He smiled, and I understood his touch to mean that he wished to lift my hand, and lay it on his breast. I laid it there, and he smiled again, and put both his hands upon it. (ch. 56)

Their unity is marked by their mutual adoption of the metaphor of light, the wordless communication, and the joining of hands. This last gesture, Pip's hands along with those of Magwitch resting on the heart, suggests that we must think of that heart not as Magwitch's failing separate organ but as the human heart in general. This union connects both with Joe and with all who suffer and are good: 'Remember reader he were that good in his hart'.

Not all images of absorption are by any means so positive in Dickens. The loss of individuality, alienating as that individuality is, can also mean a loss of all defences. Atoms can then turn into the terrifying, undifferentiated mobs of *Barnaby Rudge*:

> It was but a glimpse, but it showed them the crowd, gathering and clustering round the house: some of the armed men pressing to the front to break down the doors and windows, some bringing brands from the nearest fire, some with lifted faces following their course upon the roof and pointing them out to their companions: all raging and roaring like the flames they lighted up. They saw some men thirsting for the treasures of strong liquor which they knew were stored within; they saw others, who had been wounded, sinking down into the opposite doorways and dying, solitary wretches, in the midst of all the vast assemblage; here, a frightened woman trying to escape; and there a lost child; and there a drunken ruffian, unconscious of the death-wound on his head, raving and fighting to the last. (ch. 67)

The individuals picked out by this demonic camera-sweep seem horribly accidental, random, doomed in the face of the single monster of the mob. These rioters, figured when alive as a sea and when dead as manure-heaps, are creatures – or a creature – out of hell:

> The gutters of the street, and every crack and fissure in the stones, ran with scorching spirit, which being damned up by busy hands, overflowed the road and pavement, and formed a great pool, into which the people dropped down dead by dozens. They lay in heaps all round this fearful pond, husbands and wives, fathers and sons, mothers and daughters, women with children in their arms and babies at their breasts, and drank until they died. While some stopped with their lips to the brink and never raised their heads again, others sprang up from their fiery draught, and danced, half in a mad triumph, and half in the agony of suffocation, until they fell, and steeped their corpses in the liquor that had killed them. Nor was even this the worst or most appalling kind of death that happened on this fatal night. From the burning cellars, where they drank out of hats, pails, buckets, tubs, and shoes, some men were drawn, alive, but all alight from head to foot; who, in their unendurable anguish and suffering, making for anything that had the look of water, rolled, hissing, in this hideous lake, and splashed up liquid fire which lapped in all it met with as it ran along the surface, and neither spared the living nor the dead. (ch. 68)

More subtly, *Little Dorrit* presents both the dangers and the joys of absorption. It is a novel of reductions, radical strippings away, testing whether something can be made out of nothing. In the case of William Dorrit, Mrs Clennam, or Mr Merdle, it cannot. Stripped of trappings, they vanish. Even the hero, Arthur Clennam, thinks of mixing himself with the river in a literal, suicidal nothingness: 'And he thought – who has not thought for a moment, sometimes? – that it might be better to flow away monotonously, like the river, and to compound for its insensibility to happiness with its insensibility with pain.' (ch. 16) But he is saved by Amy Dorrit – 'I have nothing in the world', she says (pt 3, ch. 34) – and the Nothing and the Nobody coalesce. The filthy hive of individuals continue in their 'usual uproar', but Arthur and Amy are 'inseparable and blessed' (pt 3, ch. 34).

These kinds of expansive beings raise interesting questions for those such as film-makers and television adapters who seem called upon to use characters as individuals. More interestingly, they call upon us as readers to abandon some of our most cherished and comfortable notions. But literary works have never really done much in the way of ministering to habitual comfort. Dickens especially makes us squirm considerably. Who knows but that out of that squirming we might find a posture that will allow us to see and think in more radical – even more hopeful ways. Back to Yeats:

> O chestnut tree, great rooted-blossomer
> Are you the leaf, the blossom, or the bole?
> O body swayed to music, O brightening glance.
> How can we know the dancer from the dance?
>   ('Among School Children', ll. 61–64)

With Dickens, the last line, unmetrically, would be: 'How can we know the dancer, from the dancers, from the dancing, from the dance?'

Notes

1.   I would that you were all to me,
        You that are just so much, no more,
    Nor yours nor mine, nor slave nor free!
        Where does the fault lie? What the core
    O' the wound, since wound must be?

    I would I could adopt your will,
        See with your eyes, and set my heart
    Beating by yours, and drink my fill
        At your soul's springs, – your part my part
    In life, for good and ill.

    No, I yearn upward, touch you close,
        Then stand away. I kiss your cheek,
    Catch your soul's warmth, – I pluck the rose
        And love it more than tongue can speak –
    Then the good minute goes.

    Already how am I so far
        Out of that minute? Must I go
    Still like the thistle-ball, no bar,
        Onward, whenever light winds blow,
    Fixed by no friendly star?

    Just when I seemed about to learn!
        Where is the thread now? Off again!

The old trick! Only I discern –
  Infinite passion, and the pain
Of finite hearts that yearn.

Robert Browning, 'Two in the Campagna', (ll. 36–60)

2.   All quotations from Dickens's novels are from *The New Oxford Illustrated Dickens* (Oxford University Press). Citations are to chapter numbers.

3.   The authority for this oft-repeated, magnified, and simplified notion is not Dickens but Forster; and even Forster is less than plain, muddling by the passive voice the origin of the decision – perhaps it was the publisher of Forster himself – and stating (plainly enough) that the financial motive was, in any case, secondary: 'though it was believed that this resolve, which Dickens adopted as suddenly as his hero, might increase the number of his readers, that reason influenced him less than the challenge to make good his *Notes* which every mail had been bringing him from unsparing assailants beyond the Atlantic'. John Forster, in A. J. Hoppé (ed.), *The Life of Charles Dickens*, 2 vols (London: J. M. Dent, and New York: E. P. Dutton; 1966).

4.   Even here, Dickens has fun, floating past our minds this interesting syntax and the brief, impossible possibility that 'wetter' is a noun, perhaps something like a cross between a walrus and an otter. All this is grandly irrelevant, of course; but so is the entire episode.

5.   Dover may suggest 'rover', and it is, of course, a port of departure. But it seems to have figured in the Victorian (and modern) British imagination much more as a port of entry, of return: dōver/hōme. Perhaps that notorious British traveller not only carried his taste for tea and cricket (now chips and peas) to all parts of the globe, but roamed only for the great pleasure of geographical and psychological confirmation felt when coming home. Those white cliffs (whitewashed by sentiment; they are actually rather grey-mottled and ugly) have taken a place in the British stock of symbols as a kind of mother's breast. David, thus, wanting to erase one origin and claim another, naturally turns to this cradle.

3

Dickens's Theatre of Self-Knowledge

Jean Ferguson Carr

Charles Dickens often used theatrical metaphors to suggest artifice, posing, concealment – the problems of being overly self-conscious about an audience's presence. But he also returned with fascination to the metaphor of the theatre as a special forum for revealing secrets about himself and his past. He posited an image of the theatre as a space set apart from the turmoil and consequences of the ordinary world, in which 'actual truth' could be performed without the normal constraints of repression, propriety, or authorial intervention. A study of the paradoxical uses of such a performative space and the limits on its liberating powers enhances our understanding of Dickens's attitudes toward presentation of himself and his material, and of his involvement with his audience, both theatre-goers and reading public. But Dickens is also an exemplary figure whose use of theatrical metaphors illuminates more generally our desires to 'play' ourselves and to keep control of the production of play. Fascinated with himself to an extraordinary degree and eager to share with potential biographers his insights into what made him 'inimitable', Dickens struggled to articulate the contradictions of his theatrical experience. His refusal to 'understand' himself in a single autobiographical document makes his recursions to problematic issues of self-production particularly useful. This essay will examine Dickens's powerful working-through of theatre as scene and metaphor in two novels – *David Copperfield* (1849–50) and *Great Expectations* (1860–61) – and in his own intervening experience in the production of *The Frozen Deep* (1857).

David Copperfield marks the end of his school years by going to the theatre to see a production of *Julius Caesar* and a pantomime. He leaves the magical world of the theatre depressed to find himself back in the 'real' and adult world:

I felt as if I had come from the clouds, where I had been leading a romantic life for ages, to a bawling, splashing, link-lighted, umbrella-struggling, hackney-coach-jostling, patten-clinking, muddy, miserable world. . . . [I] stood in the street for a little while, as if I really were a stranger upon earth: but the unceremonious pushing and hustling that I received, soon recalled me to myself. . . . I was so filled with the play, and with the past — for it was, in a manner, like a shining transparency, through which I saw my earlier life moving along.[1]

Through the 'novel and delightful effect' of watching 'all those noble Romans alive', the play holds for David a power to focus a ceremonious order out of his past. Recalled unpleasantly to himself, David links the play to his own past, imagining a world apart from the noisy, muddy world of London in which he feels himself 'a stranger upon earth'. Through the 'shining transparency' of the play he recovers his earlier life 'moving along' as if in a procession before his eyes. David uses the *experience* of seeing a play, especially a historical play, as an orderly impetus to review his earlier life and to address his feeling of strangeness in his present. Despite David's glossing of play and past, his reaction to this particular play is curious; it is not the pantomime that attracts him, but *Julius Caesar*, with its evocation of an assassinated ruler and an ancient empire lost through betrayal and revolution. The world of ancient Rome creates an uneasy context for David's own domestic loss. Its associations seem all too similar and earth-bound — not as David claims, of 'the clouds' — to the present-day world David had experienced the day before as 'haunted', with a 'dark cloud lowering on it', a place in which an 'impending shadow' falls like a 'stain'. In his present-day world, the orderly and 'congenial' objects that once created a 'pleasure in thinking' have lost their power. The threats of adult experience seem absolute and destructive to David, razing both his past and the possibility of recuperating those passed values: 'It was as if the tranquil sanctuary of my boyhood had been sacked before my face, and its peace and honour given to the winds' (ch. 19, p. 339). Dickens's use of the theatre in this scene thus creates an uncertain relationship between the stage and the world. David describes the two realms as radically separate, one magical and romantic, the other 'miserable' and 'unceremonious'. But his analysis seems underdeveloped, defensive, naïve.

Dickens revises the scene of theatrical wonder more explicitly when he returns to a young man's experience with the theatre in *Great Expectations* (1860–61), a novel he described as written in careful comparison with *David Copperfield*.[2] Pip has as great a need as, if not greater than, David for a safe realm, magically preserved from the marshy, dangerous, class-ridden world of his present. Both David and Pip are threatened by mystifying performances in their 'real world' (David by the 'Goroo-man' and Pip by Magwitch and Compeyson), but David has a middle-class familiarity with literary performances. As a child, Pip is easily confused by the power of theatrical gestures, from Miss Havisham's elaborate tableau to Wopsle's melodramatic tragedies. Indeed Pip is so overwhelmed by Wopsle's reading of 'The Affecting Tragedy of George Barnwell' that he loses his sense of literary distance, identifying absolutely with the murderer.[3] Pip confuses the theatrical and the 'real' worlds, and his incursion into the theatre is terrifying, threatening, dark. As with his earlier humiliation of being forced to 'play', Pip finds such theatre all too 'real', revealing the dangerous psychological and economic undercurrents of society rather than providing an airy escape from such adult knowledge. Whereas David's absorption in the world of the play enabled him momentarily to evade adult awareness and complications, Pip's threatens to scrape all polite surfaces bare, to expose his own dreaded complicity in murder and sexual threat, to present the 'tragedy' he fears to find beneath his domestic farce. As an adult, Pip approaches theatre with a sceptical distance, concentrating on the responses of 'outsiders', those whose inexperience leads them to shout to the actors, to expect absolute reality from the stage. Pip has 'risen' above those naïve and lower-class responses, but does not share David's absorption or pleasure. Although he finds the theatre ridiculous, he is uncomfortable as a viewer, self-conscious of the class limitations of the production and its audience. The two times he is pressed into attending – to see *Hamlet* (ch. 31), and to see a nautical drama and a Christmas pantomime (ch. 47), Pip's attention is on the transparency of Wopsle's theatrical 'business', on the boisterous refusal of the audience to succumb to illusion, and on the jarring gap between play and production: he comments, for example, on the Danish court's elevation on a 'kitchen table' (ch. 31, p. 273), and the actor who 'ascended to the clouds in a large watch-case' (ch. 47, p. 397). He is never taken in by the illusion and never loses his sensitivity to the facts of production.

Yet despite Dickens's parodying of contemporary theatrical practices in these chapters, the larger scene of the theatre is full of ominous, strange, and revealing moments. Pip finds Wopsle's production of *Hamlet* 'droll': 'very slow, very dreary, very up-hill and down-hill, and very unlike any way in which any man in any natural circumstances of life or death ever expressed himself about anything' (ch. 31, p. 276). But that night he dreams 'miserably' that he had to 'play Hamlet to Miss Havisham's Ghost,

before twenty thousand people, without knowing twenty words of it'
(ch. 19, p. 279). The play has the power to raise a dream vision, but it is a
nightmare exposure of Pip's worst fears and repressions rather than an
innocent, pleasurable experience. More threatening is his experience of
Wopsle's Christmas pantomime, which is as ludicrous and as unmoving as
drama, but is displaced by the terrifying drama Pip performs without his
knowledge. As Pip watches Wopsle on stage, he is astonished to find the
actor staring at him, the play turned inside-out with the audience creating
the drama. The discovery that the dreaded Compeyson has sat 'like a
Ghost' behind Pip during the performance throws Pip into 'special and
peculiar terror'. The theatre makes him vulnerable, unaware of who sits
behind him or of what production he is being scripted into against his will
and knowledge. 'To think that I should be so unconscious and off my
guard after all my care', he worries, 'was as if I had shut an avenue of a
hundred doors to keep him out, and then had found him at my elbow.'
The experience leads Pip to conclude that there is no safe realm, that
'however slight an appearance of danger there might be about us, danger
was always near and active' (ch. 47, p. 399). Pip's experience of theatre
thus blurs the lines between the 'real' and the magical that David
Copperfield tried to sustain. In this later novel, the theatre evokes not an
escapist fancy, but a scene for uncovering, perhaps fatally, repressed fears
and connections.

The contradictory use of theatre explored in these two novels also
emerges in Dickens's prose and private writings. In different contexts and
times, Dickens represented the theatre as a site for exuberant comic relief
from the work and worries of his own world. At other times, he worried
about losing himself in the acting, about standing bare, revealed before
all. He wrote to Bulwer-Lytton, for example: 'Assumption has charms for
me – I hardly know for how many wild reasons – so delightful, that I feel a
loss of, oh! I can't say what exquisite foolery, when I lose a chance of
being someone in voice, etc. not at all like myself.'[4] In an essay in
Household Words in 1852, Dickens evoked the 'jocund world of
Pantomime, where there is no affliction or calamity that leaves the least
impression . . . where every one . . . is so superior to all the accidents of
life, though encountering them at every turn'.[5] Such a protected realm
would provide the 'secret' of vicarious enjoyment for an audience
Dickens described as 'vulnerable spectators, liable to pain and sorrow'. He
posits that the theatre, or at least its comic versions of pantomime and
farce, renders these spectators invulnerable and offers a controlled
experiencing of normally threatening situations. The viewer (or player)

can enact the most dangerous or sombre events, can test out the worst emotions or behaviours, without responsibility for the outcome, without having to sustain the pain or punishment beyond the limits of the play. In the context of self-examination or examination of the past, the metaphor of the play constructs a seemingly protected vantage-point from which to delve into secret places. Through the 'shining transparency', the past can be viewed as an artistic production; it can move and upset its audience, but such emotions can be offset by a more distanced aesthetic response. A villain, well-played, can be applauded; a painful confession can be admired and enjoyed.

Dickens often resorted to this theatrical frame to present emotionally-fraught material, containing the episodes within the production of a 'drama'. When, as narrator, Dickens assumed the role of stage director, he could 'call forth' the 'characters' of his 'drama' from behind a curtain raised or dropped at his direction. Such a threatrical context implies that the 'director' controls the action, that it becomes 'real' or acted out only on his cue and only when the audience is ready. Dickens used this narrative frame when he described his experience at the Blacking Warehouse, in which he suggests that no word has been uttered, that his own parents were 'stricken dumb' on the matter until he momentarily 'raised the curtain' on the scene (Forster, vol. 1, p. 32). He has David Copperfield ask 'permission' to step aside and let the performance of his past go on undisturbed by his intervention (or by his reaction or judgement). The theatrical context allows for a curious dual role, that of powerful director who oversees all things and sets the action in motion, and that of more humble stage-manager who arranges props and curtain calls, but cannot interfere with the characters' behaviour. The role creates an impression of willing observance of past scenes and avoids the narrative responsibility to comment on those scenes. It allows the narrator to maintain control over the performance, while also conveying an illusion of spontaneity, of freedom from the shaping power of the author. The role is both self-effacing – as when David asks permission to 'stand aside, to see the phantoms of those days go by me, accompanying the shadow of myself, in dim procession' (ch. 43, p. 691) – and self-aggrandizing – as when David, Prospero-like, dismisses 'the shadows' (ch. 64, p. 950).

Such a dual role might enable a narrator, as it were, to 'trick' his own repressions and fears, to distance himself sufficiently through the process of production to prevent him from censoring the play. Dickens similarly links theatricality and realism in a letter praising John Forster's biography of Goldsmith for its theatrical power:

> To read the book is to be in the time. It lives again in as fresh and
> lively a manner as if it were presented on an impossibly good stage by
> the very best actors that ever lived, or by the real actors come out of
> their graves on purpose. (22 Apr. 1848, *Letters*, vol. 2, p. 82)

Dickens admits this stage is 'impossibly' good, but praises its theatricality
as enabling us to 'be' in the time. He adds the fancy that the past itself was
theatrical, played by 'real actors' who can be called back for a repeat
performance. Of course, in the same letter, Dickens worries about the
possibilities of dramatic posturing, warning that awareness of being a
biographical subject might 'have made great men extraordinarily false,
and would have set them on always playing a part'. He thus creates a
paradoxical role for theatricality, denouncing the falseness possible when
a person acts in his world, and promoting the 'reality' evoked when that
person acts on stage. By acknowledging, even celebrating its 'illusory'
nature, the theatre prepares the audience to see 'through' it, not to accept
it as a reality in itself. Carefully set apart as a construct – scripted,
managed, performed – the play's isolation from the turmoil of daily life
offers a focused and preserved clarity. Dickens thus creates a performance
of the past that can be 'free from all hurry, nonsense, or confusion,
whatever', that is somehow protected from the 'unceremonious pushing
and hustling' of the external world. Set off thus, the theatre falls into
Dickens's category of experiences that create a 'marked stop in the
whirling wheel of life [that] brings the right perception with it'.[6] This
impossibly good stage seems to provide a way of investigating the past
(or the secrets of an individual) without the risks of self-exposure or
contagion.

Dickens thus implies that the theatrical performance has a special claim
as 'real' experience. In a letter to Mrs Cowden Clarke about the
experience of being in a play, Dickens wistfully remarked about the gap
between the play and his world: 'I begin to think *that* the real world, and
this the sham that goes out with the lights'.[7] Far from being a poor copy
or a removal from 'the real', theatre calls 'the real' forth. Dickens writes
excitedly to Forster, for example, about a 'curious dream' in which he
communicated with the ghost of his dead sister-in-law, Mary Hogarth.
He insists to Forster that he has 'rehearsed' his telling of the dream 'three
or four times over, that I might not unconsciously make it plainer or
stronger afterwards'. He suggests the value of the 'rehearsal' as fixing the
original scene, as enabling him to preserve the force and dimensions of
the dream, to try to retain the vision itself. Yet it is intriguing that he
should feel himself able to convey the 'original reality' of his dream only

after several rehearsals. He writes as if the performance will enable him to side-step the potential interference of his 'unconscious' need to alter or improve the scene. But he does not mention the 'conscious' impact of his rehearsing and dramatizing of the scene, of his translation of it from dream to narrative form. 'It was exactly this,' he claims. 'Free from all hurry, nonsense, or confusion, whatever.' He tells Forster: 'observe that throughout I was as real, animated, and full of passion as Macready' ([30 Sept. 1844]; Pilgrim *Letters*, vol. 4, p. 196). The dream seems authentic to Dickens because it was carefully staged, because he was 'as real' as an actor playing a part.

The metaphor of theatre also mitigates Dickens's ambivalence about the finality of self-expression, its tendency to freeze a person in only one role or posture, in an 'official' portrait or memorial. The play uses a script, but its text can be altered under performance; it eludes, to some extent, the awful finality of the word on a page, which Dickens described ominously in *David Copperfield* as sealing both the event and the text in an 'indelible' conclusion.[8] It can move with lightning ease from the pain of a sorrowful scene to the delights of a new role, another assumption. Dickens praised such alteration of tragic and comic scenes in *Oliver Twist* in a famous passage comparing the changes in melodrama to 'the layers of red and white in a side of streaky bacon':

> Such changes appear absurd; but they are not so unnatural as they would seem at first sight. The transitions in real life from well-spread boards to death-beds, and from mourning weeds to holiday garments, are not a whit less startling; only there, we are busy actors, instead of passive lookers-on, which makes a vast difference.[9]

The passage suggests Dickens's dream of being able to watch himself acting, to obtain a privileged vantage-point from which to observe the turmoil of 'life' without being personally implicated. He valued the involvement of the 'busy actor', but simultaneously desired a position outside that activity.

Dickens's participation in the 1857 productions of Wilkie Collins's play *The Frozen Deep* illuminates this use of theatre as self-concealment and as strategy for self-exhibition.[10] The play is based on the ill-fated expedition to the North Pole of Sir John Franklin that so fascinated Dickens and Victorian periodical readers in the 1850s. Franklin had set out on a third polar expedition and had subsequently disappeared in 1845. Rescue parties had been searching for Franklin since 1848, and in 1854 searchers claimed to have found the remains of his party and also evidence of cannibalism and mutilation. Dickens defended Franklin against the charge of such horrors in a series of articles in *Household Words*, and, as Robert Louis Brannan discusses in detail in his introduction to an edition of *The Frozen Deep*, had identified with Franklin's situation, stressing the unusual and desperate circumstances such a man would have encountered that placed his experiences beyond the understanding of normal, sheltered readers.[11]

The first production of the play was a private, amateur theatrical at Dickens's Tavistock House in January 1857 with Dickens playing the leading role and with other parts played by such friends and family as Mark Lemon, Wilkie Collins, Augustus Egg, Georgina Hogarth, Kate and Mary Dickens. In July 1857 the play was revived as a benefit for the widow of Douglas Jerrold and shown privately for Queen Victoria and then to public audiences at the Gallery of Illustration in London. And in August, the play was performed at Manchester with a somewhat more professional cast, Dickens having replaced his family with such actresses as Maria and Ellen Ternan. It was professionally staged in 1866 with a revised script, and without Dickens in the lead. In the play based on Franklin's experiences, Dickens took on the role of Richard Wardour, a man accused of heinous crimes against social codes. Although the character in the play is wrongly suspected of attempted murder or neglect of a rival in love, not of the more awful crime of cannibalism, Victorian viewers could have supplied the additional horror associated with the topic of northern expeditions and explicitly identified with Dickens. Dickens's prior role as apologist for Franklin in *Household Words* prepared his audience for a complex enactment of a man testing the limits of socially-approved behaviour and warned against a complacent judgement of such struggles.

The prologue Dickens wrote for the play invites the audience to attempt a vicarious exploration of the geographical and psychological extremes of a polar expedition, to journey into a secret and covered realm and observe the hidden depths, not only of the main character but of 'us':

> That the secrets of the vast Profound
> Within us, an exploring hand may sound,
> Testing the region of the ice-bound soul,
> Seeking the passage at its northern pole,
> Soft'ning the horrors of its wintry sleep,
> Melting the surface of that 'Frozen Deep'.[12]

Dickens appropriates for his exploration of a more personal 'vast Profound' the grandeur and danger associated with the expeditions to the

North Pole, playing out the metaphoric implications of the play's arctic landscape, whose 'frozen' surfaces must be 'melted' and 'softened', whose secret regions must be explored and tested. The audience is invited to compare the physical events experienced by the explorers with the more private and psychological events facing those at home. Dickens thus appears to offer his theatrical audience a key to self-revelation, a way of reading him through his theatrical role. Dickens, as Wardour, will stand before them, revealed, intimate, with protective surfaces melted, normally-frozen depths exposed.

The summer before he played in *The Frozen Deep*, Dickens had reluctantly sent Collins an autobiographical sketch he requested, which ended thus: 'This is the first time I ever set down even these particulars, and, glancing them over, I feel like a wild beast in a caravan describing himself in the keeper's absence'.[13]

His image of himself as wild beast, caged to protect the public from his 'free' revelations, made only when the 'keeper' is away, offers a fitting frame for the role of Wardour, the man who is suspected of having broken all bonds, having eluded his keeper and enacted his most shameful desire. The passage also conveys a more sceptical sense of performance, in which the beast *exhibits* his wildness to an invulnerable audience only because he is safely behind the frame of his cage, because his keeper is momentarily absent. Yet if Dickens is wild beast, he is also keeper, promoting certain exhibitions of himself while forestalling others. The beast, like Dickens as actor, exhibits a controlled self; he does not reveal his actual wildness.[14]

The role of Wardour and the image of 'the frozen deep' allowed Dickens to exhibit a controlled form of his restless wildness, to portray a character going 'to that white region where the Lost lie low,/ Wrapp'd in their mantles of eternal snow'. Wardour is a man from whom civilized people shrink, a man suspected of murder, of 'fury and despair' (act I; Brannan, p. 113). Furthermore, Wardour conveys, as one reviewer of the 1857 production wrote: 'A man whose constant attempts to hide the internal storm by slight simulation of good fellowship only renders more conspicuous the vastness of that which he would conceal'.[15] Like Dickens, then, Wardour asks us to see through his artifice; he 'renders conspicuous' a vastness he 'would conceal'. Forced to 'wander, wander, wander — restless, sleepless, homeless' (act III; Brannan, p. 157), he pursues 'the road that no human footsteps have ever trodden, and where no human trace is ever left' (act II; Brannan, p. 141). Wardour's very name, usually spoken to the accompaniment of ominous music in the play, suggests a mixed set of possibilities: a warden and a ward, one who wanders and is full of ardour. Wardour is the man to be watched and guarded against, but also the man who saves others, who can recover the lost from 'the Frozen Deep'.

Dickens's own sense of difference from his culture, his sense of himself as a strange and compelling mystery, must have been aggrandized by his performance of Wardour's role, and further, by his association with the explorer Franklin. His vague sense of 'something wrong' in his way of life is given a compelling solidity and form in Wardour's suffering, and is confirmed by the audience's response. As he wrote to Mrs Richard Watson:

> All last summer I had a transitory satisfaction in rending the very heart out of my body by doing the Richard Wardour part. It was a good thing to have a couple of thousand people all rigid and frozen together, in the palm of one's hand . . . and to see the hardened Carpenters at the sides crying and trembling at it night after night.[16]

Dickens's participation in the play overlapped with two major changes in his life – his decisions to leave his wife Catherine and to begin public reading tours. Both threatened to damage his reputation as a moral institution, and his letters of 1857 are full of defences against potential criticism. The letters move back and forth between exuberant descriptions of his successes as Wardour, grim concern over his domestic crises, and threats that he will do something destructive unless he distracts himself with something like the public reading tours. Next to Wardour's wildness, Dickens's much confessed quality of restlessness and his potential breaches of decorum seem more acceptable, no longer shameful secrets to conceal and hint at as a key to his darker side. What Dickens described at this time to Forster as 'the wayward and unsettled feeling which is part (I suppose) of the tenure on which one holds an imaginative life'[17] seems less aberrant by its contrast with Wardour's much more disreputable straying.

By playing the part of Wardour, Dickens performs both as himself and as a character; he gives up his own past and discourse to take on Wardour's, but his audience can recognize him through the paint and costume as 'the inimitable Boz'. His theatrical practice creates the opportunity for what Mikhail Bakhtin in 'Discourse in the Novel' calls 'double-voiced discourse', in which an author 'utilizes now one language, now another, in order to avoid giving himself up wholly to either of them'. Bakhtin argues that movement away from 'a unitary and singular language . . . open[s] up the possibility of never having to define oneself in language . . . of saying "I am me" in someone else's language, and in my own language, "I am other"'.[18] By positing himself as another person in the performance of the play, Dickens can explore dangerous emotions and desires in front of large audiences. He can display himself on stage in his most devastating posture, but in the disguise of someone else. Forster's comment that Dickens 'seemed to be always the more himself for being somebody else, for continually putting off his personality' (Forster, vol. 2, pp. 399–400), suggests just such a revelation through disguise. Yet Forster's possibility of a 'real' Dickens, 'more himself' in performance than in his own personality, is complicated by the production of such a performed self. Although Dickens can have the character Wardour say 'this *I* is Dickens', as stage-manager, ghost writer, and domineering impresario, he also says, 'this *I* is Wardour'. He thus reveals secrets, but simultaneously controls their revelation. By such combined revelation and concealment, Dickens avoids, in Bakhtin's words, 'giving himself up wholly' to either of the projected selves. He remains elusive, a staged personality. Dickens's enjoyment of the doubling of possibilities presented by the play emerges in his satisfaction over being able to turn down Queen Victoria's request for an audience after the play. 'I sent my duty in reply,' he wrote delightedly to Forster, 'but again hoped her Majesty would have the kindness to excuse my presenting myself in a costume and appearance that were not my own.' (5 July 1857; *Letters*, vol. 2, p. 859). He wrote a similar letter to Daniel Maclise: 'The Queen was undoubtedly wonderfully taken. I had a letter on Sunday, of the most unofficial and uncourtly character. She sent for me after the Play, but I beg to be excused from presenting myself in any dress but my own.' (8 July 1857; *Letters*, vol. 2, p. 859). Having won the honour of such intimacy through his presentation of himself as Wardour, Dickens then insists on his own identity (and social power) by calling attention to the artifice.

By distancing himself from the scene of Wardour's passion and self-revelation, limiting it as the experience of a 'costume and appearance that were not my own', Dickens retreats to another theatrical persona, the absolutely imperturbable impresario, who could handle all disturbance with aplomb, remain unfazed and apart despite the electricity of the production and performance. In a letter to Macready, Dickens bragged he was:

> Calm amidst the wreck, your aged friend glides away on the Dorrit stream, forgetting the uproar for a stretch of hours, refreshing himself with a ten or twelve miles' walk, pitches headforemost into foaming rehearsals, placidly emerges for editorial purposes, smokes over buckets of distemper with Mr. Stanfield aforesaid, again calmly floats upon the Dorrit waters.[19]

The producer maintains a disinterested calm, but it comes from knowing that every detail has been anticipated. As Brannan has described, Dickens insisted on direct control of the physical details of the production, writing lengthy letters to the participants about costume, sets, and props.[20] A letter to Forster about the set construction is characteristic: 'I have arranged to do it in my own way, and with my own carpenter'.[21]

But Dickens's interest in control was not limited to physical details. The previous autumn, he had declined to chair a concert committee, 'in reference to an entertainment over the arrangement of which I have no power'.[22] Similarly, he warded off a possible staging of his 1857 Christmas story unless it were done to his instruction.[23] He insisted to Bulwer-Lytton about an 1851 production that only he could play a role properly:

> But – I speak quite frankly, knowing you will not mistake me – I know
> from experience that we could find nobody to hold the play together
> . . . if I didn't do it. I think I could touch the gallant, generous, careless
> pretence, with the real man at the bottom, so as to take the audience
> with him from the first scene.[24]

The production of *The Frozen Deep* provided the opportunity for almost unlimited influence. Dickens turned the technical issues of producing a play into an opportunity for more extensive social control. He revelled in supervising the 'young people' who were to appear in the play, and commented to several correspondents (including two ministers) about the value of such 'supervised play' as a 'wonderful discipline'. His children were subjected to a 'fearful drill under their rugged parent'; 'it not only unites us in a pleasant amusement,' explained Dickens to Revd Whitwell Elwin, 'but is a wonderful discipline in punctuality, perseverance and ingenuity'.[25] In a letter to Sir James Tennent, Dickens established himself even more firmly as moral guide, describing the play as 'a remarkable lesson to my young people in patience, perseverance, punctuality, and order; and, best of all, in that kind of humility which is got from the earnest knowledge that whatever the right hand finds to do must be done with the heart in it, and in a desperate earnest'.[26] Dickens presented himself, then, as both the absorbed actor, losing himself and exposing himself in an impassioned display, *and* the distanced producer, watching the turmoil with an amused serenity, arranging for the disciplining of others. Dickens does not acknowledge that such discipline and order was for him as well as for the 'young people'; he displaces the necessity for social control onto his children and his character, leaving himself in the position of stage-manager, parent, serene overseer of the chaotic play. The doubling enables him both to risk going beyond all social barriers and to stay comfortably in charge of the mechanics of social production. It affords the illusion of invincibility, a sense that every frontier can be tried without giving up any control.

Dickens's descriptions of the pleasure the play afforded him suggest the value of such doubled experience. In his letter to Sir James Tennent (9 Jan. 1857), he wrote:

> As to the play itself; when it is made as good as my care can make it, I derive a strange feeling out of it, like writing a book in company; a satisfaction of a most singular kind, which has no exact parallel in my life; a something that I suppose to belong to a labourer in art alone, and which has to me a conviction of its being actual truth without its pain that I never could adequately state if I were to try never so hard. (*Letters*, vol. 2, p. 825)

He repeated the analysis a few months later to Daniel Maclise (8 July 1857; *Letters*, vol. 2, p. 859), adding 'I could blow off my superfluous fierceness in nothing so curious to me'. The play provided Dickens with a forum for strange and satisfying performance, for 'actual truth without its pain'; it allowed him to 'blow off' his 'fierceness in nothing so curious to me', to pursue an ordinarily private act (writing a book) in 'company', to reveal what usually remained hidden in an approved public forum. He ascribed to the excitement of performing a renewed creativity as a writer, claiming the response of the audience, 'the crying of two thousand people over the grave of Richard Wardour', enabled him to think up new ideas for a story.[27] It gave Dickens the illusion of accomplishing something 'complete', a claim he repeated in several letters describing the performance.[28] It offered him that opportunity, though, because he set the stage for his own performance.

The response of the critics focused on the sketchiness of the play itself, as well as of the play form, which enabled Dickens to infuse the part with what seemed his own energy and creativity, so that the part was both not him and was his 'true self' shining through the artificial and unconvincing, empty role. To the reviewers of the play, Dickens's performance seemed 'true', 'natural', not because he made them forget the illusion of theatre and think they were seeing Wardour, but because they felt they were seeing Dickens himself, through the disguised and assumed role. His own personality overwhelmed the sketchy character of Wardour. 'It seems to convey more than the expression of the situations can account for,' wrote the *Saturday Review*, 'and yet is free from exaggeration; it is a work of art, but the art is concealed; it is the studied embodiment of a conception, and yet appears the simple exhibition of a real character.'[29] Note the mixture of terms in this review: the performance goes beyond, yet does not exaggerate; it is studied, yet appears simple and real.

The 'truth' and 'naturalness' of the performance were, of course, produced by the apparatus of the theatre. The apparent revelation of a 'natural' self is a theatrical illusion. Dickens ruled his stage with a despotic hand, while maintaining his behind-the-scenes invisibility and his on-stage vulnerability. He got to act as if he could do nothing but perform a role he had been thrust into, yet he was his own director. A conversation Henry Merivale reported having with Dickens a few days before his death is revealing about the pleasure such indirect control provided for him. Dickens is supposed to have said:

> 'What do you think would be the realization of one of my most cherished day-dreams? . . . To hold supreme authority in the direction of a great theatre, with a skilled and noble company. The pieces should be dealt with according to my pleasure, and touched up here and there in obedience to my own judgement; the players as well as the plays being absolutely under my command. That, *that's* my day-dream.'[30]

Dickens's day-dream of controlling a grand theatre remained a dream, in more ways than merely the physical. The illusion of escape and order that the experience of the play afforded could not be sustained once the stage lights dimmed. His sense of having produced something 'complete' did not last once the production was over. In an exuberant moment during his tour with Wilkie Collins after the August performances, he described himself in a letter to Forster as an actor behaving 'melo-dramatically (Wardour to the life!)' (9 Sept. 1857; *Letters*, vol. 2, p. 880). But the satisfaction of the more earnest aspects of the role did not continue once he was 'recalled' to himself.

Dickens frequently evoked the depression he fell into after the theatrical experience ended and he was forced to abandon the roles in which he had exulted and tried to lose himself. In a letter to Collins (2 Aug. 1857), he described 'the grim despair and restlessness of this subsidence from excitement'; 'I want to escape from myself. For when I *do* start up and stare myself seedily in the face, as happens to be my case at present, my blankness is inconceivable – indescribable – my misery amazing.' (*Letters*, vol. 2, p. 873). 'I am horribly used up after [the production],' he wrote to Henry Austin (2 Sept. 1857). 'Low spirits, low pulse, low voice, intense reaction.' (*Letters*, vol. 2, p. 875). It is telling of Dickens's self-absorption that he would regard such post-production let-down, which is, after all, fairly common to actors, as special to him, as significant of some more eccentric disorder. Dickens's disappointment suggests he had hoped that the transformations of the stage would endure, that his theatre of self-knowledge could survive in the 'unceremonious pushing and hustling' of the world outside the play. The experience of acting came to represent an oasis of control in the midst of the turbulent problems Dickens faced in 1857–58. He wrote to Collins: 'The domestic unhappiness remains so strong upon me that I can't write, and (waking) can't rest, one minute. I have never known a moment's peace or content, since the last night of The Frozen Deep.'[31]

In *The History of Sexuality*, Michel Foucault argues that, in confession, the individual 'was authenticated by the discourse of truth he was able or obliged to pronounce concerning himself'.[32] That discourse involves 'the infinite task of extracting from the depths of oneself, in between the words, a truth which the very form of confession holds out like a shimmering mirage' (p. 59). Foucault shows that the confessed 'truth' is produced only in and through a highly ritualized practice. The 'authentic' confession of self does not emerge naturally, because of an individual's will or desire, but as a result of an elaborate apparatus that stages the scene in which truth may appear. Similarly, the spontaneity Dickens valued in his theatre of self-knowledge emerges because of producers, directors, scripts, and rules, over which Dickens exercised careful control. What seems to be a natural, authentic, and privileged insight into the self is called forth by an energetic direction that imposes its own forms of 'truth', although the production can never be finally controlled or complete, can never achieve its concealed ends. In his repeated uses, both actual and metaphoric, of the theatre, Dickens treated the drama as 'a shining transparency', as an illusion or disguise that would be seen through in order to catch a glimpse of the 'real actor'. But his 'shining transparency' is also a 'shimmering mirage', and his 'actual truth' must remain vulnerable to control, repression, or concealment – to art. As with the other frames for self-knowledge that Dickens explored – diary, letters, autobiography, portraiture, fiction – the theatre metaphor cannot ultimately be accorded a protected site. Its value lies, rather, in its emphasis on the artistry and artfulness of projects of self-knowledge, and on the recognition that the beast and the keeper, the actor and the impresario, are played by the same person.

Notes

1. *David Copperfield*, Trevor Blount (ed.) (Harmondsworth: Penguin, 1966) ch. 19, pp. 344–45.

2. Dickens wrote to Forster about the similarities between the two novels, adding: 'To be quite sure I had fallen into no unconscious repetitions, I read *David Copperfield* the other day'. Quoted by John Forster, in A. J. Hoppé (ed.), *The Life of Charles Dickens*, 2 vols (London: J. M. Dent; and New York: E. P. Dutton, 1966) p. 285.

3. Pip says: 'What stung me, was the identification of the whole affair with my unoffending self', *Great Expectations*, Angus Calder (ed.) (Harmondsworth: Penguin, 1965) ch. 15, p. 145. What this identification masks is the more immediate identification of Pip with Orlick.

4. 5 Jan. 1851, in Walter Dexter (ed.), *The Letters of Charles Dickens* (London: Nonesuch Press, 1937–38) vol. 2, p. 626 (hereafter referred to as *Letters*). Forster quotes this passage as a key to Dickens's personality (vol. 2, p. 400).

5. Charles Dickens, with W. H. Wills, 'A Curious Dance Round a Curious Tree', 17 Jan. 1852, in Harry Stone (ed.), *Charles Dickens' Uncollected Writings from Household Words, 1850–1859* (Bloomington: Indiana University Press, 1968) vol. 2, pp. 383–84. As Stone mentions (vol. 2, p. 381), Dickens liked this notion enough to rework it later that year in 'Lying Awake' (*Household Words*, 30 Oct. 1852) to describe the pleasure of the Christmas Pantomime: 'the secret of this enjoyment lies in the temporary superiority to the common hazards and mischances of life; in seeing casualties, attended when they really occur with bodily and mental suffering, tears, and poverty, happen through a very rough sort of poetry without the least harm being done to any one – the pretense of distress in a pantomime being so broadly humorous as to be no pretense at all' (Deborah A. Thomas (ed.), *Selected Short Fiction* (London: Penguin, 1976) p. 164).

6. In *Little Dorrit* (1855–57) this stop is ascribed to 'sickness . . . sorrow . . . the loss of the dearly loved', and is 'one of the most frequent uses of adversity' (John Holloway (ed.) (Harmondsworth: Penguin, 1967) bk 2, ch. 27, p. 787).

7. 21 Aug. 1859, in Madeline House, Graham Storey and Kathleen Tillotson (eds), *The Letters of Charles Dickens: The Pilgrim Edition* (Oxford: Clarendon Press, 1965) vol. 3, p. 117. This edition is hereafter referred to as *Pilgrim Letters*.

8. The 'indelible' event in David's memory is of the storm that kills Ham and Steerforth (ch. 55, p. 854).

9. 1837–39; *Oliver Twist*, Peter Fairclough (ed.) (Harmondsworth: Penguin, 1966) ch. 17, pp. 168–69.

10. For a historical and critical account of Dickens's involvement in the production and the authoritative edition of the play edited from the manuscript in the Pierpont Morgan Library, New York, see Robert Louis Brannan (ed.), *Under the Management of Mr Charles Dickens: His Production of 'The Frozen Deep'* (Ithaca: Cornell University Press, 1966). 'The Dickens Theatre' and SOMA Theatre of the University of Texas at Austin produced a revival of the play (directed by Alan McKendree, Utopia Theatre, University of Texas, 23 Jan. – 8 Feb. 1986) based on Brannan's edited text.

11. Brannan argues that Franklin served as a model for a new kind of hero for Dickens's fiction, a hero who would overcome 'severe inner trials' that might even be offensive or shocking to the audience (pp. 12–20). He credits the imaginative association with Franklin with allowing Dickens to create such 'negative heroes' as Sydney Carton, Pip, and Eugene Wrayburn (p. 88).

12. In the Tavistock House production of the play, John Forster delivered this prologue, but Dickens assumed the role of introducer along with his starring role for the more public performances that followed. See Brannan, p. 98.

13. 6 June 1856; *Letters*, vol. 2, p. 778.

14. For further discussion of Dickens's metaphor of himself as 'wild beast', see Jean Ferguson Carr, 'Dickens and Autobiography: A Wild Beast and His Keeper', *English Literary History*, vol. 52 (1985) pp. 447–69.

15. John Oxenford, The *Times*, 13 July 1857; quoted in Brannan, p. 82. Walt Whitman's response to Dickens's 1858 announcement in *Household Words* of his marital troubles suggests the degree to which Dickens was perceived as represented by his fictions, his various public personae. Whitman describes the surprise of finding that the author of *David Copperfield* could have written about David's final 'domestic bliss' while himself miserable at home. He comments on the strangeness of having 'the veil of sacred privacy . . . rudely swept away, and the "skeleton in the closet" . . . remorselessly exposed' ('The Private Lives of Great Men', Brooklyn *Daily Times*, 23 June 1858; rpt. in Emory Holloway (ed.), *The Uncollected Poetry and Prose of Walt Whitman* (New York: Peter Smith, 1932) vol. 2, pp. 18–19). Whitman's comment shows the kind of constraints Dickens was under to conceal or temper his 'dark' desires, or to reveal them in contorted and disguised ways.

16. 7 Dec. 1857; quoted in Brannan, p. 72. Edgar Johnson, in *Charles Dickens: His Tragedy and Triumph* (New York: Simon & Schuster, 1952), quotes Dickens's claim that he 'tore himself to pieces' performing Wardour (letter to Mrs Brown, 28 Aug. 1857, Morgan Library MS.), then comments: 'yet felt a kind of agitated relief in projecting and symbolizing an emotion not unlike his own' (vol. 2, p. 904).

17. 5 Sept. 1857; *Letters*, vol. 2, p. 877.

18. Mikhail M. Bakhtin, *The Dialogic Imagination: Four Essays*, Michael Holquist (ed.) and Caryl Emerson and Michael Holquist (trs) (Austin and London: University of Texas Press, 1981) p. 315.

19. 13 Dec. 1856; *Letters*, vol. 2, p. 815.

20. See the letters to John Thompson, 13 Aug. 1857, *Letters*, vol. 2, p. 870, and to Frank Stone, 17 Aug. 1857, *Letters*, vol. 2, p. 870. See also Brannan's discussion of Dickens's attention to details of production (pp. 50–58).

21. 18 Oct. 1856; *Letters*, vol. 2, p. 807.

22. Letter to J. Molyneux, 8 Sept. 1856; *Letters*, vol. 2, p. 798.

23. The letter to Benjamin Webster shows the various levels of control Dickens attempted to retain over his artistic productions: 'Now, I don't want it done upon the stage at all: because I never do want to see any composition there which is not intended for it. Nevertheless, I can't help its being done; and, done at all, should like it done well' (24 Nov. 1857; *Letters*, vol. 2, p. 894). Having denied his interest he then goes on to describe exactly how it could be staged and offers proofs within ten days ('It would be a three-act piece . . . ').

24. Letter to Bulwer-Lytton, 5 Jan. 1851; *Letters*, vol. 2, p. 262. The play in question was Bulwer's *Not so Bad as We Seem*.

25. 17 Oct. 1856; *Letters*, vol. 2, p. 807.

26. 9 Jan. 1857; *Letters*, vol. 2, p. 825. Versions of this comment appear also in a letter to Revd Edward Taggart, 20 Jan. 1857; *Letters*, vol. 2, p. 829.

27. Letter to Miss Coutts, 5 Sept. 1857; *Letters*, vol. 2, p. 876.

28. He wrote, for example, in a letter to Mrs Watson, 16 Jan. 1857: 'I believe that nothing so complete will ever be done again' (*Letters*, vol. 2, p. 826). The comment recurs in letters to W. F. DeCerjat, [19] Jan. 1857, and 16 Feb. 1857, and to Revd James White, 8 Feb. 1857 (*Letters*, vol. 2, pp. 827, 836 and 834).

29. 1 Aug. 1857; quoted in Brannan, p. 80.

30. Quoted in Johnson, *Charles Dickens*, vol. 2, p. 1151.

31. In this letter of 21 Mar. 1858, Dickens then suggested the 'turning notion' that doing public readings would provide 'another means of bearing it' (*Letters*, vol. 3, p. 14).

32. *The History of Sexuality, Vol. 1: An Introduction*, Robert Hurley (trs.) (New York: Random House, 1978) p. 58.

4

Pecksniff and Pratfalls

Coral Lansbury

If there is a chastening thought for academic scholars it must surely be this: Dickens is flourishing out there in the real world without any help from literary critics. Ebenezer Scrooge has long been the best friend of every advertising agent who appreciates how Dickens taught people to celebrate Christmas in the proper commercial spirit: buy the biggest and the best and do not waste time attending church when you could be more profitably employed shopping. Television and Broadway ransack Dickens's novels that seem to have been written with more than a sideways glance at the stage and screen. Dickens can be deconstructed and demythologised, he can be interpreted by Freud or Lacan, but no one can deny his popularity. Dickens does not have to be discovered. So if there is one aspect of Dickens that merits praise, it is his vulgarity: the quality that literary scholars must accept and share with advertising agents, theatrical producers and ordinary people everywhere. Some of his contemporaries regarded him as an uncultivated crowd-pleaser and spoke of him in the same terms as Pimlico and Reynolds, but even they could not deny that Dickens's vulgarity was capable of invoking moods and emotions that evaded and surpassed the calculating intellect.

Today a number of critics, including Ada Nisbet, Edwin Eigner, Paul Schlicke and A. L. Zambrano, have been looking at the pantomime and penny gaffs and the way they helped to shape Dickens's plots and characters. We know, of course, that the type of theatrical performance most people saw in Dickens's day was burlesque and parody, and what you could expect to find on the same stage was a tumbling succession of acts from performing dogs to musical Shakespeare.[1] The patent theatres had a monopoly of Shakespeare so *Hamlet* was played in the unlicensed houses as 'Methinks I see my Father', *Romeo and Juliet* as 'How to Die for Love', and *Othello* as 'Is He Jealous?'.[2] When he was twenty-one Dickens wrote his own Irish version of the latter entitled 'The O'Thello'.[3]

The powers of pantomime are still imperfectly understood, particularly its capacity to impose magical changes upon rational order: a flash of light and a rush of music, and a country scene becomes a fairy palace with Avaro – the miserly father – rolling across the stage, as Pantaloon is pursued by a Clown who seconds ago was 'Squire Bugle. Transformation lies at the heart of pantomime and when the stage and all the characters are changed 'in a moment, in the twinkling of an eye', it is a joyful prefiguration of that moment of terrible and divine mystery foretold in *Revelation* when the last trump will sound and 'we shall all be changed'. For people who were obsessed with 'the life beyond', and the 'moment of extinction', transformation scenes were a secular and consoling rendition of that final day of judgement when all will be changed as the gates of heaven open for the saved and hell gapes for the damned. Percy Fitzgerald recalls for us the nature of a pantomime transformation:

> All will recall in some elaborate transformation scene how quietly and gradually it is evolved. First the 'gauzes' lift slowly one behind the other – perhaps the most pleasing of all scenic effects – giving glimpses of 'The Realms of Bliss', seen beyond in a tantalising fashion. Then is revealed a kind of half-glorified country, clouds and banks, evidently concealing much. Always a sort of pathetic and at the same time exultant strain rises, and is repeated as the changes go on. Now we hear the faint tinkle – signal to those aloft on 'bridges' to open more glories. Now some of the banks begin to part slowly, showing realms of light, with a few divine beings – fairies – rising slowly here and there. More breaks beyond and fairies rising, with a pyramid of these ladies beginning to mount slowly in the centre. Thus it goes on, the lights streaming on full, in every colour and from every quarter, in the richest effulgence. In some of the more daring efforts, the *'femmes suspendues'* seem to float in the air or rest on the frail support of sprays or branches of trees. While, finally, perhaps, at the back of all, the most glorious paradise of all will open, revealing the pure empyrean itself, and some fair spirit aloft in a cloud among the stars, the apex of all. Then all motion ceases; the work is complete; the fumes of crimson, green, and blue fire begin to rise at the wings; the music bursts into a crash of exultation; and possibly to the general disenchantment, a burly man in a black frock steps out from the side and bows awkwardly. Then to a shrill whistle the first scene of the harlequinade closes in, and shuts out the brilliant vision.[4]

After the transformation scene has altered the stage and the characters, the pantomime relies upon knockabout harlequinade to cut the world down with laughter and impose new and less threatening artistic configurations upon the natural order of society. The music rises to a crescendo, Britannia wobbles up behind a cardboard cloud and reveals her frilly drawers as the trumpet blurts and the violin scrapes off-key. 'Squire Bugle, the rustic tyrant, threatens to bring down rack and ruin upon the young lovers in *Harlequin and Mother Goose*, and suddenly after the transformation scene he is changed into the Clown tripping over Harlequin's magic bat and landing with a gratifying thud on his backside. Of course, this is just the way we meet Pecksniff, who is blown over by a magnificent parodic invocation of romantic verse.[5] Scott's battlements glow in the fading light, Gray's ploughman wends his weary way home, Shelley's wild, west wind plays enchanter to the scared leaves, and Pecksniff, the man of feeling, is bowled over in the twinkling of an eye and left to see stars at the bottom of his own front steps. Is there any character in Dickens's world who is knocked down, or falls down with such frequency as Pecksniff? Tilly Slowboy perhaps, and Pickwick comes close, but Pecksniff surely takes the prize. He is beaten to the floor by the Martin Chuzzlewits, senior and junior, he collapses drunkenly into Mrs Todger's fireplace, and when we first meet him he has just been lifted into the air and left insensible by the west wind.

The Clown, generally Joseph Grimaldi, would often make his entrance in this fashion, spinning and turning, only to fall over Harlequin's bat. 'The spill', which became known as the 'pratfall', was an essential part of the Clown's performance. And the Clown who, as Eigner observes, 'was the only English pantomime figure who did not come directly from the Italian *commedia dell'arte*' was always interpreted differently by the actors who impersonated him.[6] He could be a knockabout buffoon, an amiable bully, or the boisterously sinister rogue of Joseph Grimaldi. One quality every Clown had to possess was an ability to tumble, and Joseph Grimaldi, whose memoirs Dickens edited, was famous for his acrobatic spills which frequently resulted in broken bones and bruises. But every Clown had to learn these acrobatic tricks as part of his repertoire, and the more the Clowns were knocked over the more the audience roared for more. There was such satisfaction in seeing the monstrous villain changed into the Clown who was then tripped up and pushed down by a superior kind of magic. As Dickens recalled:

> What words can describe the deep gloom of the opening scene, where a crafty magician holding a young lady in bondage was discovered, studying an enchanted book to the soft music of a gong! – or in what terms can we express the thrill of ecstasy with which, his magic power opposed by superior art, we beheld the monster himself

converted into Clown! What mattered it that the stage was three yards wide, and four deep? *We* never saw it. We had no eyes, ears, or corporeal senses, but for the pantomime. And when its short career was ran, and the baron previously slaughtered, coming forward with his hand upon his heart, announced that for that favour Mr Richardson returned his most sincere thanks, and the performances would commence again in a quarter of an hour, what jest could equal the effects of the baron's indignation and surprise, when the Clown, unexpectedly peeping out from behind the curtain, requested the audience 'not to believe it, for it was all gammon'! Who but a Clown could have called forth the roar of laughter that succeeded; and what witchery but a Clown's could have caused the junior usher himself to declare aloud, as he shook his sides and smote his knee in a moment of irrepressible joy, that that was the very best thing he had ever heard said![7]

The special quality of Grimaldi's Clown was a combination of trick and atrocity, an engulfing and kenspeckle selfishness that tried to claim everything for himself: Columbine, Harlequin's bat, the gold of Pantaloon and the last words of every performance. There is no excuse made for this gargantuan greed; it is the nature of the Clown to make love to every pretty woman who crosses his path, to steal, and make mischief when he cannot think of anything better to do, for the Clown is the embodiment of selfishness, and surely to say that is to describe the unreformed and unregenerate child. In a novel which is singularly devoid of children, I do not think it is Tom Pinch alone who is the child, but Pecksniff, and perhaps that is the reason why so many readers like Chesterton and Orwell have found him to be the best thing in *Martin Chuzzlewit*. However monstrous, a child is always the mirror of ourselves. Tom and Pecksniff are doubles bound together by Tom's refusal to recognize Pecksniff's real nature and Pecksniff's ability to see his own: it is only when Tom turns upon his other self and denounces him that he is able to grow up and become a man. Understanding and maturity do not come from denying the dark impulses of the spirit, but only by accepting and overcoming them. The child who wants it all and wants it now must learn to temper greed and impatience with more social virtues, but Pecksniff remains unregenerate to the end.

Of course, even old Anthony Chuzzlewit has to admit that Pecksniff can never be seen contriving his hypocrisies, much less admitting to his double dealing. If he chooses to open his front door while warbling a rustic stave, with a garden hat on his head and a spade in his hand, this rustic demeanour may simply be a reversion to the *alter ego* of Grimaldi's

Clown – the rustic yokel, 'Squire Bugle. And the lineage of the Clown stretched back to the country bumpkin who rolled around the circus ring falling over his own feet and everyone else's. Pecksniff is accused of hypocrisy throughout the novel, but he is never seen plotting his deceptions. If there is hypocrisy, it is an attribute so absolute in quality that it becomes the assertion of another moral imperative. When 'Squire Bugle is transformed into the Clown, we are bound by the dictates of magic, not reality as we customarily know it.

Pecksniff never steps forward like a Tartuffe or an Iago to weave the meshes of his guile; Pecksniff, as old Anthony grudgingly and admiringly confesses, does not let his guard down even before his daughters. The comedy of Molière's play is not Tartuffe but the inability of Orgon and his mother to read the signs that are apparent to everyone – and it should not be forgotten that in *Othello* and *Tartuffe* we are seeing actors and all their stage business. Tom Pinch may be excused for not seeing Pecksniff as a rogue, but Tartuffe is the most inept and obvious of scoundrels. The perilous irony of Iago is that we alone are made privy to the workings of his mind, but the source of Pecksniff's hypocrisy is a mystery that baffles his relations and the reader. We are told that Pecksniff is given to meditation over his bedroom fire, but those thoughts and the dreams that follow them are never revealed to us:

> 'And good night to *you*, Mr Pinch,' said Pecksniff. 'And sound sleep to you both. Bless you! Bless you!'
> Invoking this benediction on the heads of his young friends with great fervour, he withdrew to his own room; while they, being tired soon fell asleep. If Martin dreamed at all, some clue to the matter of his visions may possibly be gathered from the after-pages of this history. Those of Thomas Pinch were all of holidays, church organs, and Seraphic Pecksniffs. It was some time before Mr Pecksniff dreamed at all, or even sought his pillow, as he sat for full two hours before the fire in his own chamber, looking at the coals and thinking deeply. But he, too, slept and dreamed at last. Thus in the quiet hours of the night, one house shuts in as many incoherent and incongruous fancies as a madman's head. (Oxford Illustrated Edition, ch. 5)

The reader has the thoughts and even the dreams of Martin and Tom Pinch set out before him, but not those of Mr Pecksniff. When the transformation scene changed the order of the pantomime to the harlequinade, the audience saw only a brilliance of lights and seraphic figures; the machinery and sweating stage-hands were invisible. This is the aesthetic strategy that Dickens engages when he presents Pecksniff to his reading audience. Iago weaves his tangled web before us, Tartuffe mocks us with confessions of his shame, but if the source for Pecksniff's hypocrisy is sought, then I think we should look to the pantomime and to the Clown as unregenerate child and perhaps define that apparent hypocrisy as the quintessential expression of honesty. In a work which draws continually upon modes of parody and Shakespearian reference, Pecksniff, the constant giver of good advice, the parish pump philosopher, may well be rewriting some of Polonius's lines: 'To thine own self be true, and thou canst then be false to everyone.'

It was at this particular time that Dickens's disenchantment with romanticism, both Scottish and American, was confirmed by travel. A trip to Scott's Highlands had just given him wet feet and a cold, and the Liberty Tree of the United States had turned out to be nothing but a thorn-bush. So, in *Martin Chuzzlewit* the order of the pantomime is reversed, the harlequinade precedes the burlesque and the Clown presides over the action. Mercy and Charity are transformed into the comic sisters of burlesque where they are known as Merry and Cherry, but Pecksniff is always himself, the archetypal Clown, lord of language and master of persuasion, who knows apropos of eggs and the world at large that 'there is nothing personal in morality'.

Nobody can defeat Pecksniff in debate, no one discomfit him, not even a middle-aged gentleman at an upstairs window roaring at him to 'Come off the grass'. Like the Clown, the only way to get the better of Pecksniff, and that momentarily, is to beat him down physically. To spare the rod on this particular child is to invite a Pecksniffian foot on your neck. But even when he has felt old Martin Chuzzlewit's stick across his back, and all his plotting has been laid bare, Pecksniff rises up, hand on heart, and forgives his victim: 'If you find yourself approaching to the silent tomb, sir, think of me. If you should wish to have anything inscribed upon your silent tomb, sir, let it be, that I – ah, my remorseful sir! that I – the humble individual who has now the honour of reproaching you, forgave you.' (ch. 52) And with this sublime address he leaves them all in the certain knowledge that it is often more painful to be forgiven than to be punished.

Dickens remembered the Clown peeping out from behind the curtain when the play was over and telling the audience not to believe it, for it was all gammon. And the story of *Martin Chuzzlewit* is not left to the narrator and Tom's remarkable organ, not even to those happy families in a flower-strewn garden. There is another story being told by a 'drunken, squalid, begging-letter-writing man, called Pecksniff', who 'entertains the alehouse company with tales of . . . ingratitude and . . . munificence' (ch. 54). This was always the fate of the author of pantomimes who found that the words of his text as he wrote them were never those delivered from the stage, for the Clown would have taken charge of the performance and rewritten it to suit himself.[8] If Charles Dickens thought he had written a novel called *Martin Chuzzlewit*, he also knew he had a Clown called Pecksniff in the cast of characters, and clowns traditionally appropriated the author's text. Now that is a subtext worth considering: the whole story rewritten by Pecksniff, and it could well be a more entertaining novel than *Martin Chuzzlewit*.

Notes

1. Paul Schlicke, *Dickens and Popular Entertainment* (London: George Allen & Unwin, 1985) pp. 14–33.
2. R. J. Broadhurst, *A History of Pantomime* (New York: Arno Press, 1977) p. 218.
3. A. E. Brookes Cross, 'The Fascination of the Footlights', *Dickensian*, vol. 23 (1927) p. 87.
4. Percy Fitzgerald, *The World behind the Scenes* (London: Chatto & Windus, 1881) pp. 52–53.
5. Coral Lansbury, 'Dickens' Romanticism Domesticated', *Dickens Studies Newsletter* (June 1972) pp. 36–46.
6. Edwin Eigner, 'The Absent Clown in *Great Expectations*', *Dickens Studies Annual*, vol. 12 (1982) p. 121.
7. *Memoirs of Joseph Grimaldi*, edited by 'Boz' (London: G. Routledge, 1854) pp. vi–vii.
8. Michael R. Booth, *Victorian Spectacular Theatre 1850–1910* (London: Routledge & Kegan Paul, 1981) p. 75.

5

The Initiation of David Copperfield the Younger: A Ritual Passage in Three Acts

Carolyn Buckley LaRocque

'I am born.' Thus Dickens opens one of the finest chronicles of liminality and ritual passage recorded in the English-speaking world. These most fictional of all liminal rites, the rites which contrive to transform boy into man through the symbol and artifice of dramatic action, are nowhere more clearly drawn than in Dickens's famous account of the London-to-Dover trek of the young David Copperfield. In the boy's passage from the captivity of a childhood smothered in the clutches of Murdstone and Grinby to the halcyon prospects of an adolescence under the wing of that guardian spirit of birth and family, the androgynous Aunt Betsey, each stage of these perennial rites is brought to life by Dickens with absolute precision.

David Copperfield, like the rest of Dickens's work, has been previously discussed from the point of view of myth, fairy-tale, and archetype; but except for a passing reference in the unfinished dissertation of Lucien Pothet, 'Mythe et tradition populaire dans l'imaginaire dickensien', the presence of ritual has been passed over in silence.[1] This chapter seeks to redress this imbalance by following in the footsteps of Pothet's work and of similar studies already well under way in the field of American fiction, studies ranging from James Cox's 1954 essay, 'Remarks on the Sad Initiation of Huckleberry Finn', to Robert Daly's 1984 paper, 'Liminality and Fiction in Irving, Cooper, Cather, Fitzgerald, and Gardner'.[2]

Like Pothet and the Americans, my work is first indebted to the discussion of ritual literature by such scholars as Mircea Eliade, Victor Turner, René Girard, and Ronald Grimes; and especially to remarks by both Eliade and Turner on the nineteenth-century novel as modern genre of ritual passage.[3] Literary criticism based on the work of these anthropologists, comparatists, and religionists has been largely limited to repeatedly demonstrating the phenomenon of ritual fiction by pointing to the explicit parallels between fictional plot and ritual sequence, and to cultural affinities between literature and rite.[4] This chapter seeks to go beyond these issues to address the neglected questions of the literary crafting and composition of ritual fiction. In Dickens's work these questions lead us to recent studies and creative exercises in ritual drama, studies which have long addressed questions of the ritual community, congregation, and calendar of drama, and which have now advanced to explore the literary and theatrical crafting of ritual drama.[5]

Drawing upon work in the field of ritual drama, this chapter suggests that the ritual vigour of Dickens's art springs not from the mere coupling of liminal subject to liminal art form, nor from the precise and paradigmatic parallels of fictional plot to ritual sequence. While these may faithfully reproduce the sequence and pattern of ritual passage, it is the author's frequent infusion of Victorian stage business into his narration which finally animates these patterns into rites. In outlining the initiatory sequence, this chapter will attempt to demonstrate that Dickens's punctuation of the narrative with dramatic rhythm and measure, with theatrical timing, and with those eccentricities of figure, scene, image, and action characteristic of the Victorian stage, raises his account of liminal passage from record to rite. Tracing the leavening and finally the transformation of narrative by this infusion of Victorian stage business, this reading suggests that Dickens's art approximates rite by way of drama.

Critics and anthropologists are generally agreed on the essential outline and aims of the rites of passage marking the end of childhood; first, to remove the boy from the circle of women and children, and second, to establish him in the community of his fathers.[6] The ritual sequence falls accordingly into three acts: separation from the maternal community, a period of transition and disorientation, and final incorporation into the paternal community. The rites invariably open with the separation, often brutal and even fatal in tone, of the boy from his mother and his childhood home. The separation is immediately followed by the isolation and virtual quarantine of the initiate, now identified as an exile and outcast from his natal community. These two movements lead into the second and most critical phase of the rites: the sojourn of the initiate in the wilderness, a mysterious realm of violence and the numinous, peopled by fearsome and even supernatural beings at whose hands the boy passes through a series of painful and terrifying ordeals, most often consummated in real or symbolic circumcision. The third movement follows the return of the boy to the community and his establishment in the world of his fathers. Here final consummation of the rites is marked as representatives of the fathers and elders bestow a new name, a new wardrobe, and new prospects upon the youth, insignia of his newly-won status within the community.

David Copperfield's passage from childhood to adolescence follows precisely the pattern prescribed for these liminal rites, each phase portrayed in detail in young Davy's progress from the maternal hearth of Blunderstone Rookery to the home of his paternal aunt in Dover. While offering a complete and accurate record of initiatory passage through its selection and arrangement of plot, character, and image, Dickens's narrative is quickened into rite only by the animating force of the theatre, a force leaving its imprint on both the structure and substance of the story. The imprint of the theatre is first discernible in the narrative design, the three acts of ritual initiation each carefully divided into three scenes, a pattern showing that serial and episodic development characteristic of Dickens's work, and the measured and repetitive action characteristic of drama and essential to ritual. While the narrative falls into those rhythms and measures shared by drama and rite, its character, action, and image are animated by a theatrical and ritual stagecraft. Together, theatrical timing and measure, dramatic form and figure quicken the characters and events of the story into the forms and figures of rite.

In the first act, the boy is ritually separated from three mothers, three hearths, and three homes of childhood. The first and most violent separation, from his child-mother Clara, is overshadowed by that tone of fatality and bereavement so characteristic of this phase of the rites.[7] This decisive separation is mandated and enforced with an iron hand by Murdstone, an exemplary figure of that grim and implacable authority of the father ruling the rites, who exiles the boy from home and mother, strictly forbidding any show of maternal affection or tenderness. The child-mother, true to the ritual script, fearfully submits to Murdstone's command but grieves and wastes away. Thus Murdstone effectively destroys both the mother and the maternal hearth of childhood, and it is most fitting that he later stands accused by David's guardian spirit, Aunt Betsey, of the murder of the loving and indulgent mother of the boy's infancy. In the ritual context this is indeed his function, performed with unswerving vigour.

These first scenes of separation, scenes featuring the struggle of hapless innocence and aggrieved maternity with the tyrannical patriarch, show that codification of character peculiar to both melodrama and rite. The figures of both Edward and Jane Murdstone, proctors of the critical rites of separation and quarantine, emerge here as monolithic characters boldly drawn in that monomaniacal style of characterization Victorian theatre shares with rite. Dickens's description of the Murdstones, a description emphasizing the unrelieved severity and angularity of their demeanour, is particularly marked by that repetition, accentuation, and exaggeration of distinctive mannerism and peculiarity, that stylization and distortion of character common to popular stage and ritual arena. In a manner markedly reminiscent of the Victorian stage, these figures are reduced to a single value, often visibly and tangibly represented by a single prominent trait or sign.[8] The characteristic rigidity of the Murdstone posture and attitude, the darkness and severity of their garb and expression, reduce this sombre pair to those singular values suggested by their name, equating the Murdstones with that violence, death, and monolithic authority presiding over the rites.

The hieratic figure of Murdstone, along with that of his sister Jane, officiates throughout the opening rites of passage, drawing the boy into an ever-deepening captivity while separating him in matched stages from mother and home. The quarantine which begins as an initial effort of Murdstone to separate David from Clara explodes into violence. In a scene comically reminiscent of Freud's hypothesis on the origin of ritual, Father Murdstone beats David, and David, biting Father Murdstone in return, is locked up in his nursery.[9] Delivered from the nursery, David passes by Murdstone's order into a yet deeper quarantine among the community of his peers, fellow initiands, at Salem House.[10] Handed over to the authorities of Salem House, the boy is immediately harnessed with a placard reading, 'Take care of him. He bites.' (*David Copperfield*, ch. 5, p. 67)[11]; and he submits to the quarantine of a mad dog.[12] This phase of the rites ends formally only with the death of Davy's mother, followed by the death of his infant brother, surrogate of the initiand himself. As David himself tells us: 'The mother who lay in the grave, was the mother of my infancy; the little creature in her arms was myself, as I had once been, hushed for ever on her bosom' (ch. 9, p. 109).

The theme and rhythm of these first scenes of separation and captivity are echoed in the second set, as Davy's loss of his child-mother Clara is followed hard by his loss of her rough-and-ready surrogate, the faithful and buxom Peggotty. Mother and guardian of the later phases of Davy's childhood, Peggotty succeeds Clara Copperfield, whose role as the mother of infancy, earlier defined by the traditional stage business of dancing, singing, fainting, and weeping, is irrevocably fixed in a distinctly theatrical farewell tableau:

> I looked out, and she stood at the garden-gate alone, holding her baby up in her arms for me to see. It was cold, still weather; and not a hair of

her head, nor a fold of her dress, was stirred, as she looked intently at me, holding up her child.

    So I lost her. So I saw her afterwards, in my sleep at school – a silent presence near my bed – looking at me with the same intent face – holding up her baby in her arms. (ch. 8, p. 100)

Sharing a Christian name with her predecessor, Clara Peggotty is similarly reduced to a singularly maternal role, here visibly and even tangibly represented. This hearty Peggotty, her buttons forever bursting in gargantuan hugs, embodies the strength and vitality, the earthy qualities, which the image of the frail child-mother lacked. Her tie with the boy endures longer, but she too is finally cut from him by Murdstone as the boy is thrust into the final and deepest captivity of the opening rites, sold into perpetual bondage to the firm of Murdstone and Grinby.

    Bound to the grim precincts of the firm, the third and final scene of separation and quarantine is acted out, as the desperate initiate attaches himself to two very curious parental figures, comic surrogates for the nurturing figures of childhood. In the Micawber family we find a ritual reversal, a comic interlude sometimes found within the rites, with the benign, but irresponsible Micawbers leaning heavily on young Davy for financial and moral support. Mr Micawber, like his counterpart Mr Dick, stationed at the opposite end of the Dover Road, is a caricature, even a grotesque of the initiand poised on the brink of passage: half-child, half-man, frozen in the transitional state. Loosely drawn in the traditions of Victorian comedy and farce, the portrait of Micawber, along with that of his counterpart Mr Dick, is marked by that repetition and exaggeration of comic peculiarity, that singular distortion of character which Victorian farce shares with rite. Stylized to the point of caricature, Micawber and Dick stand as figures of warning to the initiate, totems posted boldly at either end of his passage, exemplifying the dangers of perpetual childhood. In keeping with his role, we find Micawber repeatedly warning David, whose feet now rest on the threshold of the transitional world, against following in his own sad footsteps, ending up a fugitive at odds with all the world, unfit for the duties and responsibilities of manhood and perpetually subject to the attentions of the local bailiff and the reproaches of his family.

    Mrs Micawber, like her husband, reverses the traditional parental and filial roles. Like Clara and Peggotty before her, she is clearly drawn as a mother, the vision of Peggotty's ample bodice forever bursting its buttons fading into the vision of Mrs Micawber's perpetually unlaced bodice, forever nursing the twins. Beyond the purely physical resemblance, Mrs Micawber emerges as a yet more comic figure, the most pathetic of surrogates. Leaning heavily on young Davy, she continually shares with the child the burdens, worries, and responsibilities of the distressed family, while obliquely but continually complaining of the shortcomings of her child-husband Micawber. The perpetually hysterical, perpetually nursing Mrs Micawber shows the image of the mother as she must now appear to the initiate, her old powers of nurture and protection dissipated in hysteria and comedy. Convinced now of the utter bankruptcy, both literal and figurative, of the old support system of childhood, the initiate is emotionally and mentally ready to begin his passage. With the departure of these poor surrogates, the boy resolves to attempt the passage to Dover, to seek acceptance and position in the kinship system which had excluded him at birth and so pointedly denied his manhood, to join the kindred of his father's family.

As David steps forth into the next and most critical phase of the rites, the transition and sojourn in the wilderness, he first encounters the donkey-boy, an anonymous figure paired with another at the end of the Dover road, together guarding, like Micawber and Dick, the portals of the transitional realm. While Micawber and Dick are posted as totems of the child-man, that anomaly at the heart of the rites, the teenage donkey-boys of London and Dover stand as totems of adolescence itself, typifying its salient attributes of lawlessness, aggression, and alienation. In keeping with his role, the donkey-boy of London strips David of his box and money, terrorizing and bullying the initiate, calling out all the while, 'Come to the pollis!' (ch. 12, p. 143). This brutal scene of departure offers, in microcosm, the very essence of the transitional rites, where the initiate, already stripped of family, of home, and of status, is stripped of his remaining possessions and identity, and forced into submission to the governing authorities of the rites, obliquely represented here in the donkey-boy's threats of the 'pollis'.

The unwelcome offices of the donkey-boy reduce David to the essential state required by the transitional rites. In the boy's first steps upon the road to Dover, sobbing, robbed of all his worldly goods but the clothes on his back, the memory of his birth, that most essential of states, returns, linking his flight down the Dover Road to that notion of birth and rebirth so fundamental to the rites:

> I left the young man to go where he would with my box and money; and panting and crying, but never stopping, faced about for Greenwich, which I had understood was on the Dover Road: taking very little more out of the world, towards the retreat of my aunt, Miss

Betsey, than I had brought into it, on the night when my arrival gave
her so much umbrage. (ch. 12, p. 143)

The rites of transition now opening, like the rites of separation before
them, fall into three distinct scenes, each introducing new characters while
repeating the same action and theme. Moving towards the climax of the
rites, the circumcision, we find three scenes of steadily escalating violence
and terror, as David is stripped down to his breeches by a trio of vicious
and numinous characters. These central rites of passage, marked by an
acceleration of tempo, an escalation of conflict, and an explosion of
violence suggestive of climactic stage business in contemporary theatre,
are particularly distinguished by that marked and explicit transformation
of reality common to both drama and rite. Person, place, and time,
transformed in the terms of contemporary melodrama, here achieve a
ritual intensity. Shopkeepers and tradesmen emerge as villains, thugs, and
madmen. Their shops are transformed into places of torture and
execution. Day and night alike become a span of trial and ordeal for the
bewildered initiand. These metamorphoses, conceived and conveyed in
the terms of contemporary stagecraft, detail the initiate's sojourn in the
wilderness, the realm of violence and the sacred, where the boy is
subjected to a series of ordeals at the hands of strange, and even
supernatural figures.[13]

The first such transformation is the most explicit, its metamorphosis
detailed in David's approach to Mr Dolloby, first of those fearsome
figures ranged along the Dover Road, who terrorizes the boy as he strips
him of his waistcoat. While Dolloby, dealer in rags and clothing, is an
exceedingly mild figure compared to those further down the Dover Road,
in the mind's eye of the initiate he is transformed into a figure of violence
and terror, a kind of gleeful hangman, enthroned among the trophies of
his trade:

> The master of this shop was sitting at the door in his shirt-sleeves,
> smoking; and as there were a great many coats and pairs of trousers
> dangling from the low ceiling, and only two feeble candles burning
> inside to show what they were, I fancied that he looked like a man of a
> revengeful disposition, who had hung all his enemies, and was
> enjoying himself. (ch. 13, p. 144)

The pervasive mood of terror and the threat of violence escalate as
David advances towards the second of the men stationed along his path.
The 'Goroo-man', a horrific figure of the decrepit and devouring father,

here confronts the initiate, stripping him of his jacket, while repeatedly and ritually threatening dismemberment.[14] As David moves towards this figure, Dickens narrows and intensifies the ritual field, literally marching the boy with troop and drum into the clutches of the 'Goroo-man': 'Very stiff and sore of foot I was in the morning and quite dazed by the beating of drums and marching of troops which seemed to hem me in on every side when I went down towards the long narrow street' (ch. 13, p. 146). The initiate is virtually walking the gauntlet at this point, stepping to the drums of the rites.

The narrator describes David's encounter with the 'Goroo-man' as a descent into darkness, a fearful entry into the lair of a wild beast, a common motif of the transitional rites.[15] The 'Goroo-man's' shop emerges here as a subterranean realm, a wilderness of decay, opening onto the prospect of nature run riot. Standing in the midst of that grim prospect is the figure of the donkey, totem of the transitional realm:[16]

> Into this shop, which was low and small, and which was darkened rather than lighted by a little window, overhung with clothes, and was descended into by some steps, I went with a palpitating heart; which was not relieved when an ugly old man, with the lower part of his face all covered with a stubbly grey beard, rushed out of a dirty den behind it, and seized me by the hair of my head. He was a dreadful old man to look at, in a filthy flannel waistcoat, and smelling terribly of rum. His bedstead, covered with a tumbled and ragged piece of patchwork, was in the den he had come from, where another little window showed a prospect of more stinging-nettles and a lame donkey. (ch. 13, p. 147)

The 'Goroo-man' appears at the very centre of the journey, leaping forth from the darkness at the very heart of that mythical realm. Here theatrical and ritual convention meet as the stylization and distortion of character typical of contemporary theatre merges with that fixity and transcendence of character essential to ritual. Emerging against the backdrop of the donkey, totem of the transitional rites, the 'Goroo-man' is himself furnished with the cosmic and animal qualities so often associated with mythical and ritual figures. His hands are likened to the claws of a great bird; his home to a den; his voice to wind, to a rattle, and to a whine. His repeated incantation, 'O Goroo!', interspersed with continual threats of dismemberment, 'O my eyes and limbs!', 'O my lungs and liver!', is uttered with ritual gesture and in ritual cadence, beginning in a 'fierce, monotonous whine' and falling off into 'a kind of rattle in his throat' (ch. 13, pp. 147–48).[17]

'Every time he uttered this ejaculation, his eyes seemed to be in danger of starting out, and every sentence he spoke, he delivered in a sort of tune, always exactly the same, and more like a gust of wind, which begins low, mounts up high, and falls again. . . .' (ch. 13, p. 147)

This scene is complete with all the ritual paraphernalia of transition, all the sounds and symbols customary to the rites, but there is more than the bogeyman at the heart of passage; there is violence as well.[18] Here that violence which began in the nursery battle of Murdstone and David, that violence threatened in David's vision of 'hangman' Dolloby and in the sound of troop and drum marching David into the old 'Goroo-man's' lair, escalates and spreads. The 'Goroo-man' now periodically interrupts his chants to attack David, 'mouthing as if he were going to tear me in pieces' (ch. 13, p. 148), while a crowd of boys gathers outside the shop to pelt and revile the exhausted and half-dressed initiate.

Violence explodes in the last of the three episodes, as David meets the tinker, last of the three figures stationed along the Dover road, who greets the boy with a mortal threat, 'Come here when you're called . . . or I'll rip your young body open' (ch. 13, p. 149). Here raw violence breaks out, blood is spilled, and surrogate figures of mother and son are brutally attacked by the anonymous tinker:[19]

The tinker seized the handkerchief . . . with a roughness that threw me away like a feather, and putting it loosely round his own neck, turned upon the woman with an oath, and knocked her down. I shall never forget seeing her fall backward on the hard road, and lie there with her bonnet tumbled off and her hair all whitened in the dust; nor, when I looked back from a distance, seeing her sitting on the pathway . . . wiping the blood from her face with a corner of her shawl, while he went on ahead. (ch. 13, p. 150)

Passing through this last peril of the road, David must face yet a final figure threatening ritual violence, hers the last and most critical of the ordeals he must sustain. In this character, serving as guardian and proctor of the final stage of passage, theatrical and ritual convention meet again. In Aunt Betsey, as in Murdstone and the 'Goroo-man', those hierarchs of the earlier phases of passage, that stylization, heightening, and distortion of character endemic to popular drama merge with the ascesis of character essential to rite. Like Edward Murdstone, Aunt Betsey first appears to David fixed in the postures and attitudes of inexorable authority, a hieratic figure envisioned sitting in 'awful state' (ch. 13, p. 152).

Emerging in full ritual regalia, the androgyne Aunt Betsey confronts David at the very portals of incorporation, knife in hand, barring his entry:

> There came out of the house a lady with her handkerchief tied over her cap, and a pair of gardening gloves on her hands, wearing a gardening pocket like a toll-man's apron, and carrying a great knife. I knew her immediately to be Miss Betsey, for she came stalking out of the house exactly as my poor mother had so often described her stalking up our garden at Blunderstone Rookery.
>
> 'Go away!' said Miss Betsey, shaking her head, and making a distant chop in the air with her knife. 'Go along! No boys here!' (ch. 13, p. 152)

The advent of Aunt Betsey, guardian of the portals of incorporation and toll-man of the rites, in full costume, chopping the air with her great knife while announcing 'Go along! No boys here!', points to the scene of mock circumcision marking the end of the transitional phase. David's success in sustaining this final trial, ultimately disarming Aunt Betsey and crossing the threshold of the Dover home, marks the formal opening of the final phase of the rites: the incorporation of the youth into the family of his fathers.

Guardian of the portals of incorporation, Betsey Trotwood stands too as guardian spirit of his birth and representative of his paternal kin, whose favour and protection the initiate must win. Like all guardian spirits, she presides over the critical passages in the boy's life, emerging from numinous regions trailing traces of her supernatural and sacred origins.[20] Toll-man of his birth, presiding over the first great passage of David's life, Aunt Betsey, upon hearing the forbidden tidings of the infant's manhood, vanishes as suddenly and miraculously as she had appeared: 'like a discontented fairy; or like one of those supernatural beings whom it was popularly supposed I was entitled to see. . . . Betsey Trotwood Copperfield was for ever in the land of dreams and shadows, the tremendous region whence I had so lately travelled' (ch. 1, p. 17). Now, as David travels once again through this tremendous region of birth and rebirth, Miss Betsey re-emerges from the land of dreams and shadows, preceded by strange rumour:

> I inquired about my aunt among the boatmen first, and received various answers. One said she lived in the South Foreland Light and had singed her whiskers by doing so; another that she was made fast to the great buoy outside the harbour, and could only be visited at half-tide; a third, that she was locked up in Maidstone Jail for child-stealing;

a fourth, that she was seen to mount a broom, in the last high wind, and head for Calais. (ch. 13, p. 150)

Not only this awesome figure, but another and more comic character awaits the initiate as he mounts to the scene of incorporation. Mr Dick, his head protruding from the upper story of the Dover home, his face distorted in a bizarre and enigmatic grimace, is the first sight that David's eye lights upon as he climbs the hill to his aunt's home. As the rites of incorporation proceed, Mr Dick, sheltered and protected by Aunt Betsey in his eternal suspension between childhood and manhood, emerges not only as the totem of incorporation, a figure fixed forever in the last stage of the rites, but as the surrogate of David himself, having been adopted by Aunt Betsey at the time of the boy's birth. Figure of comedy and farce, a genial caricature of the awkward and absurd figure of the child-man, Mr Dick, well along in years, retains the manners and postures of a toddler. Timid and playful, his finger forever popping in his mouth, the childish Mr Dick is, in keeping with his role, ever deferential and obedient to his patron and protector, Miss Betsey.

David, too, as he enters incorporation, takes on the manners and postures of infancy, first collapsing in tears at the feet of his aunt, bewailing his weakness and begging protection and succour. He is immediately bustled inside the house, bathed and swaddled like any new-born, and bundled on the sofa where he is spoon-fed broth and soothed, while the comical Mr Dick pokes his head in and out, winking and grinning. Strategically placed, this comic scenario mimics the traditional forms of ritual incorporation: the initiate becoming again an infant, to be reborn into the family and community as a new man.[21]

That evening David is marshalled to his bedroom 'in some sort like a prisoner, my aunt going in front and Janet bringing up the rear' (ch. 13, p. 158), and the key is turned upon him for the night. While the quarantine leitmotif of the earlier rites continues, other and more hopeful signs appear. The boy's shirt, remnant of his difficult passage, is burned as he mounts the stairs, a conflagration providing the 'only circumstance which gave me any new hope' (ch. 13, p. 158). Locked in the upstairs room, absurdly still swathed in Mr Dick's oversized shirt and trousers, with the relics of his own ragged clothing still heaped beside him on the floor, the boy sees in the blaze a faint promise of the coming extinction of the remnants of the old life and trials, and a harbinger of the final consummation of the rites, an event complete with new wardrobe and other rewards of successful passage.

Like the quarantine, the violence which reigned over the separation and transition continues but is now safely diverted from the initiand in a series of mock battles. David, resting safely now upon Aunt Betsey's divan, is a captive audience to scenes of violence vigorously re-enacted between encroaching donkey-boys and his newly-won patron and protector. In three episodes echoing those of the transition, the last being the most brutal, David, having passed through his own ordeals successfully, now merely observes the ritual violence so recently sustained:

> Jugs of water, and watering-pots, were kept in secret places ready to be discharged on the offending boys; sticks were laid in ambush behind the door, sallies were made at all hours; and incessant war prevailed . . . . there were three alarms before the bath was ready. . . . on the occasion of the last and most desperate of all, I saw my aunt engage, single-handed, with a sandy-headed lad of fifteen, and bump his sandy head against her own gate. (ch. 13, p. 155)

At last the Murdstones themselves, guardians of the old captivity of childhood, attempt the hill on another of the offending donkeys. They are driven off finally and decisively by David's new protector and guardian in a scene marking the successful conclusion of the rites. The rout of the Murdstones by Aunt Betsey accomplished, the boy is awarded new clothing, a new name, new patronage and education to mark his successful passage into manhood. Claimed now by the family of his father, joined in name and affection with his father's sister, he enters a new stage of life filled with promise:[22]

> Thus I began my new life, in a new name, and with everything new about me. Now that the state of doubt was over, I felt, for many days like one in a dream. . . . The two things clearest in my mind were, that a remoteness had come upon the old Blunderstone life – which seemed to lie in the haze of an immeasurable distance; and that a curtain had for ever fallen on my life at Murdstone and Grinbys. No one has ever raised that curtain since. (ch. 14, p. 170)

So ends the first phase in the life of David Trotwood Copperfield. In this ritual narrative, spanning four numbers in the original serial publication, the first three detailing at length the process of separation, the last packed with all the critical episodes of transition and incorporation, Dickens has given us a unified, clear, and concentrated portrait of the initiate and his ordeals. From beginning to end, the narrative offers a classic example of those rites so carefully documented and described by twentieth-century anthropology. Within this chronicle of one boy's passage from childhood to adolescence, the rites of passage stand forth true to form in each detail, each figure, each scene, each symbol, gesture, and act belonging to those rites, fully represented.

Dickens's narrative art closely approximates drama and rite in its crafting and composition. Its tripartite design and climactic crescendo mimic the form and measure of drama and rite, while its character and scene mirror ritual convention and traditional stage business. This chronicle of passage, animated within by those theatrical conventions and techniques shared by drama and rite, is animated outwardly too by that community of place, time, and person shared by ritual and theatre. In its public life Dickens's novel, like those of other mid-Victorians, partakes of the vitality and immediacy of the drama. Dickens's work transcends these in ritual vigour by the sheer density and richness of its ritual and dramatic features, and by the careful crafting of these within a chronicle of liminality and passage.

The customs surrounding the Victorian novel, most notably public and domestic oral reading and stylized dramatization, closely approximate practice and precept in the oral and performing traditions. These customs, along with serial publication, a practice suggesting in its timed release and reception both the regularity and the communal experience of the ritual calendar, together define the Victorian novel as rite and its audience as a ritual congregation.[23] Here the novel becomes, if only for the moment, a ritual arena, equivalent to the village green or city playhouse, a common ground where the great reading public of Victorian England gathers with ritual regularity, awaiting the next event, the next instalment, the next serial. Host to the rites driven from their venerable stamping-grounds by enclosure and railway, the author of narrative fiction becomes for this moment amanuensis to liminality and mythographer to his culture. *David Copperfield* is one of the greatest of these hosts, and its author, Charles Dickens, one of the greatest of the Victorian mythographers.

These dramatic rites are, of course, enacted elsewhere throughout Dickens's work. *Nicholas Nickleby*, *Oliver Twist*, and *Great Expectations* may be read as extended accounts of ritual passage. *David Copperfield* differs from these in the scope and concentration of its ritual narration. Offering within a few chapters a literary paradigm of the rites marking the end of childhood, Dickens has shaped a local model of those rites, relatively free of literary discourses, and most closely reflecting the true time-span and intensity of ritual action, its dense and symmetrical structure marking its affinity with ritual and drama. The three acts of

David Copperfield's passage, each spun into three scenes, describe perhaps the finest moment in the ritual theatre of Dickens's art.

Notes

1. Lucien Pothet, 'Mythe et tradition populaire dans l'imaginaire dickensien', Jean Burgos (ed.), unfinished dissertation at the Sorbonne (Paris: Lettres Modernes, 1979) p. 228.

2. James M. Cox, 'Remarks on the Sad Initiation of Huckleberry Finn', in John B. Vickery (ed.), *Myth and Literature, Contemporary Theory and Practice* (Lincoln: University of Nebraska Press, 1966) pp. 277–88; and Robert Daly, 'Liminality and Fiction in Irving, Cooper, Cather, Fitzgerald, and Gardner', The Critical Legacy of Victor Turner, MLA Convention, Washington, DC, 28 Dec. 1984.

3. Mircea Eliade remarks on the survival of myth and oral tradition within the nineteenth-century novel in *Images and Symbols: Studies in Religious Symbolism*, Philip Mairet (trs.) (New York: Sheed & Ward, Harvill Press, 1961) p. 11; and in *Myth and Reality*, Willard R. Trask (trs.) (New York: Harper & Row, 1963) pp. 190–92. Eliade remarks, too, on the specifically initiatory function and content of the novel and earlier narrative genres in *Birth and Rebirth: The Religious Meanings of Initiation in Human Culture*, Willard R. Trask (trs.) (New York: Harper & Row, 1958) pp. 122, 124–34. Victor Turner includes the novel in his list of the rising ritual genres of the nineteenth century in *From Ritual to Theatre: The Human Seriousness of Play* (New York: Performing Arts Journal Publications, 1982) pp. 85–86.

   For general remarks on the ritual function of literature, see René Girard, *Violence and the Sacred*, Patrick Gregory (trs.) (Baltimore, Md.: Johns Hopkins University Press, 1972); and Ronald Grimes, *Beginnings in Ritual Studies* (Washington, DC: University Press of America, 1982).

4. Works cited in footnotes 1 and 2 above are representative of work in this field.

5. The relatively greater sophistication of these studies is evident in Girard's *Violence and the Sacred*, in Grimes's *Beginnings in Ritual Studies*, and in several of Turner's works such as *From Ritual to Theatre: The Human Seriousness of Play*; and *Dramas, Fields, and Metaphors: Symbolic Action in Human Society* (Ithaca: Cornell University Press, 1974); 'Dramatic Ritual/Ritual Drama: Performance and Reflexive Anthropology', *Kenyon Review*, vol. 1 (1963) pp. 80–93; and 'Liminality and the Performative Genres', Cultural Frames and Reflections: Ritual, Drama, and Spectacle, Burg Wartenstein Symposium no. 76 (New York: Werner Gren Foundation for Anthropological Research, 1977).

6. The ritual reading of the London-to-Dover trek is based primarily on description of these initiation rites in Arnold van Gennep's *The Rites of Passage*, Monica B. Vizedom and Gabrielle L. Caffee (trs) (University of Chicago Press, 1969); in Mircea Eliade's *Birth and Rebirth: The Religious Meanings of Initiation in Human Culture*; in Victor Turner's *The Ritual Process: Structure and Anti-Structure* (Chicago: Aldine Publishing Company, 1969); and in Yehudi Cohen's *The Transition from Childhood to Adolescence: Cross-Cultural Studies of Initiation Ceremonies, Legal Systems, and Incest Taboos* (Chicago: Aldine Publishing

Company, 1964). The paper relies too on remarks by Claude Levi-Strauss in *Totemism*, Rodney Needham (trs.) (Boston, Mass.: Beacon Press, 1963) and by Girard in *Violence and the Sacred*.

7. Eliade comments on the fatal overtones of these separation rites in *Birth and Rebirth* (p. 8).

8. Quoting Ronald Grimes's description of ritual personae, a description equally applicable to the dramatis personae of Victorian drama, the Murdstones 'concretize and display values by means such as clothing, facial gesture, posture, or even objects'. The Murdstones' significance, like that of Grimes's ritual personae, is 'fully resonant in the exteriority – in the skin, demeanour, and style of action' (*Beginnings in Ritual Studies*, p. 58).

9. Sigmund Freud, *Totem and Taboo*, in *The Basic Writings of Sigmund Freud*, A. A. Brill (ed. and trs.) (New York: Random House, 1938) pp. 913–14.

10. The extrusion of males from their mother's home, followed by the co-habitation of the boys in an area set apart, is a feature common to the rituals associated both with age ten and with ages twelve to thirteen, as noted by Cohen, van Gennep, and Eliade (*Birth and Rebirth*).

11. Charles Dickens, *The Personal History, Adventures, Experience, & Observation of David Copperfield the Younger of Blunderstone Rookery*, George H. Ford (ed.) (Boston, Mass.: Houghton Mifflin, 1958). Further citations to the text will be to this edition.

12. 'The individual who is "in passage" is regarded in the same light as a criminal or the victim of an epidemic. . . . Clearly the first measure in such a situation is to isolate the victim, to forbid all contact between him and the healthy members of the community; he must be placed in quarantine . . . kept on the periphery of the community or sometimes even exiled to the forest, jungle, or desert.' Girard, *Violence and the Sacred*, pp. 281–82.

13. 'Liminal entities, such as neophytes in initiation or puberty rites, may be represented as possessing nothing. They may be disguised as monsters, wear only a strip of clothing, or even go naked, to demonstrate that as liminal beings they have no status, property, insignia, secular clothing indicating rank or role, position in a kinship system. . . . Their behavior is normally passive and humble, they must obey their instructors implicitly, and accept arbitrary punishment without complaint.' Turner, *The Ritual Process: Structure and Anti-Structure*, p. 95.

14. 'Masked figures representing gods, ancestors, or chthonic powers may appear to the novices or neophytes in grotesque, monstrous, or beautiful forms.' Turner, *Dramas, Fields, and Metaphors*, p. 239.

15. '. . . the original meaning of underground chamber . . . represents an initiatory ritual. . . . Descending into Hades means to undergo "initiatory death".' Eliade, *Myths, Rites, and Symbols: A Mircea Eliade Reader*, Wendell C. Beane and William C. Doty (eds) (New York: Harper & Row, 1976) vol. 1, p. 182.

16. The role of the donkey, linked during passage with Murdstone, the 'Goroo-Man', and the donkey-boy with his threats of the 'pollis', suggests Freud's identification of the totem with the father (*Totem and Taboo*).

17. '. . . mythical Beings, identified with or manifesting themselves through the bull-roarers, kill, eat, swallow, or burn the novice. . . . these Beings also manifest themselves in animal form or are closely connected with an animal

mythology.' Eliade, *Myths, Rites, and Symbols: A Mircea Eliade Reader*, p. 183.

18. 'Violence will determine the final result. . . . Instead of avoiding the crisis, the neophyte must advance to meet it. . . . Instead of fleeing the most painful and terrifying aspects of reciprocal violence, he must submit to each and every one of them in proper sequence. The postulant must endure hardship, hunger, even torture. . . .' Girard, *Violence and the Sacred*, pp. 282–83.

19. Continued brutality, and even violence, towards the mothers of the community, a belligerence signifying the emphatic dimunition and rejection of female authority, is a common feature of the transitional rites. The scene of David's encounter with the tinker, a scene where female interference is brutally rejected, is followed by the final eclipse of the maternal figure from the boy's heart and mind, an event marking the fulfilment of one of the primary goals of the rites (ch. 13, p. 150).

20. David Copperfield's quest for the patronage and protection of his Aunt Betsey conforms perfectly to the classic pattern described by Claude Levi-Strauss in his study of initiation ritual (*Totemism*, p. 23).

21. Van Gennep and Eliade particularly note the infantile behaviour required of the initiate during incorporation (*The Rites of Passage*, p. 81; *Birth and Rebirth*, p. 31).

22. See Cohen for remarks on the key role awarded the paternal aunt in the education of the initiate (pp. 76–77), and for remarks on the adoption of the initiate by foster-parents living at a distance from the parental home (pp. 171– 72).

23. In the circumstances of its public release and reception, as in the stylization of its character and action, the novel fulfils all the terms of anthropologist Ronald Grimes's definition of evolving ritual form: 'Ritualizing transpires as animated persons enact formative gestures in the face of receptivity during crucial times in founded places' (*Beginnings in Ritual Studies*, p. 55).

6

Lady Dedlock Prostrate: Drama, Melodrama, and Expressionism in Dickens's Floor Scenes

Mary Saunders

Prostitutes, women with illegitimate children, women who are illegitimate children, women who almost engage in adulterous affairs, or who are enmeshed in their own schemes of revenge: such seriously troubled women comprise a large group of Dickens's characters. Many of these, if memorable, are minor figures. There is Annie Strong, for instance, whose fears of violating the trust of her much older husband occupy only a few pages of *David Copperfield*. Or there is the briefly appearing Tattycoram in *Little Dorrit*, who exchanges her subjugation within the Meagles family for virtual imprisonment at the hands of Miss Wade. Some of these women, however, like Nancy in *Oliver Twist* and Lady Dedlock and Esther in *Bleak House*, are at the very heart of the novels in which they appear. These major characters share with their secondary sisters a tendency to manifest their distress in a manner that has proven highly distressing to critics: they fall to the floor, and it is rare when they do so quietly.

Here is Lady Dedlock, after revealing herself to Esther as her mother and after being on her knees for several pages: 'My child, my child! . . . For the last time! These kisses for the last time! These arms upon my neck for the last time! We shall meet no more.'[1] This effusive interlude from chapter 36 is damned by Robert Garis in *The Dickens Theatre* as being the 'nadir of imaginative inventiveness' in *Bleak House*, and Garis is only one of many Dickens readers and critics who have shuddered at those scenes which reveal the novelist's immersion in the melodramatic theatre of his day: his fondness for stunning effects which seemingly belie the complexity of life. In the heyday of melodrama, too, readers were recoiling from Dickensian histrionics. The reviewer in the popular *Bell's New Weekly Messenger* complained about the 'spasmodic aside' from Lady

Dedlock when she goes on her knees in chapter 29 (p. 364) after learning that Esther is her daughter.[2]

Like Dickens's scenes of dying innocents (Little Nell, Paul Dombey, Jo in *Bleak House*) and victorious angels (Nicholas Nickleby pummelling Squeers, Betsey Trotwood defying the Murdstones), the floor scenes *are* stunning effects, undeniable evidence of Dickens's theatrical bent. Unlike the death or justice scenes, however, the floor scenes involve women only (that is, only women fall; male characters may watch) until the sufferings of Bradley Headstone in *Our Mutual Friend*, when, late in the novel, he is rejected by Charley Hexam: Bradley 'drooped his devoted head when the boy was gone, and shrank together on the floor, and grovelled there, with the palms of his hands tight-clasping his hot temples, in unutterable misery, and unrelieved by a single tear'.[3]

Citing Bradley Headstone as the first male character in Dickens's fiction to express his distress in a manner previously the prerogative of women points to the need for clarifying the boundaries of my study. I am not considering characters who contribute vaguely to the boiling of the pot, figures like Monks who, in chapter 33 of *Oliver Twist*, has an epileptic fit.[4] If some characters in Dickens's novels do deserve to be dismissed as melodramatic flops, surely Monks is one of them. Furthermore, I am excluding the comic floor scenes, like Pecksniff's 'pratfalls' in *Martin Chuzzlewit*, and the swoonings of children.[5] I am looking instead at that fairly large group of Dickens's adult characters, always women until *Our Mutual Friend*, who are troubled in sometimes extraordinarily pressing ways and who express themselves through means that have come to be dismissed as melodramatic: floor scenes. Yet there is more to these characters than their emotional gyrations and more to these gyrations than recognized by Garis or the *Bleak House* reviewer in *Bell's*. These fictional women are sympathetic figures whose sufferings are recognizably human. After giving an overview of the floor scenes and ways of describing their significance in the novels, I shall use the example of Lady Dedlock to argue that the expressiveness of these scenes is an essential element in Dickens's portrayal of his characters' humanity and his attempt to engage the reader in understanding that humanity.

That Dickens in *Our Mutual Friend*, his last completed novel, finally allows an adult male to display utterly vulnerable helplessness might be offered as evidence of his maturing ability to transcend sexist stereotypes, as might the decreasing number of times, in the course of his career, that his female characters descend to the floor or its equivalent. The following is a brief (and representative) body count of Dickens's falling women: Nancy falls six times, counting her horrible death scene (ch. 16, p. 101;

ch. 39, p. 244; ch. 40, pp. 257–58; ch. 44, p. 285; ch. 46, p. 298; ch. 47, p. 303); counting her death, Lady Dedlock falls four times (ch. 29, p. 364; ch. 36, pp. 449–52; ch. 55, p. 666; ch. 59, p. 713), and Esther, four, all quiet descents except when, recovering from the smallpox, she reunites with Ada Clare in chapter 36 (ch. 3, p. 19; ch. 36, p. 456; ch. 57, p. 688; ch. 59, p. 711). Appearing some seventeen years after Nancy and her sufferings, Louisa in the 1854 *Hard Times* falls three times.[6] Although Tattycoram has two frenzied floor scenes, the remarkable Miss Wade in *Little Dorrit* never descends; neither does Estella in the 1861 *Great Expectations*. Mrs Clennam in *Little Dorrit* drops down once, in a scene of repentance shortly before her death. Similarly, Miss Havisham has two floor scenes of repentance.[7] It should be noted, of course, that both Mrs Clennam and Miss Havisham do spend most of their time in chairs.

This decreasing number of floor scenes might be taken – and is probably best taken not too seriously – as evidence of Dickens's changing perspective as a creator of men and women. I am more interested in arguing, however, that we can be misled by the label of 'melodramatic' when examining such scenes and that they should be taken seriously as essential to Dickens's characterizations. I do not question that the scenes are melodramatic; I disagree, and strongly, with the use of 'melodrama' as a dismissive or an exclusive label.

In insisting that the melodrama which dominated the nineteenth-century stage must be taken on its own terms, Michael R. Booth has pointed out that those who fault such theatre for its lack of developed characters and psychological penetration 'might as well . . . abuse a milkmaid for not being a fashion designer'.[8] Following Booth's lead, I am not going to fault Lady Dedlock for not being a heroine from the novels of Eliot or James – nor, I hope, shall I try to turn her into one – but I am going to examine her melodramatic scenes as they function within Dickens's dramatic and expressionistic techniques of characterization. And it is to later in the century, to the visual arts and expressionism with its emphasis on innerness, that I turn for help in appreciating the nature and function of Dickens's floor scenes. That expressionism, at least for literary study, does not have the pejorative connotations of melodrama, suggests its usefulness in an attempt to take a fresh look at what has been a troublesome problem in assessing Dickens's art.

As exemplified in the works of such late nineteenth-century painters as Vincent van Gogh and Edward Munch, expressionism attempted to go beneath the surfaces of impressionism and naturalism, seeking through hyperbolic forms to portray the inner being; the word was first used in 1880 to describe those artists 'who undertake to express special emotions or passions'.[9] Both melodrama and expressionism are media of sensational effects, but where melodrama projects moral clarity – the loudly clashing forces of good and evil, with the former triumphing in the resolutions of the plot – expressionism suggests unfathomable depths. Polish novelist Stanislaw Przybyszewski, who became close to Munch in Berlin in the early 1890s, described the intense depths of individuality that he saw in Munch's art:

> His paintings are virtually chemical preparations of the soul created during that moment when all reason has become silent, when every conceptual process has ceased to operate: preparations of the animalistic, reason-less soul as it winds and curls upward in wildest storms, and shrinks in dusk-filled states of retreat, and screams in wild cramps of pain, and howls for hunger.[10]

Such intense subjectivity often conveyed the despair of the individual soul in isolation, as in Munch's famous *The Scream* (1893 – 95). A sound of agony beyond solace that the audience for the art can only imagine: surely this is the 'sound' of Dickens's floor scenes.

Steven Cohen has used the example of Lady Dedlock to suggest that such scenes are metaphors for the characters' mental disorders.[11] These collapses do expressionistically confirm that something is badly amiss in the characters' psyches, but I also stress that the wildness without does more than indicate wildness within. The effect of these explosive moments for both character and reader is one of brief but necessary relief: the character has her moment of crying in the night, of trying to make connection with someone outside of herself, while the reader is invited to make that sort of human connection with the character, to approach the centre of innerness beneath the dramatic layers of mystery.

'Dramatic', if it is understood as not necessarily excluding intense expressive moments – be they labelled 'theatrical', 'melodramatic', or 'expressionistic' – may be the single most important word in discussing Dickens's techniques of characterizing women, and by it I mean that there is an absence of a clear narrative guide to the recesses of character and to judgements about character. Dickens typically gives multiple visions of Nancy or Louisa Gradgrind Bounderby or Lady Dedlock, or even of Esther, whose insecure depiction of herself does not match the way that others respond to her; and the effect of these different perspectives is at once distance and intimacy. With no consistently reliable narrative vision, the focus becomes suspensefully intense as the reader sees the characters through many eyes – Mrs Sparsit's view of Louisa, Guppy's or

Tulkinghorn's of Lady Dedlock – and becomes involved in imagining what these characters are like inside. The 'drama' of Dickens's novels in this sense has long been acknowledged, with critics from different eras and orientations emphasizing the necessity for a working, involved reader participating in the Dickens world.[12] For the frequent absence of a clear narrative guide means that the focus is as much on the interpretative work of the reader as it is on the characters themselves. The floor scenes are thus crucial to the drama of the relationship between character and readers because without the expressive ventilations of these scenes, our view of Louisa in *Hard Times* might be as short-sighted as the malicious Mrs Sparsit's, who actually believes that Louisa might run away with the empty James Harthouse. But we, who have seen Louisa on her knees beside her brother's bed (bk 2, ch. 8, p. 145) and know that she will stand (or kneel) beside him whatever his wretched nature and behaviour: we should know better. Similarly, we might believe in chapter 48 of *Bleak House* that Lady Dedlock has shot her nemesis, Tulkinghorn, the family solicitor who has relentlessly stalked her secrets; but we have seen both the power of her feelings for Esther and her devotion to Sir Leicester. We know, as much as we can know anything about anybody, that she is not a murderess.

Because of the limitations of space and because Lady Dedlock has so often been considered as little more than a shadowy figure of melodrama, I have chosen her as my focus in examining Dickens's apparent intentions for his readers' responses to his complicated, troubled women as they express themselves in floor scenes. Her feelings are not destroyed, and that they survive and even strengthen (after all, she chooses to die near the grave of her lover) becomes one of the important mysteries of *Bleak House*.[13] But Lady Dedlock must have some way of communicating these feelings, and in this world of the imaginatively dead, of social strictures so binding that they led Honora Barbary to forswear her love for Captain Hawdon and to become Lady Dedlock, she must, as she tells Esther in their only interview, sustain her mask and continue to appear 'proud and disdainful' (ch. 36, p. 450). It is with the audience of readers that Dickens seems to have hoped that Lady Dedlock could make a lasting emotional connection. He wanted to draw from his readers that imaginative understanding denied her by the myrmidons of society; by the sharp-eyed and variously motivated representatives of the law – Tulkinghorn and Mr Guppy and Inspector Bucket – who track her past; and denied her even by Esther and her young maid Rosa, who, despite their caring, must remain ultimately distant because of social dictates. (After learning the identity of her mother, Esther's obsession is that she might 'bring calamity upon the stately house' of Dedlock [ch. 36, p. 454].)

It is the reader who witnesses all of Lady Dedlock's floor scenes, and these moments confirm the depth of her innerness, a depth which is suggested in more dramatically rendered interactions between Lady Dedlock and other characters as she tries to mask her interest in the law-copier's handwriting (ch. 2, p. 16) or to pretend that in asking for an account of his death (ch. 12, pp. 148–50) she is merely curious to hear a bizarre story. Something dark and complicated involving this dead man and Esther has obviously been part of Lady Dedlock's past, and it is the floor scenes that not only clarify the literal pieces of her story, but also expose her as more than a melodramatic lady with a menacing past. All of the floor scenes turn upon some revelation for Lady Dedlock or Esther – learning from Guppy that Esther is still alive, for example, sends Lady Dedlock into her first frenzy in chapter 29 – but the greater revelation is always for the reader: the revelation of complex human suffering that demands an effort of imagination, an effort denied Lady Dedlock within the world of the novel itself.

Slowly and carefully, before chapter 29 and the first floor scene, Dickens generates sympathy for Lady Dedlock in a variety of ways. While evoking suppressed passion surrounded by blindness or hostility, he also shows the warmth and admiration Lady Dedlock can inspire within her chilly circle at the centre of the fashionable world. There is of course the devotion of Sir Leicester and of her maid, Rose. Even Lawrence Boythorn, full of comically delivered diatribes agains Sir Leicester, softens in praise of Lady Dedlock as 'the most accomplished Lady in the world' (ch. 9, p. 109). Her first floor scene confirms for the reader that she is a character worthy of sympathetic attention. This emotional prostration is part of the terrifying thickenings of plot half-way through the novel when everything seems subject to disease and destruction – in chapter 31, Esther falls victim to smallpox; in chapter 32, Krook combusts – and when the reader needs the relief of some answers. At the end of chapter 29, the 'young man of the name of Guppy' has told Lady Dedlock that he has pieced together the truth about her affair with Nemo-Hawdon and the identity of Esther as their daughter. The reader, piecing together the many strong clues, has suspected this for some chapters, but what is news is that Lady Dedlock had been deceived by her sister into thinking that the child died soon after birth. In other words, the reader learns that Lady Dedlock did not wilfully abandon her daughter. Furthermore, the violence of Lady Dedlock's reaction reveals just how intense her emotions are, and that they are directed towards her daughter, not towards Guppy as a potential blackmailer.[14]

Mr Guppy leaves, and the narrator describes Lady Dedlock as going to pieces; it is the reader who must imagine her agony and sympathize, for as the narrator says, the 'air is so shut in and shut out throughout the house in town, that sounds need be uttered trumpet-tongued indeed by my Lady in her chamber, to carry any faint vibration to Sir Leicester's ears'. And yet, the narrator continues:

> This cry is in the house, going upward from a wild figure on its knees. 'O my child, my child! Not dead in the first hours of her life, as my cruel sister told me; but sternly nurtured by her, after she had renounced me and my name! O my child, O my child!' (p. 364)

The scene can unquestionably be called melodramatic and theatrical, most obviously from the standpoint of giving the reader information about Lady Dedlock's deception by her sister. The language, except for her invocations of 'my child', is scarcely the language of wild torment: it is the language of an actress conveying an important piece of information to her audience. And yet the passage, I maintain, has an emotional resonance which comes from several sources. At last and for certain the passion within Lady Dedlock is evident; tangible, too, is the killing entrapment of the Dedlock world where 'the air is so shut in and shut out'; in such an atmosphere, screaming and writhing on the floor seem inevitable. She wants to make a connection of some kind with her daughter, but at this point in her story, only the reader can hear her cries and render her sympathetic understanding. As a passage of necessary communication between character and reader, the floor scene serves its purpose. And what should the language and behaviour of passionate torment be like in fiction? How can strong emotion be conveyed without recourse to scenes that can be dismissed, at least by the tough-minded of the late twentieth century, as 'melodramatic'?

Strong emotion can of course be conveyed through narrative reticence, through dramatic scenes like those in which Lady Dedlock's innerness is conveyed through gestures and through responses which do not directly reveal her feelings but instead intriguingly suggest them. The scenes between Lady Dedlock and Tulkinghorn in chapters 41 and 48, in which she struggles to maintain self-control while Tulkinghorn turns his torturing screws, are perhaps the most brilliant examples of Dickens's dramatic art in *Bleak House*.[15] And strong emotion can be conveyed through descriptions of innerness that do not require the character to verbalize a 'horror that is . . . unutterable'. I am quoting here from chapter 55 (p. 666), Lady Dedlock's last floor scene before her death. All is up with her by this point; her secrets are out; and she believes that she will be charged with the murder of Tulkinghorn. Przybyszewski's description (those 'dusk-filled states' of retreat and 'wild cramps of pain') of the soul in agony in Munch's art might be of Lady Dedlock:

> She has thrown herself upon the floor, and lies with her hair all wildly scattered, and her face buried in the cushions of a couch. She rises up, hurries to and fro, flings herself down again, and rocks and moans. The horror that is upon her, is unutterable. If she really were the murderess, it could hardly be, for the moment, more intense.

But Dickens does not linger long over her frantic realization that 'there is no escape but in death'. The secrets of her heart find no expression in wild cries. We read instead the note she leaves for Sir Leicester in which she asserts her innocence in the murder, but also admits her guilty past and the shame with which she hurries from both her husband and herself. The language of this note combines informative theatricality with simplicity. She tells Sir Leicester, and also the reader, that she did attempt to see Tulkinghorn with 'one last petition' on the night of his death, and she quietly commands Sir Leicester, after declaring her innocence in the murder, to 'Believe no other good of me'. But she also describes herself as 'racked' by 'dreadful suspense' and petitions Sir Leicester in her 'last adieu', 'to forget the unworthy woman on whom you have wasted a most generous devotion' (pp. 666–67).

It is the fact of Lady Dedlock's communicating by notes in her last appearances that seems to express – like her cries, after Guppy's first visit, that no one but the reader hears – not that the author is going too far in creating melodramatic effects, but that Lady Dedlock can go nowhere in terms of her relations with others: she is completely alone. Her notes are read by those who love her, but this can make no difference to her. Sir Leicester forgives her fully; Esther reads the messages addressed to her that Lady Dedlock has left at Snagsby's and prays 'a long time . . . for my unhappy mother' (ch. 59, p. 710). Lady Dedlock never hears Sir Leicester's forgiveness nor Esther's prayers; it is the reader who serves as an imaginative intermediary between these characters, participating in this drama in which sympathetic communication is impossible, except in so far as the reader grows in understanding of the character.

I hope I have suggested the reader-involving rhythm that Dickens creates in his characterization of Lady Dedlock: narrative reticence and mystery concerning her situation and feelings alternate with scenes in which she expresses herself; drama alternates with the melodrama and expressionism of the floor scenes. It seems appropriate now to turn finally to the scene at the centre of this rhythm, that occurring in chapter 36 between Lady Dedlock and Esther which Garis finds so embarrassing.

Lady Dedlock goes down on her knees on page 449 (Esther describes her as 'at my feet . . . in her great agony of mind') and although Esther raises her up on the same page, Lady Dedlock shrinks down again in Esther's embrace on page 450, 'as if she were unwilling that I should touch her'. She does not rise until her departure on page 452 in a torrent of self-debasement and exclamation marks:

> My child, my child! . . . These kisses for the last time! . . . If you hear of Lady Dedlock, brilliant, prosperous, and flattered; think of your wretched mother, conscience-stricken, underneath that mask! Think that the reality is in her suffering, in her useless remorse, in her murdering within her breast the only love and truth of which it is capable!

The scene is filled with cries, embraces, and with Esther's description of her own responses as 'broken incoherent words' (p. 449).

It is the only time in a very long novel in which either Lady Dedlock or Esther expresses herself with anything like fullness or passion to each other, or to anyone for that matter, and this is the simplest way to justify the scene: in the unravelling story of Esther's insecurity and Lady Dedlock's secret shame, there must come a moment of emotional openness lest the tension become unbearable. But beyond this justification, the scene serves a deeper revelatory function for the reader. Beneath the surface of intense responsiveness between mother and daughter, no saving communication is really possible. Lady Dedlock does not believe that Esther forgives her, or if she does believe this, she says that 'it is far too late' (p. 449). She shrinks from and within Esther's embrace; she has no idea of her daughter's own needs and self-denial, for Esther feels 'a burst of gratitude to the providence of God that I was so changed [through her disfiguring illness] as that I never could disgrace her by any trace of likeness' (p. 449). In the midst of the cries and embraces there is an absence of communication; the scene projects emotional relief but it is also one more instance of the failure of communication in *Bleak House*. The watching, listening reader, however, should receive the message, understanding the love expressed and feeling horrified at its hopelessness. The cries are as penetrating and as futile as the wordless voice of Munch's *The Scream*.

The BBC television serialization of *Bleak House* offers an alternative way of playing this scene. In Episode 6, the encounter lasts for about two minutes, with Lady Dedlock going on her knees before Esther and declaring herself her mother. The scene shifts to Esther relating the experience to Mr Jarndyce; all is as muted and dignified as the sophisticated twentieth-century viewer could desire.[16] But what is missing is what I maintain is integral to Dickens's art in the novel: the drama, as well as the melodrama and expressionism, of solipsistic innerness that draws the reader into a world in which sympathetic communication is possible only in the imagination of the reader. Although perhaps the last thing needed in a discussion of Dickens's techniques is the use of another label or term, 'expressionism' does seem to offer valuable assistance in seeing and hearing the floor scenes as something other than histrionics. Denoting the outer signifying the inner, expressionism elucidates these scenes in which drama fuses with melodrama. The outer – the expressiveness of words and gestures – has its most powerful meaning in *Bleak House* in what is unsaid, the revelation of an innerness that can never be communicated in the stifling air of the Dedlock mansions or even the open air of the Lincolnshire countryside where Lady Dedlock and Esther come together as mother and daughter. It can, however, be communicated, as much as the secrets of the heart ever can be, within the drama of author, narrator, character, and reader.

Notes

1. *Bleak House*, George Ford and Sylvère Monod (eds) (New York: W. W. Norton, 1977) ch. 36, p. 452. Subsequent references to *Bleak House* are to this edition.

2. Robert Garis, *The Dickens Theatre: A Reassessment of the Novels* (Oxford: Clarendon Press, 1965) p. 140; 'Reviews of New Books', *Bleak House*, *Bell's New Weekly Messenger*, 6 Feb. 1852, no. 9, p. 6. The large subject of Dickens in relation to the Victorian theatre has had many investigators. See, for example, William F. Axton, *Circle of Fire: Dickens' Vision and Style and the Popular Victorian Theatre* (Lexington: University of Kentucky Press, 1966) pp. 139–62, on Dickens's melodramatic scenes. Also see George Worth, *Dickensian Melodrama: A Reading of the Novels* (Lawrence: University of Kansas Press, 1978). For a catalogue of British and American performances of *Bleak House*, see Philip H. Bolton, '*Bleak House* and the Playhouse', *Dickens Studies Annual*, vol. 12 (1983) pp. 81–112; over a period of twenty years in America, from 1873–1894, there were over forty productions of *Bleak House* – including one staged in Cleveland.

3. *Our Mutual Friend*, Stephen Gill (ed.) (New York: Penguin, 1971) bk 4, ch. 7, pp. 781–82.

4. *Oliver Twist*, Kathleen Tillotson (ed.) (Oxford University Press, 1982) p. 207. Subsequent references to *Oliver Twist* are to this edition.

5. For a discussion of 'Pecksniff and Pratfalls', see Coral Lansbury's essay, included in this volume. In '*Oliver Twist* as Heroine', Dickens and Others, University of California at Santa Barbara (22 Feb. 1986), Cheri Larsen finds that Oliver's fainting scenes, along with his self-effacing virtue, place him 'in the circle of Dickensian angels' with Rose Maylie and Agnes Wickfield. I agree with Larsen that the boundaries separating Dickens's fictional males and females need a closer look, and that such a look at Dickens's children probably signals the inadequacy of viewing his characters stereotypically according to gender. My subjects, however, are obviously not the characters in that charmed 'circle of Dickensian angels', and their floor scenes are usually more expressive than swoonings.

6. *Hard Times*, George Ford and Sylvère Monod (eds) (New York: W. W. Norton, 1966) bk 2, ch. 8, pp. 145–46; bk 2, ch. 12, p. 167; bk 3, ch. 1, p. 172. Subsequent references to *Hard Times* are to this edition.

7. *Little Dorrit*, John Holloway (ed.) (Harmondsworth: Penguin, 1967); for the floor scenes of Tattycoram, see bk 1, ch. 2, pp. 65–66, and bk 2, ch. 33, pp. 879–80; Mrs Clennam, bk 2, ch. 31, p. 858. *Great Expectations*, Angus Calder (ed.) (Harmondsworth: Penguin, 1965); Miss Havisham falls in ch. 38, pp. 324–25, and in ch. 49, pp. 410–13. A longer study of Dickens's seriously troubled female characters and what is revealed in their floor scenes (or their lack of floor scenes) would also include Edith Dombey; Rosa Dartle, Little Emily, and possibly Betsey Trotwood from *David Copperfield*; and Bella Wilfer from *Our Mutual Friend*.

   In *Dickens and Women* (Stanford University Press, 1983), Michael Slater groups many of these women together because of their sharing 'a passionate nature and a strong intelligence' (pp. 259 and 260–61). Slater finds that Dickens's 'women's novels', with the exception of *Oliver Twist* and Nancy, come from the period between *Dombey and Son* (1846–48) and *Little Dorrit* (1855–57). Here are the largest number of female characters and a significant focus on the condition of women (p. 243). With *Little Dorrit*, Slater observes that Dickens's central concern shifted to the male protagonists and their experiences of hopeless love (pp. 277–97). Slater seems to have missed, perhaps mercifully so, a fascinating opportunity to draw a parallel between Dickens's men and his women, for it seems to me that beginning with Arthur Clennam and culminating in Bradley Headstone and Eugene Wrayburn, Dickens's adult male characters become more and more like (and are developed through similar techniques as) his troubled women. With the appearance of *The Androgynous Trollope*, can *The Androgynous Dickens* be far behind?

8. Michael R. Booth, *English Melodrama* (London: Herbert Jenkins, 1965) p. 186.

9. Quoted in R. S. Furness, *Expressionism*, The Critical Idiom Series, John D. Jump (ed.) (London: Methuen, 1973) no. 29, p. 4. Furness's primary subject is the continental Expressionist writers of the late-nineteenth and twentieth century who, like Dickens's admirer Dostoyevsky, limned the 'soul under stress, racked and burning' (p. 9).

10. Przybyszewski, 'Psychischer Naturalismus' (1894), quoted in Reinhold Heller, *Munch: His Life and Work* (University of Chicago Press, 1984) p. 106.

11. Steven Cohen, 'Figures Beyond the Text: A Theory of Readable Character in the Novel', *Novel*, vol. 17 (1983) p. 15.

12. John Forster, *The Life of Charles Dickens* (London: J. M. Dent, 1927) vol. 1, p. 338; vol. 2, pp. 116–17, 275; F. W. Boege, 'Point of View in Dickens', *Publications of the Modern Language Association of America*, vol. 65 (1950) pp. 90–105; Susan Horton, *The Reader in the Dickens World* (London: Macmillan, 1981); Rosemary Mundhenk, 'The Education of the Reader in *Our Mutual Friend*', *Nineteenth-Century Fiction*, vol. 34 (June 1979) pp. 41–58. For a useful discussion of 'The Bonds of Reading', see Janice Carlisle, *The Sense of an Audience: Dickens, Thackeray, and George Eliot at Mid-Century* (Athens: University of Georgia Press, 1981) pp. 12–64. Also see John Kucich, *Excess and Restraint in the Novels of Charles Dickens* (Athens: University of Georgia Press, 1981) pp. 36–46. Kucich stresses Dickens's extraordinary ability to shock and move his readers, involving them with his characters without entering into some nether world of the unacceptable. In *The Act of Reading: A Theory of Aesthetic Response* (Baltimore, Md.: Johns Hopkins University Press, 1978) pp. 191–92, Wolfgang Iser more or less dismisses Dickens as having exploited the interruptions in serial reading for commercial purposes. Yet it is in Iser's discussion in *The Implied Reader: Patterns of Communication in Prose Fiction from Bunyan to Beckett* (Baltimore, Md.: Johns Hopkins University Press, 1974) of the 'variety of cunning strategems' (p. xiv) that a novelist employs to stimulate reader involvement that I find support for my exploration of Dickens's techniques of characterization. Iser stresses the importance of '*interruptions*' (italics his; p. 288) in the reading process: 'We look forward, we look back, we decide, we change our decisions, we form expectations. . . .' Dickens's readers were compellingly invited by the interruptions of serialization to participate in this dynamic process of questioning and piecing together, and Dickens of course was aware of the nature of the serial experience (he popularized it) and of his audience's expectations.

13. Hillis Miller notes Lady Dedlock's choosing her destiny and finding in death the only freedom possible for her: 'to accept oneself as what one already irrevocably is'. *Charles Dickens: The World of His Novels* (Cambridge, Mass.: Harvard University Press, 1959) p. 205. Also, Miller's judgement (p. 222) that Lady Dedlock is 'someone who has had a chance at the broad, imaginative moral life with all its complexities. But Lady Dedlock's struggles with the kind of moral problems which will command the center of Henry James's novels, and even of Meredith's, are only at the periphery of *Bleak House*.' Critical aloofness towards Lady Dedlock is beginning to be replaced by some warm attention. Marilyn Georgas, for example, has given a sympathetic reading of her importance in the novel in 'Dickens, Defoe, the Devil, and the Dedlocks: The Faust Motif in *Bleak House*', *Dickens Studies Annual*, vol. 10 (1982) pp. 23–42. And Susan Horton calls attention to the mystery of Lady Dedlock's character by noting the tentativeness with which the third-person narrator describes what *may* be going on behind the eyes of Tulkinghorn and Lady Dedlock as they watch each other; Horton believes, and I agree with her, that Dickens reserves the secrets of the heart and that the reader must work hard to glimpse them (p. 49).

14. Lady Dedlock has made a gesture of offering Guppy something from her 'rich bauble of a casket' (ch. 29, p. 364), but Guppy refuses; when she is alone, fears of blackmail seem absent from her mind.

15. Robert Garis says that the emphasis in confrontation scenes like those

between Lady Dedlock and Tulkinghorn is not on 'what these two are thinking and feeling' but rather on the *'frisson* of mystery, the thrilled apprehension of hidden motives and plans' (pp. 56–57). Garis warns that if we 'ponder privately on Lady Dedlock's inner life, we are simply making up our own novel' (p. 56). Of course we are 'making up our own novel'; we to an extent construct our own fantasy fictions whenever we encounter a novel or play that engages our imaginations. I am also arguing, however, that Dickens's concept of Lady Dedlock's character and his method of presenting her have a deeper, parallel purpose: inviting the reader to help him create Lady Dedlock and her story, Dickens is at least as interested in the reader's effort at imaginatively understanding her psychology as he is in unfolding a tantalizing tale of surface and reality.

16. 'Bleak House', *Masterpiece Theatre*, British Broadcasting Corporation; Public Broadcasting Service, 1 Dec. 1985–19 Jan. 1986.

7

Dickens and Acting Women

Nina Auerbach

In 1858, Dickens wrote to John Forster in wonder at the nineteen-year-old transvestite actress, Marie Wilton. Her 'saucy and amusing' portrayal of the boy Pippo in H. J. Byron's burlesque, *The Maid and the Magpie*, did not merely simulate masculinity: it stole the thing itself. Such thefts entranced Dickens, though he punished his own thieving characters unremittingly.

> There is the strangest thing in it that ever I have seen on the stage. The boy, Pippo, by Miss Wilton. While it is astonishingly impudent (must be, or it couldn't be done at all), it is so stupendously like a boy, and unlike a woman, that it is perfectly free from offense. I have never seen such a thing. Priscilla Horton, as a boy, not to be thought of beside it. She does an imitation of the dancing of the Christy Minstrels — wonderfully clever — which, in the audacity of its thorough-going, is surprising. A thing that you *can not* imagine a woman's doing at all; and yet the manner, the appearance, the levity, impulse, and spirits of it, are so exactly like a boy, that you cannot think of anything like her sex in association with it . . . I call her the cleverest girl I have ever seen on the stage in my time, and the most singularly original.[1]

As man and author, Dickens needed women to be meltingly womanly: an 'unsexed' woman, like his own Miss Murdstone, is an unholy affront to all he commands us to cherish. One wonders what he felt as he saw Jo, his beloved martyr in *Bleak House*, transformed on the stage into a popular breeches role. Long after Dickens's death, Jo continued to provide a show-case for shapely actresses. The metamorphosis that delighted Dickens, the credulous spectator, would no doubt have appeared to the thundering legislator as Jo's final, most blighting, martyrdom.

But as Pippo, Marie Wilton is not only a boy–girl; she is an adult–child, a still more resonantly recurring figure in Dickens's canon. He describes her quite properly as 'a woman', not 'a girl'. As Pippo, she defies not only her gender, but her adulthood. In his novels, Dickens stigmatizes such a trespass still more emphatically than he does that of the boy-girl: whether they are adult children or infantine adults, the creature who is simultaneously old and young is pitied as a victim (if society blights him, as it does wizened little Paul Dombey) or damned as a predator (if, like Harold Skimpole and young Smallweed, he acts a role that denies his age). In his novels, Dickens makes Time and Nature absolute arbiters; they blight those who deny their rhythms. The stage can twist them beyond recognition; in fiction, they take their revenge.

In *The Life and Adventures of Nicholas Nickleby*, Dickens enlists Time and Nature to mock the curl-papered Infant Phenomenon, an ageing child actress stunted by gin and water, who simpers, kicks, pirouettes, and shrieks her way through her juvenile routines in her father's company. Unlike Marie Wilton in 'the audacity of [her] thorough-going', the Infant Phenomenon transcends nothing, for she is a comic monster. As consummately as the self-sacrificing Madeline Bray who will elicit our tears later in the novel, the Phenomenon is in thrall to her father's commands. Like the pathetic heroine of 'Gaslight Fairies', the stern exposé of theatrical exploitation Dickens wrote in 1855 for *Household Words*, the Phenomenon is warped into performing.[2] The twenty-three-year-old 'Miss Fairy' is pure as a child; her drunken, delusion-ridden father forces her to play a pantomime fairy so that she may care for her younger siblings. Actresses are thrust into the company of factory hands, paupered outcasts, weary seamstresses, and other stunted victims of a careless society. Dickens saw in Marie Wilton a wealth of forbidden things, but he wrenched the Phenomenon and Miss Fairy into degraded roles. He blames these roles on their fathers' misgovernment, but in fact it is the author himself who cripples and shrivels their potential to become all things.

In *Nicholas Nickleby*, the Phenomenon's role is illuminated by that of another old child who is sadder still than she: the stunted Smike. His child's costume dramatizes the many tragedies inflicted on him:

> Although he could not have been less than eighteen or nineteen years old, and was tall for that age, he wore a skeleton suit, such as is usually put upon very little boys, and which, though most absurdly short in the arms and legs, was quite wide enough for his attenuated frame . . . Heaven knows how long he had been [at Dotheboys Hall], but he still wore the same linen which he had first taken down; for round his neck was a tattered child's frill, only half concealed by a coarse, man's handkerchief.[3]

At Smike's age, Marie Wilton would play Pippo, irradiating her boy's costume to Dickens's delight by impudent self-transformation. As a novelist, though, he finds only pathos and neglect in young adults who wear children's costumes. Both Smike and the Phenomenon join Dickens's host of damned and distorted souls who are exiled from the light of the sun. Describing 'the sunburnt faces of gypsy children' in Hampton, the narrator reminds us of more somber childhoods that are warped or lost:

> It is a pleasant thing to see that the sun has been there, to know that the air and light are on them every day, to feel that they *are* children, and lead children's lives; that if their pillows be damp, it is with the dews of Heaven, and not with tears; that the limbs of their girls are free, and that they are not crippled by distortions, imposing an unnatural and horrible penance upon their sex [like that of the Phenomenon]; that their lives are spent from day to day at least among the waving trees, and not in the midst of dreadful engines which make young children old before they know what childhood is, and give them the exhaustion and infirmity of age, without, like age, the privilege to die. God send that old nursery tales were true, and that gypsies stole such children by the score! (ch. 50, p. 748)

The Phenomenon becomes a type of the pathos and mutilation bad fathers and cruel authors inflict on all old children. It is not in her to dream of the transcendence of a Marie Wilton. Perhaps, though, the Phenomenon is not so much maimed by her role as, simply, untalented. If she were gifted enough to transform herself into Pippo, would Dickens allow us to applaud rather than pity her?

When Dickens conceived *Nicholas Nickleby*, he withheld himself, it seems, from the very possibility of an Infant Phenomenon. According to the theatre historian Eric Wollencott Barnes, Dickens's grotesque stage child was based on a juvenile actress named Jean Davenport who in the 1830s was as remarkable an adult-child as Marie Wilton would be in the late 1850s. Jean Davenport too was eerily versatile. Dickens's Phenomenon is a machine of monotonous shrieks and twirls, but Miss Davenport graduated from playing stereotyped juvenile roles like Little Pickle in *The Spoil'd Child* to thrilling audiences as Richard III (though she limited herself to the evil king's soliloquies).[4] In Portsmouth, in 1837, she entranced with her versatility a stage-struck entrepreneur named Ben Terry:

> Miss Davenport played Shylock, in scenes from *The Merchant of Venice*, and, in conformity with the monopolies, regaled her public with songs

('The Rose of Lucerne', 'Since Now I'm Doom'd', 'I'm a Brisk and Sprightly Lad just come Home from Sea', 'Poll Dang It, D'y' Go') and danced the Sailor's Hornpipe. She played six characters, male and female, in a piece called *The Manager's Daughter*; all of which suggests that Miss Davenport was a performer of virtuosity . . .[5]

Dickens and Ben Terry probably saw Miss Davenport in the same year, and *Nicholas Nickleby* began to appear in 1838, a year after she enthralled Ben Terry. But she inspired the two men to different dreams. Her mercurial ability to become male and female, old and young, in turn, lured Ben Terry to the stage. He was not much of an actor, but the theatrical dynasty he conceived and managed allowed him to live — vicariously at least — as many lives as Miss Davenport. In the decade of Marie Wilton's success, the 1850s, Ben's daughters Kate and Ellen became Infant Phenomena more popular than Miss Davenport, the model Ben trained them to emulate. Like her, they danced incessant hornpipes; like her, Ellen, Ben's favourite, made herself male and female, comic and tragic, old and young. Like Miss Davenport herself (but unlike Dickens's Infant Phenomenon), Ellen Terry survived her childhood success. After years of forced retirement, Jean Davenport returned to the stage as 'a lovely and winning actress of considerable talent'.[6] Ellen Terry grew up to become the foremost actress of the late Victorian stage. She was born in her father's mind as 'the manager's daughter' when he saw Jean Davenport becoming the entire cast of characters in an ephemeral play of that name. The adult-child Dickens would mock inspired in the shrewder, more generous Ben Terry a vision of performance that, through his many descendants, glorified the British theatre for generations.

Like many nineteenth-century stage children, Jean Davenport transmitted promises of infinite potential, defying the constraints of a single identity. Dickens understood this audacity thoroughly in Marie Wilton, but *Nicholas Nickleby* turns kaleidoscopic performers into prisoners, wrenched, like other child victims, into unnatural and deforming postures. In this early novel, Dickens began to insist upon the primacy of the theatre within him, one that dwarfed actual theatrical troupes like the seedy Crummles family. He sets out not only to surpass the versatility of professional actors, but to attract the middle-class family audience who shunned, in 1838, the disreputable metamorphoses of the professional theatre. He aims to replace the actual theatre he could not help loving with the one-man performances that composed his own novels, performances that were not only pyrotechnically brilliant, but impeccably family-minded. His Infant Phenomenon is deformed less by her life as

stage child than she is by the theatrical energy of her author, who brooks
no rivals.

With no struggle, Dickens won the game and became a theatre in
himself. No management could rival his. In 1870, when he died, the
British theatre was inching towards general acceptability: Henry Irving
had not yet elevated himself and his profession by assuming Dickens's
own inimitable amalgam of satanic virtuosity and rigid respectability. In
Dickens's later, triumphantly authoritative and expansive novels, what
becomes of the adult-child? Having proved that he can better any actor
by becoming all people, places, and times, does Dickens become more
generous towards the Infant Phenomena who continue to inhabit his
novels?

His later works hover with intensifying tenderness over a series of
scarred, father-blighted heroines whom he asks us to love all the better for
their various stigmas. The fond appellations 'Little Nell' and 'Little Dorrit'
reverse the proclamation of the Infant Phenomenon: like her, they are old
children, and sadly false ones. Little Nell is fourteen; Little Dorrit is
twenty-two; their parasitic grandfather and father have blocked their
growth. The Infant Phenomenon twirled for her life; Little Nell borrows
her charismatic virtuosity to die with. Evolving into sadder, more muffled
characters, the Infant Phenomenon anticipates Dickens's most poignant
heroines, but she is never allowed to fulfil the boast of her name. Finally,
she realizes herself in Jenny Wren, the alluringly crippled adult – child of
Our Mutual Friend; she is still preyed upon by a warping father, who is a
surrogate for the jealous author. Those who love Jenny Wren are invited,
not to extend their beings with Jean Davenport and Marie Wilton
beyond the boundaries of time, but to embrace time's constraints; Jenny
beckons her audiences to 'Come up and be dead!'

The theatrical energy that defies boundaries comes to rest, in Dickens's
novels, in stricken harbingers of doom, as the author, playing the role of a
wicked father, stunts mobile audacity into pathos. He surrounds with
deniers his vehicles of infinite expansion. At the beginning of Little
Dorrit's story, 'the supposed child' encounters one of Dickens's self-
flagellating prostitutes:

> 'Kiss a poor lost creature dear,' she said, bending her face, 'and tell
> me where's she taking you.'
> Little Dorrit turned towards her.
> 'Why, my God!' she said, recoiling, 'you're a woman!'
> 'Don't mind that!' said Little Dorrit, clasping one of her hands that
> had suddenly released hers. 'I am not afraid of you.'

'Then you had better be,' she answered. 'Have you no mother?'
'No.'
'No father?'
'Yes, a very dear one.'
'Go home to him, and be afraid of me. Let me go. Good night!'
'I must thank you first; let me speak to you as if I really were a child.'
'You can't do it,' said the woman. 'You are kind and innocent; but
you can't look at me out of a child's eyes. I never should have touched
you, but I thought you were a child.'
And with a strange, wild, cry, she went away.[7]

Even the fallen woman, Dickens's arch-trespasser, cries sternly to the
child-woman, 'You can't do it'. Dickens, the spectator who in the theatre
believed all he saw, surrounds his young-old performers with fallen
sceptics who reduce their wonder and mutilate it into innocence.

Notes

1. Letter of 17 Dec. 1858; quoted by John Forster, in A. J. Hoppé (ed.), *The Life of
    Charles Dickens*, rev. edn (London: J. M. Dent, 1969) vol. 2, pp. 440–41.
2. 'Gaslight Fairies', *Household Words*, vol. 11 (10 Feb. 1855) no. 255, pp. 25–28.
3. *The Life and Adventures of Nicholas Nickleby*, Michael Slater (ed.) (Harmonds-
    worth: Penguin, 1978) ch. 7, p. 143. Hereafter cited in the text.
4. Eric Wollencott Barnes, *The Lady of Fashion: The Life and the Theatre of Anna
    Cora Mowatt* (New York: Charles Scribner's Sons, 1954) p. 246.
5. Marguerite Steen, *A Pride of Terrys: Family Saga* (London: Longman, 1962)
    pp. 13–14.
6. Barnes, *The Lady of Fashion*, p. 246.
7. *Little Dorrit*, John Holloway (ed.) (Harmondsworth: Penguin, 1967) ch. 14,
    p. 218.

8

'The Mimic Life of the Theatre': The 1838 Adaptation of *Oliver Twist*

Regina Barreca

Theatrical versions of *Oliver Twist* seem to be as ubiquitous as they are successful. Looking at the novel in the light of one of its earliest stage adaptations will help to suggest some of the reasons why this is so, however little consensus exists concerning the theatrical merits of the 1838 version of *Oliver Twist*. In 1838 George Almar adapted and produced a version of the text which was, according to A. Nicholas Vardac, performed in both London and New York. Almar's adaptation, says Vardac, was used throughout the century as the basis for other theatrical versions of this Dickens novel.[1]

It should be noted that Dickens himself seemed rather less than enthusiastic about Almar's production; according to Forster, 'in the middle of the first scene he laid him down upon the floor in a corner of the box and never rose from it until the drop-scene fell'.[2] Nevertheless, as in the case of numerous adaptations of Dickens's novels, the whole-hearted approval of the audiences made the theatrical versions of Dickens's novel so popular during the nineteenth century that one critic was driven to enquire, 'What will become of the English stage when the public has grown weary, if it ever does grow weary, of dramatic versions of the stories of . . . Mr Dickens?'[3] Obviously Dickens himself was one of the play's few critics.

It is not surprising that Dickens's novels were so readily adapted for the stage. 'Their strong situations and fierce contrasts of characters', writes George Rowell, made them attractive to theatre managers. He continues, 'shorn of much of their humor and all of their original observation, Dickens's novels emerged on the Victorian stage as melodramas, crude, sensational – and tremendously successful'.[4]

Oliver Twist is itself a self-consciously theatrical book; 'life' is often compared to the theatre with various results. In a brief, disturbing scene embedded in chapter 5, we have one of the first important mentions of theatre. An old woman, ragged and toothless, listens to her son-in-law describe the agonizing death of her daughter. Oliver, apprenticed to the undertaker, has virtually no role in this scene; as mute observer, he simply provides a convenient pretext for its telling. The dead woman's husband falls into a swoon while describing his wife's slow starvation and wasting illness in horrifying and enraging detail. 'There was neither fire nor candle,' he cries, 'She died in the dark.' After he falls unconscious, the woman's mother narrates the death of her child to the undertaker in the following terms: 'She was my daughter. . . . Lord, Lord! Well it is strange to think that I who gave birth to her, and was a woman then, should be alive and merry now, and she lying there so cold and stiff! Lord, Lord! – to think of it; it's as good as a play – good as a play!'[5]

The comparison of the apparently 'genuine tragedy' of a woman's death is presented to us in this scene in direct comparison to the 'illegitimate tragedy' or melodrama of the stage. This interplay between supposedly realistic action and theatrical action works in a complex manner during this moment of the text and, I intend to argue, during much of *Oliver Twist*. The old woman has no natural context in which to inscribe the death of her daughter; the best she can do, 'mumbling and chuckling' in her garret, is to compare it to the cheap theatricality with which she is somehow familiar. This scene offers the crystallized pathos associated with Victorian tragedy (the death of the young wife and mother from starvation, the grief of her children and husband) but is ultimately undercut by the old woman's leer and her disconcerting phrase 'good as a play'. It is the theatrical and melodramatic aspects of *Oliver Twist* which argue for a reading which links it to the theatrical adaptations that flourished after (and, in some cases, even during) its serial publication in 1837–38.

'Actors', wrote Dickens, are in 'the mimic life of the theatre'.[6] The preface to the playbill accompanying George Almar's adaptation and production of *Oliver Twist* at the Surrey Theatre in 1838 reinforces this idea of theatre as 'mirror of life'. Perhaps one of the most crucial points concerning the text is that *Oliver Twist* was regarded as a public idea rather than the product of a private imagination.

Oliver Twist, then, was held up as a documentary account of a social situation peculiar to the time, as an unexaggerated portrayal of actual events only moderately altered to protect the names of the innocent. Dickens was compared to Hogarth and defined as chronicler rather than artist. The stage itself is meant to function as classroom, pulpit and

' "mirror up to nature", albeit in its worst light'. The Surrey bill is unreserved in its testimony to the potential good of the theatre and makes, among a host of others, the following claims:

> The Stage is never devoted to a more noble or better purpose than when it lends its powerful aid to improve the morals and correct the vices of the age. It is this conviction which has led to the adaptation of the impressive Work upon which this Drama was founded, opening one of the darkest volumes of life, and revealing facts that must startle. . . . It is possible that many persons may conceive the striking pictures presented to them in this Drama have not their parallel in real life but are exaggerated, wrought up and coloured merely for the sake of effect. . . . such is not the case.[7]

In addition, and perhaps with most emphasis, the playbill claims that the *Oliver Twist* will 'forcibly inculcate the great moral lesson that vice . . . will sooner or later meet with punishment and disgrace, while virtue, whatever be its trial and temptations, will ultimately secure a lasting and just reward'.[8]

Yet one thing becomes apparent even from a reading of the play's preface and the scene synopsis provided before the script-text begins: despite the protestations to the contrary, the play focuses completely on the emotionally basic and intellectually simple aspects of Dickens's novel. The impact of this evening in the theatre would hardly be one of an uplifting moral message delivered through a socially delicate medium. Instead, the 1838 adaptation of *Oliver Twist* is a full blown 'murderous melodrama', of the sort that Dickens discusses in an important passage on theatre included in the novel.

The opening paragraphs of chapter 17 of *Oliver Twist* deal with the long-standing theatrical custom of permitting the 'regular alternation' of comic and tragic scenes 'as the layers of red and white in a side of streaky bacon'. The paragraphs catalogue a number of stage conventions, including the despair of the hero, followed immediately by the miraculous appearance of castle halls, followed by the victimization of the heroine. Dickens suggests, however, that life simply imitates art on this point: 'Such changes appear absurd; but they are not so unnatural as they would seem at first sight. The transitions in real life from well-spread boards to death-beds, and from mourning weeds to holiday garments, are not a whit less startling.'[9] The old woman from chapter 5 suggested a similar interpretation of events; here the narrator offers us a chance to see life once again as 'good as a play'.

The adaptation of *Oliver Twist* for the stage does narrow the moral and intellectual complexity of Dickens's text in so far as it appropriates only the most forceful and inherently interesting scenes from the novel for its own purposes. Drama must translate undercurrents into action, must make feelings into events, into visible, tangible 'realities' in order to draw the audience fully into the world created on the stage. The 1838 adaptation serves to underline the fact that it is, all philosophical apologies aside, the dark underworld of Dickens's London that fascinates. We turn to Fagin's den and Sikes's room for the real action contained in the tale; Mr Brownlow's study offers only the blandest dialogue and we are anxious to return to the more unfamiliar Other-ness of, for example, Jacob's Island.

What *Oliver Twist* provides, above all else, is an inoculation against evil. Perhaps that is the true implication of the playbill's preface: we satisfy our desire for interaction with evil through Oliver's association with it, while remaining as untainted as the title character himself. It is the preacher describing vice in full detail so that we might shun it when we meet it, a description both titillating and threatening, fulfilling needs on two levels. The play, however, eclipses the moral lesson it purports to teach through graphic portrayals of violence, as well as through the seductive nature of the underworld against which it is supposedly warning its audience.

It becomes apparent as we study the adaptation that the play makes manifest the melodramatic aspects of *Oliver Twist* that the novel, theatrical as it is, still only implies. This is particularly noticeable in the case of Nancy, one of Fagin's girls and the mistress of Bill Sikes. In dealing with Nancy, Dickens himself is treading very gingerly, balancing the character between vice and virtue. Dickens states in the preface to his novel that 'the girl is a prostitute', and yet it is obvious in her final scene that Nancy is 'saved': ' "Then spare my life for the love of Heaven, as I spared yours," rejoined the girl, clinging to him. "Bill, dear Bill, you cannot have the heart to kill me . . . for dear God's sake, for your own, for mine. . . . It is never too late to repent." '[10]

Despite her moving appeal, which offers him a chance at salvation, Bill begins to beat her. In a final gesture, Nancy holds up Rose Maylie's handkerchief (Rose acts purity and goodness to Nancy's degradation and vice) and raises her eyes and arms towards heaven. The gesture, in fact, forms a sort of tableau for the end of the chapter: 'It was a ghastly figure to look up. The murderer . . . seized a heavy club and struck her down.' This entire final scene offers the moral complexity that characterizes the best of Dickens's work, since it forces the reader to see Nancy both as a prostitute and as a good woman. Nancy's reconciliation with the forces of goodness, in fact, is precisely what the adaptation, in its necessary whittling down of moral middle-ground, cannot accommodate.

The undeniable climax of the 1838 adaptation occurs at Nancy's murder. Like Dickens's own adaptation of Nancy's murder for his public readings, the articulation of this scene into any dramatic form must heighten the emotionally hysterical aspect which is tempered in the novel by the dead-pan, cautious narration. The novel allows us to project our own horror on to the events described as if by a journalist. In contrast, the dramatic versions absorb the horror and transform the scene into the catalyst that turns *Oliver Twist* into a revenge tragedy better titled *Nancy's Vindication*. In fact, re-titling a work for the theatre in such a manner was not unprecedented: the stage version of *David Copperfield* was renamed *Little Em'ly*.

In making Nancy's murder one of the most central and sensational parts of the play, relegating the Oliver story to a position of secondary importance for the entire final act, the adaptation still denies Nancy the possibility for goodness given her by Dickens. The murder scene (VII, iii.) omits any reference to prayer, heaven or God; Nancy clings to Bill as she does in the novel, but her entreaties remain entirely secular. 'Spare my life as I spared yours,' she cries, without reference to heaven. 'We will lead better lives, and forget how wicked we have been –' she begs. The adapted Nancy lacks a spiritual dimension and appears to want to continue her unlawful association with Bill. This is in great contrast to the Nancy created by Dickens who, once again, has the potential to be a fully realized and fully salvageable soul. The parallel speech of Nancy's in the novel reads: 'let us both leave this dreadful place and *far apart* lead better lives, and forget how we have lived, *except in prayers*, and *never see each other more*' [my emphasis].[11]

The adaptation's refusal or inability to make Nancy as complex as she is in the original is not altogether surprising. It is, as Joseph Donohue noted in *Theatre in the Age of Kean*, an aspect of melodrama that: 'since the moral posture of the characters is initially clear, the play itself is occupied essentially with a series of events which will cumulatively and finally demonstrate the justness of these characterizations. The ethical purpose of melodrama is to reorder the material world so that it mirrors inherent truths.'[12] Nancy might be the centre of attention in the play but she cannot become a good woman; the structure of melodrama would not permit it. She can no more be changed by good than Oliver can be changed by evil and he, as we know, remains the same whether he is in a den of thieves or sitting in Mr Brownlow's study.

It is perhaps one of Oliver's weaknesses that he does not grow in emotional stature or evolve despite his constant exposure to the vicissitudes of life. He does not grow into a new place in the world; the world alters in order to fit Oliver. Events take place around him, and it is with the events rather than with the characters that we are concerned. As George Orwell remarked in his essay on Dickens, '[Dickens's novels] always exist round a framework of melodrama. The last thing anyone remembers about these books are central stories. . . . there is little attempt at development – the characters simply go on and on, behaving like idiots, in a kind of eternity.'[13]

Such is the nature of melodrama. In contrast to Nancy, it is important to note, Oliver remains a fairly static character in the novel. Oliver is created, as Dickens writes in the preface of the novel, to illustrate 'the principle of Good surviving through every adverse circumstance, and triumphing at last'.[14] That Oliver is an inert element in the play does not, therefore, delete any important aspect of the novel. That Nancy remains static considerably alters the presentation and subsequent interpretation of her character. Nancy becomes the catalyst for the remaining action in the play, certainly, but without challenging any social conventions and without raising questions concerning the problematic relationship between revenge and punishment raised by the novel.

Victorian theatre was characterized by the catastrophe, according to Michael R. Booth. Nineteenth-century melodrama had its 'own apocalyptic character and its own titanic conflict between good and evil – which manifested itself in physical as well as moral symbols . . . [Melodrama] was obsessed with catastrophe.'[15]

The 'sensation scenes' in *Oliver Twist* are the murder of Nancy and the hanging of Sikes. Only Nancy's death, however, is the catastrophe. It is her end which sets the stage in motion. Because of the brutal nature of her murder, we are given *carte blanche*. We seek to avenge her death in the play although we have not been given the opportunity to reconsider the manner of her life. One of the last lines of the play is 'poor Nancy is avenged'. Those who did not protect or defend her in life offered money to secure the capture of her assailant and are pleased by telling themselves that they have secured justice on her behalf. There is no place for irony in melodrama; this is one reason Dickens's novels lose a dimension when translated into this form. In addition, the loss of irony perhaps helps to account for melodrama's inability to thrive in the twentieth century except in its most drastically curtailed forms.

That Dickens has difficulty with matters concerning women and sexuality has been noted by many critics, yet I think that he must be given credit for his attempts to portray morally complex women in *Oliver Twist*. Critics have argued about Nancy from the day she appeared. Thackeray, in a review titled 'Going to See a Man Hanged', which appeared in *Fraser's Magazine* in 1840, wrote that 'Miss Nancy is the most unreal fantastical personage possible'. Thackeray went on to say that '[Dickens] dare not not tell us the truth concerning young ladies. . . . He has no right to present us one or two favourable points as characterising the whole; and therefore . . . had better leave the picture alone together.'[16]

Critics today still find Nancy problematic. Interesting to note that in his introduction to what must be the most popular edition of *Oliver Twist* – the Penguin edition, known for its wide use in schools and universities – Angus Wilson agrees with Thackeray, finding Nancy 'devoid of charm . . . sensuality, so finally null'. Wilson asserts that her speech 'has never been heard outside theatrical one-night stands', and he sees this as part of the 'emasculating debt' Dickens 'paid to his beloved public'.[17] (But then Wilson states later on in the same essay that Mrs Rochester in *Jane Eyre* is emblematic of the 'cheap melodrama' novelists of the period used in their texts. If Bertha Rochester is cheap melodrama, it is only our loss that authors did not, in fact, make fuller use of it.)

In contrast, some critics, such as Wilkie Collins, thought Nancy one of Dickens's best creations.[18] I believe this is the case. Nancy, as we have seen, is a character too fully developed in the book to play effectively on stage, and she must be subsequently narrowed until she does fit the stereotype of the stage victim. In the book, her pitiful, bitter life bears little resemblance to the stage prostitute: perhaps that is why she seems to lack 'sensuality'. What Nancy does, she does for money; that much Dickens makes clear in his preface ('the girl is a prostitute'). It is to Dickens's credit that he did not make her a charming, voluptuous creature but rather a terrified, enraged victim.

In a similar manner, Dickens presents Agnes, Oliver's mother, as a victim of circumstance, as an abandoned unwed mother who is not damned by her sin. Granted, the two women who are sexually active in this novel – Nancy and Agnes – die horrible, lonely deaths. Since they suffer for their sexual sins on earth, is it therefore safe for us to assume that, at least, they have paid the necessary price for heaven? In much the same way as Nancy dominates the final scene of the play, Agnes dominates the final scene of the novel. Agnes is a woman without a last name, a sort of Virgin Mary figure; one must go to a church to seek her out. Cruikshank's last illustration for the text shows Oliver and Rose Maylie at Agnes's tomb where Dickens believes Agnes's spirit hovers, believing it 'none the less because that nook is in a Church and she was weak and erring'.[19] It appears that Agnes, like Nancy, has won her right to be forgiven. Paralleling the character of Nancy in the novel, the figure of Agnes provides a dimension of moral complexity which the theatrical adaptation must reduce to its most easily accessible form. Oliver's mother, according to the adaptation, believed that she was married, and imagined herself to be conceiving a child in wedlock. Perhaps this occurs so that Oliver is presented as somehow less of an illegitimate child, if indeed degrees of illegitimacy are possible.

With all the difficulties of transferring *Oliver Twist* from the page to the proscenium, which included a number of changes in addition to the ones I have already discussed – making Oliver Mr Brownlow's nephew, for example – it is no surprise that Dickens ended up face down in the corner of the box. What is surprisingly important, as we have seen, is the illuminations theatrical versions can provide for readers of the novel because of, rather than in spite of, the alterations in the scripting of the text. Dickens's novels were embraced as much for their inherent theatricality as for their exclusively novelistic strategies; they were, and remain, 'as good as a play'.

Notes

1. A. Nicholas Vardac, *Stage to Screen: Theatrical Method from Garrick to Griffith* (New York: Benjamin Blom, 1968) p. 258.
2. Quoted in Alexander Woolcott, *Mr Dickens Goes to the Play* (New York: G. P. Putnam's Sons, 1922) p. 229.
3. Allardyce Nicoll, *History of Nineteenth Century Drama 1850–1900* (Cambridge University Press, 1924) vol. 1, p. 2.
4. George Rowell, *The Victorian Theatre 1792–1914: A Survey* (Cambridge University Press, 1978) p. 51.
5. *Oliver Twist* (Harmondsworth: Penguin, 1983) ch. 5, p. 83. All subsequent references to the text are from this edition.
6. *Oliver Twist*, ch. 17, p. 169.
7. This quotation is from the playbill (of the Almar version of *Oliver Twist*) to the Surrey production of 19 Nov. 1838. It was reprinted in the bound text of the play, published by Thomas Hailes Lacey of London. The playbill appears on pages 2 and 3.
8. Playbill, p. 3.
9. *Oliver Twist*, ch. 17, p. 169.
10. *Oliver Twist*, ch. 47, p. 422.
11. Almar's adaptation of *Oliver Twist*, VII, iii.
12. Joseph Donohue, *Theatre in the Age of Kean* (Totowa, N.J.: Rowman & Littlefield, 1975) p. 110.

13. George Orwell, 'Charles Dickens', *A Collection of Essays* (New York: Harcourt Brace Jovanovich, 1953) p. 83.

14. Dickens's preface to *Oliver Twist*, p. 33.

15. Michael R. Booth, *Victorian Spectacular Theatre: 1850–1910* (Boston: Routledge & Kegan Paul, 1981) p. 12.

16. William Thackeray, 'Going to See a Man Hanged', *Fraser's Magazine*, vol. 22 (Aug. 1840) pp. 154–55.

17. Angus Wilson, 'Introduction' to Penguin Edition of *Oliver Twist*, p. 22.

18. 'The character of Nancy is the finest thing he ever did. He never afterwards saw all sides of a woman's character – saw all around her.' Quoted in Wilson's 'Introduction', p. 22.

19. *Oliver Twist*, ch. 53, p. 480.

9

Melodrama and the Working Class

Michael R. Booth

When we recollect some of the great moments and events of nineteenth-century theatre, the new stars created overnight, the hit play, the outstanding production, our minds go to Edmund Kean's Shylock at Drury Lane in 1814, Madame Vestris at the Olympic in the 1830s, the four-year run of the comedy *Our Boys* at the Vaudeville in the 1870s, Henry Irving's first night as Mathias in *The Bells* at the Lyceum in 1871 and later his production of *Faust* there in 1885, *Charley's Aunt* at the Royalty in the 1890s, and Mrs Patrick Campbell in *The Second Mrs Tanqueray* at the St James's in 1893. All these successes of the nineteenth century had one thing in common: they all occurred at West-End London theatres (although it is perhaps anachronistic to refer to Drury Lane in 1814 as 'West-End'). Not surprisingly, then, we think of the West End of London when we discuss 'the Theatre' in the nineteenth century. The best-known dramatists of the Victorian period – Boucicault, Robertson, Gilbert, Pinero, Jones – all wrote for the West End; the best actors performed there, and the best plays opened there, touring to the West-End-thirsty provinces and Empire and the United States after a long London run. We also know that the backbone of the Victorian West-End audience was the middle class, a class that strengthened its hold on the West-End theatre as it strengthened its own respectability and that of the actor-managers who served it.[1]

In 1866 the critic Henry Morley declared, 'In our provinces and colonies the form of entertainment will be, as it is now, mainly determined by the example of the eight or nine theatres in or near the West End of London of which I hold the performances to be worth serious attention.'[2] A model manager, he said, should take as a standard of the audience he wishes to please 'an honest Englishman of the educated middle-class'.[3] This middle-class audience lavished box-office success upon such melodramas as *The Lady of Lyons* in 1838, *The Corsican Brothers* in 1852,

96

The Ticket-of-Leave Man in 1863, and the *Sign of the Cross* in 1896. One wonders, then, if melodrama had any special identity with or origins in the entertainment needs of the working class, or if anything of its character was determined by working-class taste? Clearly melodrama was just as attractive to the West-End middle-class audience as to anybody else; indeed, the only melodramas whose titles most of us can remember were first performed in the West End. If this is true, can the content of melodrama, melodrama's relationship to its audience, and the nature of that audience tell us anything that is socially accurate and meaningful about the Victorian working class, or can we only perceive this class on the melodramatic stage and in the theatres through the lens of the Victorian middle-class eye?

Some kind of answer to these questions is attempted in this chapter, which deals primarily with three aspects of the subject of melodrama and the working class: the audience for melodrama, the manner in which the critics of the day perceived the working-class segment of that audience, and the way in which the content of melodrama itself reflected working-class life and experience. I want to deal with the questions that arise from this problem, and begin by approaching melodrama through its audience.

Research into nineteenth-century theatre audiences is in a very primitive state; there is virtually no significant modern scholarship, and historians write happily about plays, acting, theatre architecture, production methods, the actor-manager, and so on, without paying the slightest attention to what kind of audiences went to what theatres at what period of time, what their class status was, what jobs they had, where and how they lived, and what their tastes and interests were. However, we do have one interesting set of statistics. In 1866, the same year in which Morley denied the existence of any worthwhile drama outside a narrow coterie of West-End theatres, the *Report from the Select Committee on Theatrical Licenses and Regulations* included an appendix on the audience capacities of twenty-seven metropolitan theatres.[4] If we omit Covent Garden and Her Majesty's, which were opera houses, we find that the nightly audience capacity of the remaining twenty-five theatres is 51 263, and sixty-three per cent of that capacity is taken up by theatres outside the West End. The capacity of six East-End theatres alone – the City of London, the Effingham, the Pavilion, the Grecian, the Standard, and the Britannia – amounts to 17 600 places nightly or thirty-four per cent of the total, a percentage that would have been higher if a seventh East-End theatre, the Garrick, which had a capacity of 500, had not been temporarily closed. The *Report* does not mention the numerous penny theatres or gaffs and the large saloon theatres like the Albion in

Whitechapel, which would have added substantially to this figure. Even if the gaffs and saloon theatres are excluded, the capacity of theatres in primarily working-class districts outside the West End is about one half of all places in the twenty-five metropolitan theatres listed. The staple dramatic fare in all these theatres was melodrama.

After 1866 the number of East-End theatres declined, but in 1884 – when Clement Scott complained of a dearth of theatrical amusements in the East End – there were still four major theatres open and several music halls. Indeed, it is clear that all through the Victorian period the East End possessed a major and virtually self-contained entertainment industry. At the end of the century the population of the East End was about 2 000 000, and Charles Booth in 1889 estimated that ninety-five per cent of its population was working-class (in his categories A to F) as compared to eighty per cent in Central London. The suburban, provincial, and overseas tourist audience which poured into the West End, then as now, did *not* visit the East End in search of entertainment.

We know far too little about the West-End audience and even less about the audience in the East End and other working-class areas of London. Henry Mayhew informs us that thieves living in an East-End lodging house went to the Britannia, the City of London, the Albert Saloon, and the Standard, as well as to the Surrey and the Victoria on the other side of the river. He also notes that the galleries of the City of London, the Garrick, and the Pavilion were popular with dustmen who preferred melodramas with 'plenty of murdering scenes in them', and that costermongers attended the Surrey-side theatres, some of them going three times a week. A scavenger told him that he attended the theatre at Christmas, especially the Victoria, and especially pantomime. A rubbish carter whom Mayhew interviewed went to see Phelps at Sadler's Wells.[5] Dickens is very specific about the prowlers, idlers, mechanics, dock-labourers, costermongers, petty tradesmen, small clerks, milliners, stay-makers, shoe-binders, and slop-workers in the Britannia's audience.[6] Jews went to the Pavilion in Whitechapel, sailors and Jews to the Effingham. But all this information is in little bits and pieces and is almost useless as evidence.

Part of the problem of gathering reliable evidence about melodrama and its audience in theatres outside the West End has been a class problem, not unique to theatre history. We have been accustomed to looking at Victorian theatre through middle-class eyes rather than our own. Publishers like Lacy, French, and Dicks printed relatively few plays performed outside the West End, perhaps not more than 200 first given in the East End, for instance. Out of the thousands of nineteenth-century plays printed not only were the best-known plays of the period written by middle-class playwrights and done at middle-class theatres, but the records of Victorian theatre available to us were compiled by middle-class journalists and historians. Detailed and colourful as they are, they operate from a point of view socially and morally restricted, and it may be difficult to trust them when these critics write of popular performance outside their normal theatre-going experience. Critics like Morley and William Archer, who never visited working-class theatres, at least for reviewing purposes, disliked the healthy but vulgar energy of the popular melodrama and, indeed, all forms of theatre not patronized by a fairly select and educated audience. Others had wider views, and ventured outside the theatrical centre. Dickens has left us two vivid accounts in *Household Words* of the Britannia in 1850;[7] Henry Mayhew visits the gallery of the Victoria about 1851;[8] Shaw thoroughly enjoys the British pantomime in 1897.[9] On a visit to a Marylebone penny gaff in 1881, the *Sunday Times* representative found it expedient to conceal himself in a greasy overcoat and choker, old boots, and a battered white billycock hat. Almost all such visitors, even Dickens, treat the theatres and the performances they visit as material for comedy or moral disapproval, or both: the audience offers striking but distasteful local colour – like a tribe of savages engaged in strange ritual in the presence of a visiting High Church tourist of anthropological inclinations.

What are we to think, for instance, about the truthfulness of T. W. Erle's accounts in *Letters from a Theatrical Scene-Painter* (two series were first published in 1859 and 1862) of performances at the Effingham, Grecian, Britannia, Marylebone, Surrey, and Victoria? Erle describes eleven melodramas and their acting style, with occasional comments on audiences. His information, especially about melodramatic acting and costuming at these theatres, is invaluable. Yet Erle is so relentlessly amused, condescending, patronizing, and downright contemptuous of his subject matter that one wonders how reliable he is. For example, in *Adelbert the Deserter* at the Effingham, a speech against capital punishment is 'warmly applauded by the house, the matter being one of individual interest to a large portion of the audience, seeing that every execution at the Old Bailey diminishes the RE (Royal Effingham) audience by one'.[10] Of *The Foundlings of the Sea* at the Victoria, Erle writes concerning the character of a vagabond scoundrel:

So conversant indeed must the members of the establishment be with the ragamuffin aspect of humanity, that there can be no one from the manager to the callboy who would not be competent to undertake a

part of the kind at the shortest notice and feel comfortably at home in
it. The Victoria audiences are competent critics in a case of this
description, since the house is largely graced by the presence of
embryo and mature convicts, and of gentlemen on tickets of leave
during their transient intervals of sojourn in the bosom of Lambeth
society.[11]

Do we conclude with Erle that the *majority* of the audience at these two
theatres were criminals? Do we credit the moral indignation of James
Grant, Mayhew, and other contemporary writers about the penny gaff as
having an absolute basis in fact when they declare that such places were
only nurseries for young criminals and prostitutes? The difficulty is that
much of our evidence comes from these sources, from the intrepid middle-
class explorer in the jungle of working-class culture, delighting in the
strange sights and sounds around him, minutely recording the incon-
veniences of his situation, fearful but proud of the hazards of his
expedition, keeping a sharp look out for dangerous animals lurking in the
densest growth.

Vast numbers of melodramas were performed for Victorian working-
class audiences, and since comedy, burlesque, and comic opera were
virtually unknown in their theatres, melodrama constituted – as it did
not in the West End – a very significant majority of all theatrical
entertainment. The number of melodramas they saw – to confine our
scope to London (to say nothing of theatres in the manufacturing towns
and the fairground theatres, whose appetite for melodrama was immense)
– must have far exceeded the numbers performed for middle-class
audiences. From the audience point of view, melodrama – and pantomime
at Christmas – *was* the Victorian working-class theatre. Our sense of
the working-class experience of Victorian theatre comes to us by courtesy
of diligent middle-class observers, journalists, sociologists, and
parliamentarians. Finally, the content of that melodrama was essentially
the same, whatever theatre it was played in and to whatever class, with, of
course, variants of subject matter and differences in style. The feeling for
working-class life in melodrama may be stronger in the plays performed
outside the West End, but the structure of melodrama has class conflict so
built into it that something of this feeling permeates the whole genre.

We simply do not know where the first audiences for melodrama came
from or who they were. We do know that melodrama grew up almost
simultaneously, at the end of the eighteenth century and beginning of the
nineteenth, in the patent theatres of Drury Lane and Covent Garden, in
the dumb-show theatres and circuses of the Surrey side of the Thames,

and in the aquatic spectacles at Sadler's Wells in remote Islington. Certainly, the taste for it was universal and cut across all classes. By the time the Gothic romanticism of early melodrama passed into a domestic and material mode in the 1830s and 1840s, the basic structure and character of melodrama were forever fixed, and the melodramatic world was sharply divided into good and evil, oppressor and oppressed, the heroic and the villainous, the ideal and the base. Because melodrama was always in touch with the social concerns and cultural tastes of its audience, it quickly absorbed the new industrial proletariat into its structure; indeed, it was the only kind of English drama to do so. Industrial discontent, unemployment, machine-smashing, the theme of master-against-man enter melodrama as early as 1832 in John Walker's *The Factory Lad* at the Surrey Theatre, which has a subsidiary but powerfully expressed theme of the injustice of parish welfare. The moral polarity of melodrama easily shaped industrial themes into a bitter conflict between rich mill owner and villainous foreman on the one hand and employees or poor starving ex-employees on the other. (Not always: a few such melodramas looked favourably upon the master and opposed strikes.)[12] A long line of descent runs from *The Factory Lad* to Galsworthy's *Strife* in 1909 to Howard Brenton's *The Weapons of Happiness* at the National Theatre in 1976.

One could argue that the new subject matter of the workman, his place of work, and his economic dependence upon his employer strongly reinforced the innate class bitterness of melodrama, a noteworthy aspect of its character demonstrated in a variety of social and personal relationships: squire and peasant, landlord and tenant, peer and cottager, seducer and heroine, workman and master or foreman. The tension and hostility in such relationships were apparent well before 1832, but they are much stronger after. Here is the hero of *The Factory Lad* telling his wife that steam has been their ruin:

> Instead of five-and-thirty good hands, there won't be ten wanted now, and them half boys and strangers. Yes, steam be now going to do all the work, and poor, hard-working, honest men, who ha' been for years toiling to do all for the good of a master, be now turned out o' doors to do what they can or what they like. And you know what that means, and what it must come to.[13]

The overt hostility and implied threat of that last statement is countered, not unreasonably, by the factory owner:

> Science has opened to us her stores, and we shall be fools indeed not to take advantage of the good it brings. The time must come, and shortly,

when even the labourer himself will freely acknowledge that our improvements in machinery and the aid afforded to us by the use of steam will place England on a still nobler eminence than the proud height she has already attained.[14]

In melodrama, however, such things never remain a matter of business. The nature of melodrama is to individualize and personalize, to treat all ideas, all social problems in terms of individual conflict, courage, weakness, and vice. The whole world is seen in the microcosm of the struggle between evil and good, as incarnated in the villain on the one hand and the hero and heroine on the other.[15] Just before he discusses economics, the factory owner of Walker's play has scornfully dismissed the pleas and threats of his ex-workmen by crying, 'Is England's proud aristocracy to tremble when brawling fools mouth and question? No; the hangman shall be their answer.'[16] About seventy years later, at the turn of the next century, a play by Arthur Moss, *The Workman's Foe*, was performed on a music-hall bill at the Peckham Theatre of Varieties, South London. The plot of *The Workman's Foe* concerns the attempt of a ruthless factory foreman to seduce a workgirl under his supervision (as he has others). The girl's fellow-worker and sweetheart, a former strikeleader, tells the foreman, 'I spoke for the weak and defenceless against your tyranny and wickedness; yes, and against your villainy. It is men like you who cause revolutions among workers. You are a *heartless sweater*. Human life is nothing to you.' The foreman replies, 'I've climbed to power, despite the envy and hatred of the working-man. And now I'll sweat as I please. I'll put the workman's head under my heel, and crush it with as little remorse as I would you.' The worker is dismissed from employment and the foreman gloats:

I'll discharge all the men who took part in the strike, one by one, and get fresh men in their places at half the price. Why should I care how little the workers earn, so long as I'm successful? I made my position here by learning the art of riding rough-shod over my fellows. I've climbed the ladder of fortune by hypocrisy and cunning, and by sweating the workers that I and my employers may revel in luxury. Men of brains and cunning must rule the world.[17]

There is nothing about working conditions in this play, nothing but an elemental class hatred that can be so simply and powerfully stated because the hero-villain dichotomy of melodrama is the perfect vehicle for its expression.

The growth of the metropolis in the nineteenth century, from 900 000 in 1800, to 6 000 000 in 1900, is of course an integral part of the growth of a melodrama that occupies itself with the working class of that metropolis. The East End of London did not really exist until the great period of dock building early in the century, the first stage of which was completed with the opening of the St Katharine Docks in 1828. In the same year the Brunswick Theatre and the Pavilion Theatre were opened: the first East-End theatres proper. In the next fifteen years seven more theatres and saloon theatres opened in the East End. New theatres were also built across the Thames and on the fringes of the West End. These theatres belonged to the working and lower middle classes. They sat, not in the galleries of West-End theatres, but in the boxes and pit of their own neighbourhood theatres. Part of the extensive melodramatic repertory they watched was concerned with the lives of their own class of people in their own city. When this happened, they saw on stage the rooms, taverns, and public places which they inhabited, and in which they congregated. The middle-class theatres were doing much the same thing: urban verisimilitude in scenery and setting and the presence of the urban poor and humble as central characters in the drama marked both East-End and West-End theatres alike, although in the West End the fearful fall into poverty rather than the habituation to it was a prominent theme. Since West-End theatres had more money to spend, their version of the reality of the London scene was visually more detailed and convincing.

What all this means is that for the first time in English drama the working class appeared in serious plays, not always as comic characters, in a recognizable and contemporary domestic environment. Daily life, the ordinary family under stress, the attempt to find work, and the battle against poverty, crime, drink, and homelessness comprise the subject of numerous domestic melodramas. In *England and the English*, published in 1833, Bulwer-Lytton called on playwrights to be more modern, to use 'tales of a household nature, that find their echo in the heart of the people . . . awakening an interest common to us all; intense yet homely, actual – earnest – the pathos and passion of every-day life.'[18] What he wished for was already happening in domestic melodrama. Furthermore, the setting for this 'pathos and passion' is often London itself: the domestic melodrama is the first environmental drama to be written, and the first about life in a big city. Not only is this a matter of domestic and public settings on stage faithfully imitating real life, as far as stage art allowed, but it is also the deliberate thematic use of London as a moral symbol as well as a spectacle of life and an all-enclosing urban jungle.

An early form of stage naturalism, of the kind found in the first production of Tolstoy's *The Power of Darkness* (1889), Gorki's *The Lower Depths* (1902), and Hauptmann's *The Weavers* (1892), is strongly marked in English melodrama of the 1840s. This was partly French in origin, influenced by *Les Bohémiens de Paris* (1843), the stage version of Eugène Sue's novel *Les Mystères de Paris*; probably it was also influenced by the urban and topographical realism of *Oliver Twist* and *Nicholas Nickleby*, which were instantly and widely adapted for the stage. Urban melodrama divided the stage into two nations, and showed scenes of high life and low life alternately, the elegant villa interior in Regent's Park and the squalor of a drinking hole in St Giles's, as in this setting in T. W. Moncrieff's *The Scamps of London* (1843): *'Interior of miserable room in Rat's Castle, the Rookery, Dyot Street, St. Giles. At the back of the bagatelle board NED BRINDLE, JOE ONION, DICK SMITH, CADGERS, and VAGABONDS of every description divided into groups, sitting, smoking, drinking, &c.'*[19] This sort of play specialized in showing the busy new railway stations, the homeless poor underneath the dry arches of Waterloo Bridge, and the interiors of pubs where workmen gathered to drink. The unfortunate hero of *The Bottle* drinks in the High Mettled Racer in Finsbury Square, and just such a pub occurs in one of the best and best-known melodramas of the century, Tom Taylor's *The Ticket-of-Leave Man*, where the out-of-work hero seeks employment by the foreman of a gang of navvies in an East End pub, the Bridgewater Arms. Both stage detail and clientele are carefully authentic. *The Ticket-of-Leave Man* was produced in 1863 at the Olympic, a West-End theatre of some reputation; in 1881 *The Lights O' London* at the Princess's, a leading West-End melodrama house, contained a colourful and completely naturalistic scene of the Borough Market on a Saturday night, a scene which Clement Scott in the *Telegraph* found 'too real, too painful, too smeared with the dirt and degradation of London life'. The author of *The Lights O' London*, George R. Sims, had written about the East End and continued the occasional occupation of journalistic commentator upon London life which he had held before becoming a dramatist, but the presence of a scene like this in West-End melodrama is a sign of the ubiquity of the realistic mode in urban melodrama, wherever it was performed.

The crowds that thronged the stage of the Princess's for the Borough Market scene indicated that accurate topography alone was insufficient for the presentation of that urban environment in which the working class lived and moved. The life of the streets as well as the humble domestic and commercial interior was reproduced in melodrama, which required serious and comic characters pursuing a variety of avocations, characters entirely recognizable to audiences who met them every day. In T. P.

Taylor's two temperance melodramas, *The Bottle* (1847) and *The Drunkard's Children* (1848), both based upon Cruikshank's temperance engravings and both performed at the City of London Theatre in Bishopsgate, the settings are domestic parlours, lodging-houses, beer-shops, gin-palaces, and the streets of London: in *The Bottle*, Finsbury Square, Chick Lane, Moorfields, and 'A View Near the Bank'. The characters are multifarious and multitudinous at the same time: a mechanic (the hero of *The Bottle*), a master engineer (his employer), a recruiting sergeant, a constable, a bailiff, a thief, a needlewoman, a lodging-house keeper, a shoe-binder, a pieman. These are some of the dramatis personae of *The Bottle*. *The Drunkard's Children* is even more thronged: coster-mongers, dancers, publicans, a safe-cracker, thimble-rigger, casino manager, prison chaplain, gaoler, barmaid, threepenny lodging-house keeper, dog fancier, prize-fighter, dustman, lascar, and others. Many domestic melodramas bear no relation to the life of the streets, but the ones that stress the problems of life in London frequently do, and these usually include street people and workers. *Lizzie Lyle, or The Flower Makers of Finsbury* (1869) has its artificial flower makers; *Mary Edmonstone* (1862) possesses a carpenter, a needle seller, a milkmaid, and a hawker of dying confessions; *The Negro of Wapping* (1838) contains a crossing-sweeper, a chair-mender, a rush-maker, and stonemasons.

To live in London, to keep body and soul together, and to provide for one's family is as difficult for the poorer characters of melodrama as it is for those in Dickens's novels. The number of plays that include the word 'London' in their titles is remarkable: *The Heart of London* (1830), *London by Night* (1845), *The Poor of London* (1864), *Lost in London* (1867), *The Streets of London* (1857), *The Great World of London* (1898), *The Work Girls of London* (1864) – these are only a few examples. The cumulative impression derived from such titles and from a reading of their content is of a life lived at the edge of survival, of the loss of innocence, of the dangers of drink and crime, of size and numbers and sickness and weariness. The tired coal-miner of Watt Phillips's *Lost in London*, searching endlessly for his wife in the great city, says that 'it be a dreadful and a dreary place, this Lunnon, for them as are weak an' wi' no hand to guide 'em'.[20] Urban environmentalism in melodrama is not merely a veri-similitude of scene and character, but it also carries a thematic and symbolic significance which sees London as an image of a dark and difficult existence.

There is one curious feature of urban melodrama that needs further investigation. The coal-miner's wife in *Lost in London* has fled with her seducer from her Lancashire village to London. The contrast between rural virtue and urban vice, and the theme of the loss of innocence, is very strong in domestic melodrama, and it commonly concerns the working class in the city and the peasant class in the countryside. Virtuous members of the latter leave their villages, come up to London, and are either seriously endangered by vice or actually succumb to it, or find their dreams broken by poverty and moral squalor. Such themes are sharply dramatized by a structure which first portrays the blissful village home and then the perils and sorrows of life in the city. The village of domestic melodrama is a fantasy, a never-never land of ideal beauty, tranquillity, and innocence; it contains the old home – often a rose-embowered cottage – and the church, two powerful reminders of a lost world in the degradation of the city. Incidentally, the song 'Home, Sweet Home' was written for just such a village melodrama, *Clari, the Maid of Milan* (1823). The good village girl of Douglas Jerrold's *Martha Willis, the Servant Maid* (1831) goes into domestic service in London and unpacks her box upon arrival; it contains 'the picture of our church and village, that Mr Carmine painted for me, and told me always to keep by me'.[21] It is not long before Martha, falsely accused of theft, languishes in Newgate under sentence of death. In *The Bottle*, Ruth, the wife of the drunken hero, pleads with the bailiff to be allowed to keep one possession:

> I must beg you not to take that; it is the picture of the village church where I worshipped as a girl, that saw me wedded in my womanhood; there are a thousand dear recollections connected with it, humble though they be. There was a meadow close by, over whose green turf I have often wandered, and spent many happy hours, when a laughing merry child; and dearer far it is to me, for beneath a rude mound in that sad resting-place poor mother and father lie.[22]

Later, sick and starving and looking for work, Ruth is assisted by her friend Esther, who is a seamstress doing piece-work at home. Esther has no money for her rent, and complains:

> Work, work, work, and yet of no avail; it will not clear away the poverty by which I am surrounded. The dreadful threat of the few things I have got together being taken from me, the fear of being thrust forth homeless, checks every zealous intention, defies all industrious efforts. Well, well, I must try – still struggle on.[23]

Esther has rescued Ruth's picture of her village church from the sale; when Ruth sees it she cries, 'Why does it hang there, as if to remind me of the past – to tell me what I might have been?'[24]

One can only explain such scenes and such themes – a whole sub-class of domestic melodrama is involved – in terms of the lives and theatrical needs of urban audiences. Did the emigration of country people into the cities create a class of audience that retained some memory of its rural origins, perhaps softened and idealized by the passage of time? Or was this kind of writing designed to appeal to those who knew nothing of the countryside, who were born in cities, and who longed for something different, for an ethos as well as an environment? The homesickness in such plays is not just for the village, the old parents at home, and the peace of the countryside, but it is also for a simpler and purer life, a return to a Garden of Eden that never existed. Whatever the explanation, and there must be one if we knew more about the social origins and lives of urban theatre audiences, the village theme is strikingly prominent.

What, then, can we say in conclusion about melodrama and the working class? That English melodrama provides us with the first drama that takes this class seriously is clear. It is also the first environmental drama in the sense of offering a setting of urban life as real as stage art can make it, and peopling that stage with characters who are a living part of the environment. Melodramatic urban life rises to the theme of dark metropolitanism so familiar in Dickens, where London on the stage, as in his novels, takes on a character and meaning of its own. To those who have claimed, as they still sometimes do, that nineteenth-century drama, and melodrama in particular, has no relevance to the social realities of life[25] – the charge makes just as much sense levelled at Dickens – one can reply by asking them to examine without prejudice and with some care the melodramas that treat of the life of the drunkard, the factory worker, the poor, and the destitute. They might also reflect upon the enormous working-class audience, especially in the East End, that filled its own local theatres and at least equalled and probably outnumbered the middle-class and West-End audience. Of course there are hundreds and hundreds of melodramas that have nothing whatever to do with the working class or with urban life or even with the modern world; a great many of these were performed with success in working-class theatres. Even this fact, however, tells us something about the taste of working-class audiences. In any consideration of English drama, the popular Victorian working-class theatre should be treated with no less respect and no less seriously than the novels of Dickens in the development of English fiction.

Notes

1. See George Rowell, *The Victorian Theatre*, 2nd edn (Cambridge University Press, 1978) pp. 82–83; John Pick, *The West End* (Eastbourne: John Offord, 1983) especially chs. 4–6; Michael R. Booth, 'The Theatre and its Audience', in Clifford Leech and T.W. Craik (eds) *The Revels History of Drama in English: Vol. 6, 1750 – 1880* (London: Methuen, 1975) pp. 13–19, 28.

2. Henry Morley, *The Journal of a London Playgoer*, Michael R. Booth (ed.) (Leicester University Press, 1974) p. 14.

3. *Ibid.*, p. 20.

4. *Report from the Select Committee on Theatrical Licences and Regulations* (1866) p. 295.

5. See the articles 'Habits and Amusements of Costermongers', 'Of the Dustmen of London', 'Statement of a "Popular Scavager" ', 'Of the Rubbish Carters', and 'Cheap Lodging-Houses' in vols 1–3 of Henry Mayhew, *London Labour and the London Poor* (London: Griffin, Bohn, 1861; rpt. New York: Dover, 1968).

6. Charles Dickens, 'Two Views of a Cheap Theatre', *The Uncommercial Traveller and Reprinted Pieces* (Oxford University Press, 1958) p. 32.

7. *Household Words*, 30 Mar. and 15 Apr. 1850.

8. 'Victorian Gallery', *London Labour and the London Poor*, vol. 1, pp. 18–20.

9. *Saturday Review*, 9 Apr. 1898.

10. T. W. Erle, *Letters from a Theatrical Scene-Painter* (London: Marcus Ward, 1880) p. 16.

11. *Ibid.*, pp. 100–101.

12. For example, G. F. Taylor, *The Factory Strike* (1838), in which the villain is a strike leader who burns the factory and murders his generous employer, and Tom Taylor's *Arkwright's Wife* (1873), which attacks machine-smashing and mob violence. On industrial melodrama, see Michael R. Booth, *English Melodrama* (London: Herbert Jenkins, 1965) pp. 136–39, and Michael R. Booth (ed.), *English Plays of the Nineteenth Century* (Oxford University Press, 1969–76) vol. 1, pp. 204–05.

13. *The Factory Lad*, in Booth (ed.), *English Plays of the Nineteenth Century*, vol. 1, p. 215.

14. *Ibid.*, p. 218.

15. See, for instance, the chapter on domestic melodrama in Booth, *English Melodrama*, pp. 118–44.

16. *The Factory Lad*, in Booth (ed.), *English Plays of the Nineteenth Century*, vol. 1, p. 218.

17. Arthur Moss, *The Workman's Foe* (London: Heywood, [n.d.]) pp. 11–12.

18. Edward Bulwer-Lytton, *England and the English* (London: Richard Bentley, 1833) vol. 2, p. 145.

19. T. W. Moncrieff, *The Scamps of London* (London: Dicks Standard Plays, [n.d.]) no. 472, p. 15.

20. Watt Phillips, *Lost in London*, in Michael R. Booth (ed.), *Hiss the Villain* (London: Eyre & Spottiswoode, 1964) pp. 244–45.

21. Douglas Jerrold, *Martha Willis, the Servant Maid* (London: Dicks Standard Plays, [n.d.]) no. 420, p. 7.

22. T. P. Taylor, *The Bottle* (London: Samuel French, [n.d.]) p. 22.

23. *Ibid.*, pp. 30–31.

24. *Ibid.*, p. 31.
25. Such as, to take a representative sample, Dutton Cook, *Nights at the Play* (London: Chatto & Windus, 1883) pp. 13–14; Leonard Ashley (ed.), *Nineteenth-Century British Drama* (Glenview, Ill.: Scott, Foresman, 1967) p. 7; Terry Otten, *The Deserted Stage* (Athens, Ohio: Ohio University Press, 1972) vol. 1, pp. 3–4.

10

Little Dorrit as 'Poor Theatre': Dickens through Grotowski

John J. Glavin

During the autumn of 1985 I adapted Dickens's novel *Little Dorrit* for the stage according to the principles of the 'Poor Theatre' created by the great contemporary Polish director, Jerzy Grotowski.[1] A little while before we opened our adaptation, I asked the cast if they thought, as I had begun to fear, that the audience might have trouble following our adaptation. 'Only,' one of them cheerfully answered, 'only if they've read the novel.' Readers of Dickens's great novel may indeed feel some bewilderment, and even animosity, as I outline what we did to Dickens's text, and why. The novel's multiple plots we diminished to one story, Arthur Clennam's. We reduced the novelist's massive cast to eleven characters, performed by eleven actors and a broom. The broom was Little Dorrit herself, an idea adapted from Grotowski's staging of the story of Jacob and Rachel in his play *Akropolis*. All of the speeches did come from Dickens's text but the speeches were not often given in the play by those who had said them in the novel.

If these changes constitute a betrayal of *Little Dorrit*, then such a betrayal seems to be inevitable if the imprinted page is to be transformed into embodied speech and enacted gesture. In *Contra Petilian* Augustine puns crucially on the Latin *traditor*, which means, he reminds his readers, both traitor and transmitter. It is a pun fundamental to the history of all texts, but especially to the history of texts in and for the theatre. As I shall argue in the pages that follow, the adapter-director who transmits fiction to the stage must betray the inscribed text to bring it to another kind of life. Not to betray is, in effect, to embalm.

Jerzy Grotowski (b. Rzeszow, Poland, 1933) emerged during the late sixties as the most influential figure to have appeared in the Western theatre since Bertolt Brecht. Continuing, and in a sense completing, Stanislavski's epochal revision of acting technique, Grotowski combined European with Eastern theatre styles, notably Indian, Chinese and

Indonesian, to form a radically new kind of theatre, stripped of every technological accretion which could come between the performer and his audience. This theatre, which he called 'Poor Theatre', lasted roughly from 1959, when he became the director of the Theatre of Thirteen Rows in Opole, until 1968 with the final production of his Laboratory Theatre in Wroclaw, *Apocalypsis Cum Figuris.*[2] The ideas developed during this extraordinarily productive decade Grotowski published in *Towards a Poor Theatre* in 1968, a book which has had profound influence throughout the western theatre, and which served as our paradigm in adapting Dickens's text.[3]

The essential poverty of this radically new form of theatre is of two kinds, formal and thematic. Formally, Poor Theatre strips away every-thing drama has borrowed from the other and, to the stage, ancillary arts, retaining only 'the actor–spectator relations of perceptual, direct "live" communion' (Grotowski, p. 19). Centred thematically on 'the archetype of the savior-martyr', Poor Theatre also dismisses 'conventional images of harmony, aspiration and spiritual nobility as the deceptive values of a false civilization'.[4] In their place Grotowski creates an 'auto sacramentale' in which the central figures come to realize their 'spiritual potential through the mortification of the flesh that directly parallels the self-transcendence aimed at in Grotowski's acting techniques'.[5] Radically stripped, this impoverished theatre can yield the audience performances of unrivalled psychic richness, performances which, Grotowski argues, allow us 'to cross our frontiers, exceed our limitations, fill our emptiness – fulfill ourselves' (Grotowski, p. 21).

This emphasis on the audience is rooted in Grotowski's sense of theatre as a 'scalpel, enabling us to open ourselves, to transcend ourselves, to find what is hidden within us and to make the act of encountering others' (Grotowski, p. 57). The text to be adapted to the theatre he sees essentially as a catalyst. From this point of view the 'best adaptations are those that have repudiated a timorous fidelity to the letter of the text'. Grotowski thus invites the adapter, as Raymonde Temkine suggests, 'To rethink the work, even to inflect it, transpose it, and pour it into a new structure . . . bypassing, eliminating, in order to seize what attracts . . . what resists . . . the core of the work'.[6]

Grotowski's own theatre is – or rather was, since he has devised no new plays since 1968 – a theatre of adaptation, relying either on master-texts of Renaissance drama, by Calderón, Shakespeare, and Marlowe, or the great works of Polish Romanticism: Michiewicz, Slowacki and Wyspiański. These texts, which seem to him 'the voices of my ancestors', 'fascinate' Grotowski. He insists 'they give us the possibility of a sincere

confrontation' – confrontation emerges as the cardinal term in Grotowski's theatre-lexicon – 'a brutal and brusque confrontation between . . .
the beliefs and experiences of life, of previous generations and . . . our
own experiences and our own prejudices' (Grotowski, p. 58). And yet,
despite the fact that his plays, especially from his Polish sources, adapt
works written on the largest scale, Grotowski's own plays never last more
than seventy minutes. His casts are never larger than eight. He insists that
his audiences be limited to between forty and sixty persons at each
performance. Only that kind of scale, Grotowski argues, can retain for the
theatre the essential feature that supports its claim on the audience in an
age of film – the immediate, personal contact of spectator and actor.

   With Grotowski's eyes I thus came to see that *Little Dorrit* contains as
many theatrically viable plays as there are players challenged to stage it.
His practice showed me that a play does not have to be epic in staging to
be epic in impact, to be authentically Dickensian. He thereby released us
from both the desire and the obligation to stage an entire novel, as the
Royal Shakespeare Company did *Nicholas Nickleby*, complete with
hundreds of characters, multiple plots, narrative and authorial comment.
Rather than aspiring to such comprehensive coverage – and inevitably
failing to provide it, because all adaptation from novel to play must
transgress the text it takes from – Grotowski invites us to treasure and
conserve the text we adapt.

   Our *Little Dorrit* became a play about Arthur Clennam. But we could
just as successfully have made a play about the Dorrits, without Arthur.[7]
Or we could have made a play about the Merdles, in which there need
have been no mention of the Clennams. There is a superb play in Bleeding
Heart Yard by itself. And a very great play indeed – one to which I hope
to return in the next few years – in the Meagles and Tattycoram, the
Gowans and Miss Wade. All of these plays are possible because the
adapter's task is not the replacement of novel with play, a task as
impossible as it is not worth doing. Nor should the adapter merely
bounce the theatre-piece off the prose text, as though the first text were
a sort of fictive trampoline, another image of Grotowski's. Instead
Grotowski urges us to confront ourselves with the source-text, and then
follow the lines that confrontation provokes. And that is exactly how we
began to adapt *Little Dorrit*.

   Grotowski suggests 'we start working on a theatre performance . . . by
violating our innermost selves, searching for the things which can hurt us
most deeply' (Grotowski, p. 42). I therefore asked each of the eleven
members of the cast, the number of people who elected to stay with the
production after they read Grotowski's 'Statement of Principles', to tell

me, as they finished reading each quarter of the novel, which two characters, irrespective of sex, they would hate to play on the stage and why. These nominations it seemed to me would establish, for our group, the emotional fault-lines of the play, the points from and along which deeply situated emotions were most likely to erupt. The play that emerged, perhaps not surprisingly in a university setting, was about Mrs Clennam and her son.

We found, and uncovered, in Clennam the story of a mind forced by its early history to live as fully as possible outside the body, a mind that can desire now only in an elegiac, ghostly echo of libido. His early experiences leave Clennam longing for incarceration because imprisonment represents fundamental embodiment, radical enclosure in time and space. Only by clinging to this ultimate form of enclosure can Dickens's hero re-root himself, a willed martyrdom of his old ephemeral self, in order to mother out of his imagination and into time the new self of desire.

This version of the plot of *Little Dorrit* seems to me a powerfully and authentically Dickensian story. In Dickens's universe each man finds himself, like the imprisoned debtors in the Marshalsea, caged by claims upon the self from the structures of family, unjust and duplicitous claims he can never adequately repay. These claims we see in *Little Dorrit* not only in the stories of Arthur and Amy but in those of all the secondary characters: Flora, the Flintwinches, the Meagles and the Gowans. (It is indeed the essential falsity of these claims that guarantees the success of the quintessentially false Barnacle clan.) Such demands can be disclaimed only, and temporarily, by figures like the uxoricide Rigaud/Blandois. Nevertheless, Rigaud too is ultimately destroyed, like all those who reject prison, by the inevitable and ubiquitous powers of enclosure. To refuse imprisonment is to reject what is for Dickens the essential reality of human experience.

At the same time, from *Pickwick* onwards, places of imprisonment emerge in the novels as the locus of true knowledge and psychic rebirth. Radical enclosure extirpates the false self engendered by genealogy and supported by society's unreliable fictions. But the potential for self-liberation through physical enclosure evades those who like Mrs Clennam merely imitate gaoling, pretending to be immured but having her own power of command intact. True and profitable imprisonment for Dickens must be accompanied by the entire surrender of the will, except for the will to suffer entire loss. It was in this drive towards self-gaoling, that particularly Dickensian form of the ubiquitous Romantic nostalgia for the gutter, that we found the spine of our dramatic action.

We were fortunate in being able to stage our manifold prison in a small and low, more Gothic than Revival, stone crypt. Four central columns, supporting the crypt's pattern of vaults, divided the space into three equal areas — roughly, a nave with aisles to the north and south. A shallow, raised apse to the east ended with a stone altar surmounted by a stone crucifix. On its north side, a small door opened out of the apse into a labyrinthine corridor that gave access to the principal entrance of the building. Through this door the audience entered the darkened crypt, having been guided through the entrance corridor by a member of the cast. They faced across the full extension of the central playing space to a larger, western, rounded space, dominated by the crypt's principal, heavy wooden doors. In this western apse we placed a wooden second altar table. Between the two apses the audience found its seats, two long rows in the crypt's aisles, in front low stools, behind them low chairs.

On the wooden, western altar table the arriving audience found Clennam lying supine. Scattered throughout the rest of the darkened space the other members of the cast crouched or huddled, calling out in an increasing cacophany broken phrases from the novel's text. Suddenly, the man who had led the audience in clapped for silence. As the other figures crept out of sight, he intoned from a lectern a passage from Dickens's preface to the 1857 edition, informing the spectators of their location and their role.

Grotowski insists on the spectator's role in the play. In shaping Poor Theatre one must also cast the audience: the actors must determine their performances in response to a role they imagine the audience is playing in response to the acting it watches. Taking our cue from Dickens's preface, we projected an audience of pseudo-psychical tourists, unwitting participants in an unplanned and personal seance. In our playing space they find what Dickens in the preface insists will happen to anyone who happens into 'Marshalsea Place', what happened to him when, after many years' absence, he made his way back to the site of his family's imprisonment. Our visitors suddenly looking 'upon the rooms in which the debtors lived' unexpectedly found themselves, as Dickens predicts, among his and their own 'crowding ghosts of many miserable years':

Whosoever goes into Marshalsea Place, turning out of Angel Court . . . will find his feet on the very paving-stones of the extinct Marshalsea jail; will see its narrow yard to the right and to the left, very little altered if at all, except that the walls were lowered when the place got free; will look upon rooms in which the debtors lived; and will stand among the crowding ghosts of many miserable years.[8]

These haunting lines began our play. They counterpointed this passage from the beginning of volume 2, chapter 30: 'far aslant across the city struck the long bright rays, bars of the prison of this lower world' (p. 831). Together, they echoed and re-echoed throughout the production, insistently identifying the playing space as a synecdoche for all the structures of the human situation, universal and inevitable forms of imprisonment.

To embody in this playing space the terrible power Mrs Clennam seems to her son, she was played by three actors, two women and one man, imprisoned round a heavy bench in the eastern apse, backed by the stone altar and the stone crucifix. One of the women was the bridal Mrs Clennam (Mrs Clennam/1), veiled, standing to one side, supporting herself against the bench's arm, trapped forever in the terrible moment of betrayal when she found the 'guilty creature' in her newly-wedded husband's arms. The other woman was the mad Mrs Clennam (Mrs Clennam/3), who in the novel's final scenes runs into the streets, desperate to protect her secret from Rigaud/Blandois's exposure. Blindly, guided by her hands against the blank stone wall, she paced ceaselessly back and forth in the little apse, desperate to discover some form of release. Seated in the bench, heavily draped and hooded in black, the man offered the Mrs Clennam of the wheel chair (Mrs Clennam/2), the stern and unyielding mother who does 'not forget'. Mid-way through the play, the same actor suddenly appeared as Mr Dorrit, thereafter switching rapidly between the two identities, Arthur's sought-after and denied parent.

Arthur was also tripled, but – until his ultimate, ironic prison triumph – his three parts were separated. The detached identities were portrayed by two actors, a black and a white man, identically dressed, inseparably bound to each other, speaking the lines the novel gives to the mysterious Rigaud/Blandois. Blandois's reason for being in the novel is never made explicitly clear, though the careful reader never doubts his necessity. In our play, centring on the crucial scene where Mrs Clennam dismisses Arthur from the house in order to deal with Blandois (vol. 2, ch. 10), we made this double-figure the 'Purpose' and 'Hope' Arthur rejects in the opening sequence in Marseilles (vol. 1, ch. 2, p. 59). Separated from his imagination, this purpose and hope transform inevitably into the greed and lust that propel Blandois through the novel.

As the audience enters, they see the pair endlessly circle underneath the wooden altar on which Clennam is lying, reaching out to trace the edges of the table with their grasping hands, somehow unable to rise up from beneath the platform to touch and confront him. In the silence after the preface, they freeze. The reader of the preface, the audience's initial guide, takes a seat among the spectators. He then becomes the Mocker, from time to time hurling at Arthur Mr F's Aunt's jeers and gibes, beginning the 'dialectic between mockery and apotheosis' crucial to Grotowski's theatre.[9] But, at the start, he is silent, watching Arthur slowly inch himself forward on the slab until, palms pressed to the stone floor, he slowly somersaults backward to crouch at the bottom of the nave.

From the aisles, voices sing out the sad song of a London Sunday, 'Come to Church, Come to Church/They won't come. They won't come' (vol. 1, ch. 3, p. 68). Rigaud and Blandois stand. They are now ferrymen. To the dismal psalmody they begin to ferry Clennam home, his hands resting on their shoulders as they propel him into the theatre. But almost at once he rejects their begging, somehow threatening, claims for his attention. He thrusts them out of his way, crying out as they slink back Tattycoram's reproach, 'I am ill used. I am ill used' (vol. 1, ch. 2, p. 65). Thereafter, they dog him, mocking his initial search for freedom, his subsequent idealizing of Little Dorrit, and his ultimate self-immolation in the prison cell.

Throwing off purpose and hope, proclaiming from the start that he has no will, Clennam enters our play as a broken Odysseus, returning not to a faithful wife but an all-too-faithful mother. In the early scenes he attempts to impose on his tripled parent the history of guilt he imagines her to bear. 'Grasping at money. Driving hard bargain. Some one may have been injured. Ruined. If reparation can be made. Let us make it, mother.' (vol. 1, ch. 5, p. 88). He returns to her room repeatedly, trying to force her to accept his version of her life. But her triple voice continually drowns out his claims, literally throwing him over in his demands to be noticed and deferred to, denouncing him with the curse which comes true at the play's conclusion: 'Better you had been motherless from your cradle' (vol. 1, ch. 5, p. 90).

Forced to accept the defeat of his initial scheme, 'giving up the business', he begins to substitute, for the failed biological relation of parent and child, his own invention and inversion. He becomes the loving parent to this 'child', the servant Little Dorrit – a veiled broom propped at the side of the playing space which Clennam gradually invests with character and history. The spinning of this fiction is counterpointed against Rigaud/Blandois's mocking delivery of Flora, in our play a similarly veiled, squatting, bird-like revenant, circling round and round Clennam as she unwinds the babble of their failed past romance. Rejecting with horror her all-too-palpable reality, he increasingly identifies himself instead with the Dorrit family's prison cell. And he discovers, when he returns to his mother's room for what will be the last time, that he has indeed, and to his shock, effectuated that psychic transfer.

This sequence conflates volume 2, chapter 10, 'The dreams of Mrs Flintwinch thicken' (p. 600) and chapter 23, 'Mistress Affery makes a Conditional Promise, respecting her Dreams' (p. 747). In his mother's room Clennam discovers that Rigaud/Blandois have taken the son's place he had earlier resigned. He has successfully purged the past by having himself purged from it:

Clennam: Sir, whoever you are, I would lose no time in placing you outside this house, if I were master here.

Mrs Clennam/2: But you are not master here.

Blandois: It appears to me, madame, that Monsieur your son is disposed to complain of me.

Rigaud: He is not polite.

Mrs Clennam/1: You separated yourself from my affairs.

Mrs Clennam/3: It was not my act.

Mrs Clennam/2: It was yours. . . . You abandoned me.

Mrs Clennam/3: To them.

Mrs Clennam/1: He abandoned me.

Mrs Clennam/2: Now he occupies —

Mrs Clennam/3: — your place.

Mrs Clennam (All): Your place — he occupies — your place.
    (*Echo*)

Rigaud/Blandois, boasting of the murder of Madame Rigaud, 'dashing herself to death upon the rocks below' (vol. 1, ch. 1, p. 50), drag off their first victim, Flintwinch. The tripled-mother disappears in the opposite direction, murmuring 'Let it be, let it be.' And Clennam, through what he will later call his 'reserve and self-mistrust' (vol. 2, ch. 29, p. 828), is left entirely alone, as he has now willed himself – alone except for the veiled broom, stuck in the corner of the eastern apse, to whom he tenderly whispers, 'My child'.

This crucial mid-play passage, from the genealogical reality of his family's house, to the preferred fiction of the prison, we marked with his long crossing of the Iron Bridge, a bridge composed out of all the members of the cast but Clennam himself. Creeping into the central space in postures taken from the Damned in Michelangelo's *Last Judgement*, they suddenly, slowly rise up in two parallel lines, stretching themselves into the iron struts of the long bridge. And as Arthur approaches with his 'child' and passes between them, they seductively murmur to him the superb beginning of volume 2, chapter 23 (p. 742):

> As though a criminal should be chained in a stationary boat on a deep clear river, condemned, whatever countless leagues of water flowed past him, always to see the body of the fellow-creature he had drowned lying at the bottom, immovable, and unchangeable, except as the eddies made it broad or long, now expanding, now contracting its terrible lineaments, so Arthur —

At the same time, Clennam speaks to his companion the lines associated in the novel with his surrendering Pet Meagles, describing how 'the flowers, pale and unreal in the moonlight, float away upon the river', like 'the greater things that once were in our breasts and near our hearts' (vol. 1, ch. 28, p. 387). At that moment reality too floats from him.

Abruptly, his reverie is shattered. Rigaud and Blandois, breaking from their places in the bridge, have seized Little Dorrit. The others collapse, rocking back and forth in howls of laughter. Rigaud grasps Clennam, forcing him to watch, as Blandois tauntingly, grotesquely rapes the broom. All Clennam's discarded libido surges into the action, forcing him to witness what he has displaced from the course of his own nature, 'a bursting . . . of the smouldering fire so long pent up' (vol. 2, ch. 30, p. 842) – the novel's description of Mrs Clennam's desperate flight from her house to the Marshalsea. Writhing in horror, he cannot break from Rigaud's grasp; in fact, it is the grasped, not the grasper, who is rocking the pair from and towards the violation before them. And then, as suddenly as it began, the rape has ended. A shocking silence follows the screams of laughter. Arthur has broken from Rigaud, not to rescue Little Dorrit, but to hurl himself also to the ground, a fellow victim. As the rest slink away, Clennam, prone, murmurs a slightly varied quotation of Dickens's own words recalling the 'grief and humiliation' of his Marshalsea days: 'I often forget, forget in my dreams, that I am a man. They have broken my heart.'[10]

The male Mrs Clennam enters, now the benevolent patriarch, Mr Dorrit, extolling the quiet of the prison in speeches originally given to the doctor and nurse at Little Dorrit's own birth (vol. 1, ch. 6, p. 101): 'The flies trouble you, don't they, my dear? Perhaps they're sent as a consolation, if only we knew it. How are you now, my dear? No better? No, my dear, it isn't to be expected. You'll be worse before you're better, and you know it, don't you?' The actors playing Flintwinch and Affery reappear, now Tip and Fanny. The trio extols the 'freedom' and 'peace' of the prison, but they are at the same time the matador and picadors of a corrida in which Arthur is the bull, the first of those pain-filled 'genteel fictions' (vol. 1, ch. 7, p. 114) that mask the bitter truths of the Marshalsea. From the aisles voices warningly call, 'The Lock, the Lock' (vol. 1, ch. 8, p. 125). Bells ring. But Arthur on hands and knees continues to charge Dorrit's ripped, red smoking-jacket, until stabbed by the concealed broom, which he at the same time painfully, ecstatically grabs to his groin. Entirely felled, he is made 'welcome to the Marshalsea'.

The prison scenes that follow, and which make up the second half of the play, conflate Clennam's early elective visits to the Marshalsea with his later self-imposed imprisonment for debt. The playing-space, which earlier could be anything, he has now narrowed to his stone cell, empty except for a single low stool, a copy of the stools on which half the audience sit. At the same point, the Mocker leaves his place among the audience outside the action and joins Clennam as the ultimate inside figure, the Turnkey, modelled on Bob, the child Amy Dorrit's friend. But this Turnkey is only the apparent keeper of the prison. It is in fact Clennam who, to accomplish the deepest experience of psychic liberation, refuses all physical liberty. Instead, in both the novel and the play, he insists, to the dismay of the other characters, on going through an apparently unnecessary askesis. 'I must take', he insists, 'the consequences of what I have done' (vol. 1, ch. 26, p. 783). In a perverse exercise of indomitable will that copies and parodies his mother, he condemns himself not simply to the prison but to an unrelenting regime of solitude and starvation. Like Grotowski's own 'holy actor', he is both saint and 'self-willed martyr controlling his own torture and *using* his persecutors to destroy his body in order to purify his spirit'.[11] The prison's 'iron stripes' he, not 'the early glowing sun', turns 'into stripes of gold' (vol. 2, ch. 30, p. 831).

In the first half of the play the Mocker, seated among them, voiced the audience's initial bewilderment and then gradual hostility to the difficult style of the play, and especially their hostility to the insistence on self-transgression which Grotowski substitutes for the conventional drama's demand for identification with the characters. But now, as the audience is forced to confront Clennam's brutal agony, they become increasingly pained by his suffering. It is their growing sympathy that the ex-Mocker/now-Turnkey proffers to the action. His bitter taunts give way to a genuine, foolish kindness, the characteristic Dickens associates with the Chiverys and with Maggy. The Turnkey emerges as, in effect, the kindly sacristan of so many chancel-centred plays, sweetly and not very smartly helping to further mysteries whose depths elude him. Thus, even as the play moves towards its apotheosis, it remains rooted in mockery.

The audience's hostility transfers to the other figures in the play. They now resist Clennam. They disbelieve. First, Fanny and Tip offer him 'something green' (vol. 2, ch. 27, p. 791), in our play not lettuce but a bunch of grapes. In a comforting which is also a torture they slowly roll the grapes across his hands, press them to his nostrils, force them against his tongue. He is barely able to spit out what he has already half swallowed. Later, when the Turnkey offers him a toy, a furled band of crêpe paper, Clennam uses it to gag and bind himself, to bind and rebind his limbs in even stricter confinement. At the same time Mr F's Aunt, his particular nemesis, rips away the bands, denouncing him in a speech that begins with Panck's abuse of Casby (vol. 2, ch. 32, p. 869), and concludes with Flintwinch's denunciation of Mrs Clennam: 'All Pride, all Spite, all Unforgiveness' (vol. 2, ch. 30, p. 851). At the conclusion of each ordeal, he calls out for Little Dorrit, who has been lost to him since his entrance into the prison. He can hear her voice, far off, whispering passages that come from her letters to Clennam in volume 2, chapters 4 and 11. But he cannot, yet, make her visible.

Finally, broken, exhausted, deserted, Clennam finds himself approached by Mr Dorrit. In a whispered parody of the confessional, Dorrit gives Clennam the counsel he offers his brother Frederick in the novel (vol. 1, ch. 19, p. 267):

Dorrit: Do you think your habits are as precise and methodical as – shall I say mine are?
Clennam: But I am not like you.
Dorrit: Oh but you might be, my son, you might be like me, if you chose.

In the proposition of that model, Clennam finds the clue to the ultimate surrender of will that leads to his final, equivocal freedom. Using Dorrit's own language, drawing Dorrit's torn red jacket round himself, he forces himself to stand, proclaiming, in a speech that derives from Mr Dorrit's deluded boasting at Mrs Merdle's Roman dinner, that he is 'the Father of the Marshalsea, if I may establish a claim to so honourable a title'. He insists that, like Little Dorrit, he has been 'Born Here, Bred Here, the child of an unfortunate father' (vol. 2, ch. 19, p. 709). His fellow debtors crowd around him. Pushing him to the ground, kicking him back and forth from one to another, they turn him into the ball in a violent, prolonged soccer match. But he invites their kicks, crying out repeatedly Dorrit's levee boast, 'Ladies and gentlemen, God bless you all. I accept the conferred distinction.'

This final degradation allows Clennam the ultimate act of renunciation, the dismissal of Little Dorrit. His tormentors now venerate him, genuflecting as they approach to kiss his wounds, murmuring a conflation of the comments on the enriched Dorrit and the impoverished Clennam: 'He both spoke and acted very handsome. Very handsome indeed!' (vol. 2, ch. 27, p. 790). 'Anybody might see: the shadow of the wall is dark upon him' (vol. 2, ch. 28, p. 803).

The worshippers withdraw. Bells ring. All the women in the cast carry in, high above their crouching forms, the broom. Clennam drags himself a few steps forward, collapses. Speaking through the women, Little Dorrit begs, 'Let me lend you all I have' (vol. 2, ch. 29, p. 838). Clennam refuses and, following closely the scenario of volume 2, chapter 29, 'A Plea in the Marshalsea', dismisses her. She must, he insists, 'see me only as I am. A ruined man far removed from you, whose course is run while yours is but beginning. . . . Abandon all hope' (p. 829). Her sight confirms the self he has created. Imposing it on her, he imposes it on the world. He has become, in fact, the Nobody of desire he termed himself in the earlier parts of the novel (the Nobody of the novel's original title 'Nobody's Fault'). This absolute negation culminates the *via negativa* central to both Dickens and Grotowski. Both artists insist that only an entire kenosis of self can produce the deeply desired escape from what the novel knows as 'the prison of this lower world'. Little Dorrit, to the sound of bells, withdraws.

But as she goes, Rigaud and Blandois appear. Throughout Clennam's ordeal they have capered on the stone altar, aping his agony. Now they find themselves dragged back towards him. Hope entirely abandoned, purpose completely denied, the negated self can summon back the separated, repressed elements it requires to complete its fiction. Against their protests, Clennam forces them to support him in his ultimate triumph. Through a complex series of movements, the trio gradually transform from the writhing forms of the Laocoön to a stance suggesting Christ, the Virgin and the Baptist at the centre of the Sistine *Last Judgement*: Rigaud and Blandois balancing and supporting the heroic and resurrected hero, returned in judgement. He cries out, 'I have done what it was given me to do' – a version of his mother's blasphemous *Consummatum Est* (vol. 2, ch. 30, p. 849). And all three voices cry out her claim for recognition, 'I will be known as I know myself' (p. 845).

In response, his doomed mother crawls forward, her three forms fallen and separate. She attempts to refuse his powerful demand. But, finally, she must call out against her will the truth of his parentage: 'I am not your mother'. Clennam thus achieves explicitly in his moment of triumph the dream that undergirds so much of Dickens's major fiction: the child's replacement of the imposed, unfeeling, inadequate mother by a benevolent, beneficent and chosen father. His mother's original curse he has transformed into benison.

Now, on the verge of death, in delirium, he takes Little Dorrit as his bride. Mr Dorrit rises up from the fallen form of Mrs Clennam/2. He proffers the broom. Towards this pair Clennam makes his way, faltering, and finally falling, speaking Pet's speech when she intercepts Clennam by the river, to tell him she has accepted Gowan: the speech beginning 'You wonder to see me here by myself', and ending 'Passing along this deep shade, out at that arch of light at the other end, we come upon the ferry, and the cottage, by the best approach, I think.' (vol. 1, ch. 28, pp. 382–83). No longer able to stand, Clennam is lifted by Mr Dorrit and the attendant Turnkey, and carried out through the opened doors of the theatre, doors that sprang open as his mother died before his reunited form. And as he is carried out of the audience's sight he proclaims: 'I am rich now. Proud now. Happy now,' Little Dorrit's own speech when Clennam finally consents to accept her love (vol. 2, ch. 34, p. 846). The novel's running title for those pages is 'ALL LOST, AND ALL GAINED'.

Rigaud and Blandois, the two remaining Mrs Clennams, the only figures left in the playing space, curl up and quietly, human tumble-weed, roll away. From the distance come the last whispered echoes of the crucial phrases: 'Far aslant across the city strike the long bright rays, bars of the prison of this lower world.' There were no curtain calls. The audience, after a few uncertain moments, followed the performers out through the western doors, into a landscape they had not seen when they entered. The actors had disappeared. The spectators were left to find their way back to the point from which they had started.

Through its poetics of radical deprivation, Poor Theatre protects *Little Dorrit* from two forms of menace. First, it frees the adaptation from the danger of localization in the nineteenth century. For the most part, Dickens's novels are now trapped on the stage into a dead past, a kind of *faux*-Victoriana of fog-machines, mob-caps and music-hall bawdy. But the 'fierce August day' with which the novel begins is both 'Thirty years ago' and perduring; the debts it chronicles, ontological and periodless. To strip the production of every *merely* historical sign and gesture, we were careful, adapting Grotowski's practice, to costume the play from second-hand shops, in bridal and evening gowns, morning suits and uniforms.

These cast-offs the actors wore to every rehearsal for two months, until their finery had been reduced to the faded rags of debtors' fantasy. In this way we enable the stage to touch the audience with the same urgent, contemporary power Victorian and all subsequent readers have found in the novel itself. The play becomes like the saints on which Grotowski models his actors 'neither ancient nor modern . . . simply true, always true, carriers of that truth that captures the crucial questions of existence in every age'.[12]

At the same time our staging frees the play from the novel's necessary evasion of its own implications. It is the business of fiction to evade crystallization, to distend, to postpone, to submerge. That is the glory of its form.[13] But it is the business of the stage to embody, to clarify, to present. That which in the novel is all suggestion in the powerful emptiness between the markings on the page must, on the stage, make itself seen to be felt. One cannot stage a novel. One can only stage one reading of that novel. This seems to me to be the single most significant lesson Poor Theatre teaches the adapter. A successful stage-adaptation cannot, in any significant way, reproduce the novel it follows. To try to do so violates not only the particular economy of the parent text, in this case, of extended prose narrative, but also, just as inevitably, the particular economy of the stage.

To successfully adapt, Grotowski shows us, we must entirely subvert. Instead of copying, the adapter must find those forms in the theatre consonant with the vision of the parent-text. Only by this radical process of confrontation and subversion can the adapter realize the aim generic to every work of art: to give us what we had prized in the original text, what Stefan Brecht calls 'real information': what life 'might have been, could not be, might be, or cannot become'.[14]

Notes

1.   The adaptation was first performed on 8 Dec. 1985, in Copley Crypt, Georgetown University, Washington, DC, with the following cast: CLEN- NAM, Paul Kennan; MRS CLENNAM/1, Stacy Plavoukis; MRS CLENNAM/2, Drew Davis Poling; MRS CLENNAM/3, Jacqueline Cantwell; RIGAUD, Richard Heffernan; BLANDOIS, Aaron Ashby; AFFERY-FANNY, Teresa Stoughton; FLINTWINCH-TIP, Paul Fallon; FLORA, Heidi Daniels; MR F'S AUNT, Therese M. Wegmann; MOCKER-TURNKEY, Alec W. Farr.
2.   During, and immediately after, the Poor Theatre period, Grotowski's work was covered extensively in America by the theatre periodical, *The Drama Review*. See vol. 8 (1964) pp. 120–33; vol. 9 (1965) pp. 53–171 and

172–89; vol. 13 (1968) pp. 10–45; vol. 14 (1969) pp. 172–77 and 178–83; vol. 14 (1970) pp. 178–211; vol. 15 (1971) pp. 36–46; vol. 19 (1975) pp. 58–69; vol. 22 (1978) pp. 67–76. Recently there have appeared two useful full-length studies devoted to him: Jennifer Kumiega, *The Theatre of Grotowski* (London and New York: Methuen, 1985) and Zbigniew Osiński, *Grotowski and His Laboratory*, Lillian Vallee and Robert Findlay (trs) (New York: *Performing Arts Journal* Publications, 1985). Timothy J. Wiles offers a brilliant analysis of Grotowski and his place in the development of western theatre in *The Theatre Event* (University of Chicago Press, 1980). For a strong dissenting voice, see Jan Kott, 'Why Should I Take Part in the Sacred Dance?', *The Theatre of Essence* (Evanston: Northwestern University Press, 1984).

3. Jerzy Grotowski, *Towards a Poor Theatre* (New York: Simon & Schuster, 1968). All citations from *Towards a Poor Theatre* appear in the text as (Grotowski,   ) with page number.

4. Christopher Innes, *The Holy Theatre: Ritual and the Avant Garde* (New York: Cambridge University Press, 1981) p. 164.

5. *Ibid.*, p. 170.

6. Raymonde Temkine, *Grotowski*, Alex Szogyi (trs.) (New York: Avon Books, 1972) p. 71.

7. The Library of Congress copyright roles list what seems to be just such a play, the 1909 *The Dorrits*, a comedy in 3 acts by Margaret Mayo, itself adapted from a German play by Franz von Schoenthan.

8. *Little Dorrit*, John Holloway (ed.) (Harmondsworth: Penguin, 1967, rpt. 1976) p. 36. All references to Dickens's novel appear in the text with volume, chapter and page number for this edition. I quote the playing text of the adaptation which, because of the requirements of performance, frequently elides or alters tense and person.

9. Jerzy Grotowski, 'Doctor Faustus in Poland', *TDR*, vol. 8 (1964) p. 121.

10. Edgar Johnson, *Charles Dickens: His Tragedy and Triumph* (New York: Viking, 1977) p. 33.

11. Innes, *The Holy Theatre*, p. 172.

12. Leonardo Boff, *Saint Francis*, John M. Diercksmeier (trs.) (New York: Crossroad, 1982) p. 1.

13. Bert O. States makes a similar point in terms of the novel's use of *delay*: 'it is part of the liberty of the novel form to put perspectives on top of perspectives, to reach out in philosophical, biographical, societal, and, most commonly, descriptive directions that lie behind the scene and the action. From the dramatic point of view, these are delays, but from the narrative, or thematic, viewpoint they are enrichments of the novel's projection of its universe. It is exactly because the novel is not fastened in the world that it can take virtually anything in the world as its subject. Thus the reading of a novel is a continual act of suspension of some part of the scene or action while another is being developed.' *Great Reckonings in Little Rooms: On the Phenomenology of Theater* (Berkeley: University of California Press, 1985) p. 136.

14. Stefan Brecht, Peter L. Feldman, Donald M. Kaplan, Jan Kott, Charles Ludlam and Donald Richie, 'On Grotowski: A Series of Critiques', *TDR*, vol. 14 (1970) p. 189.

11

Action, Character, and Language: Dickens, His Contemporaries, and the Lure of the Stage

James Redmond

> *The purely romantic drama . . . owes no allegiance to time or space . . . and although the illusion may be assisted by the effect on the senses of . . . complicated scenery and decorations. . . . yet this sort of assistance is dangerous. For the principal and only genuine excitement ought to come from within — from the moved and sympathetic imagination; whereas, where so much is addressed to the mere external senses of seeing and hearing, the spiritual vision is apt to languish, and the attraction from without will withdraw the mind from the proper and only legitimate interest which is intended to spring from within.*
>
> (S. T. Coleridge, notes on *The Tempest*, 1818)

> *Yes — oh dear yes — the novel tells a story . . . and I wish that it was not so, that it could be something different — melody, or perception of truth, not this low atavistic form. . . . It is immensely old — goes back to neolithic times, perhaps to palaeolithic. Neanderthal man listened to stories, if one may judge by the shape of his skull. The primitive audience was an audience of shock-heads, gaping round the camp-fire, fatigued with contending against the mammoth or the hairy rhinoceros, and only kept awake by suspense. What would happen next? The novelist droned on, and as soon as the audience guessed what happened next, they either fell asleep or killed him.*
>
> (E. M. Forster, *Aspects of the Novel*, 1927)

Dickens played a leading role in the long, energetic attempt to reconnect the London stage with dramatic literature, and among his personal friends he acted out the conflicts that were central to the vigorous and at times violent debate. At the heart of the controversy was the question of how far the conventional dominance of stage action ought to yield to what was regarded as a 'modern' fascination with the intricacies of a sensibility, with internal psychological subtlety expressed through introspective lyrical verse.

The issue was argued at great length in the cultural journals. In the course of 1823, for example, six long letters, signed 'John Lacey' had appeared in *The London Magazine* making the traditional demand for broad Aristotelian action, and disparaging the avant-garde taste for passive, inward-looking reflection. The author arraigned contemporary playwrights in general, and in particular James Haynes for his *Durazzo*, in a spirit of nagging grievance:

> Action is the essence of drama; nay, its definition: business, bustle, hurly and combustion dire, are indispensable to effective drama. . . . But that essence and these indispensables, you, Gentlemen, seem, with one consent, sedulously to avoid meddling with. . . . You seem to think that the whole virtue of tragedy lies in its poeticity; and the softer, the sweeter, the more soul-soothing, the more hushing the poetry is, the better you think it, though the audience go to sleep under your noses. . . . Oh! so as we deliver forth poetry enough, what a-plague have we to do with plotting?
>
> The tragedy under consideration is deplorably meagre in the item of story. It has no interest whatever of plot or construction. There is no one great or absorbing action to engross our attention by its magnitude or intensity: neither is there any ingenious perplexity of incidents, to be unravelled by the catastrophe, and keep the mind actively suspended during the process of disentanglement. Terror and Pity, without one at least of which tragedy is a farce, are neither of them excited. Curiosity is not roused, nor anxiety solicited. Sir, the author of Durazzo, will you allow me to ask, what you mean by expending so much excellent poetry on such a miserable plot?[1]

Already in the early 1820s the accusation was that the majority of literary Englishmen attracted to the playhouse were writing with contempt for essential theatrical interests and offering dramatic texts which were eager to be 'beautiful as poetry but as nothing else'. 'Ay, on this very principle of sacrificing everything, plot, action, character-ism . . . to puling, pitiful, emasculate poetry, do the dramatists of the day construct their pieces.'

The forcefulness of this plea for a traditional 'Aristotelian' approach to play-construction was prompted not only by the practice of aspiring dramatists, but also by a considerable body of critical theory, which in the following decades added weight and stridency to its demand for lyrical texts untrammelled by stage vulgarities that make the judicious grieve and the unskilful throw up their sweaty night-caps. John Henry Newman, with typical intellectual boldness, directly challenged the most venerable of all authorities in an important review article in 1829. His ostensible subject was a volume entitled *The Theatre of the Greeks*, but he used the opportunity to indicate the direction he wanted modern drama to take. He was speaking for those in his generation who had absorbed romantic convictions so naturally that they were held to be self-evident truths: art, above all else, is concerned with the poetic sensibility and Aristotle could not have been more misleading:

> The Greek tragedians are not generally felicitous in the construction of their plots. . . . Seldom does any great interest arise from the action; which, instead of being progressive and sustained, is commonly either a mere necessary condition of the drama, or a convenience for the introduction of matter more important than itself. It is often stationary – often irregular – sometimes either wants or outlives the catastrophe. . . . The action then will be more justly viewed as the vehicle for introducing the personages of the drama, than as the principal object of the poet's art; it is not in the plot, but in the characters, sentiments, and diction, that the actual merit and poetry of the composition are found. . . .
>
> E.g. in neither the Oedipus Colonus nor the Philoctetes, the two most beautiful plays of Sophocles, is the plot striking. . . . the beauties . . . are almost independent of the plot; it is the chorus which imparts grace and interest to the actionless scene. . . .
>
> Let us listen to their harmonious and majestic language – to the voices of sorrow, joy, compassion, or religious emotion – to the animated odes of the chorus. Why interrupt so divine a display of poetical genius by inquiries degrading it to the level of every-day events? . . . The very spirit of beauty breathes through every part of the composition. . . .
>
> Aristotle treats dramatic composition more as an exhibition of ingenious workmanship, than as a free and unfettered effusion of genius. The inferior poem may, on his principle, be the better tragedy.[2]

Newman goes on to defend the modern poet's right to be obscure. In the most crucial set of experiments in the century, Macready was soon to be driven to despair by Browning's wilful use of dramatic language that would not stoop to lucidity. Newman is eager to argue that obscurity is in itself a true note to know a poet by:

> As the poet's habits of mind lead to contemplation rather than to communication with others, he is more or less obscure. . . . He will be obscure, moreover, from the depth of his feelings, which require a congenial reader to enter into them – and from their acuteness, which shrinks from any formal accuracy in the expression of them. And he will be obscure, not only from the carelessness of genius, and from the originality of his conceptions, but it may be from natural deficiency in the power of clear and eloquent expression, which . . . is a talent distinct from poetry.
>
> Another talent necessary to composition is the power of unfolding the meaning in an orderly manner. A poetical mind is often too impatient to explain itself justly; it is overpowered by a rush of emotions, which sometimes want of power, sometimes the indolence of inward enjoyment, prevents it from describing.

The poetic mind contemplates itself and is not primarily concerned to communicate: easy clarity is a more vulgar achievement. Enterprisingly, Homer is cited as the classical guarantor of these modern values in art: Homer's 'is the style of one who rhapsodized without deference to hearer or judge, in an age . . . before the theatre had degraded poetry into an exhibition'.

It is necessary to see that there was intransigent partisan commitment on both sides. 'John Lacey' wanted to subordinate the lyrical disposition so central to the literary ethos of the period, and Newman wanted that lyrical urge to dominate so utterly that plot, staging, even emotional and intellectual clarity would yield.

The modernist argument was developed importantly by John Stuart Mill in a related pair of essays in 1833.[3] Concern with dramatic action, with story-telling, with 'mere outward circumstance' is destructively inimical to the poetic disposition; they come from and appeal to 'two distinct . . . and mutually exclusive characters of mind'. Story, event, plot appeal to children, to primitive peoples and, in modern Europe – in 'this most grown-up and unchildlike age' – to 'the shallowest and emptiest' of minds and hearts. The most commonplace and superficial minds 'take a natural delight in fictitious narrative; the excitement it affords is of the kind which comes from without'. Poetry, whose source is the fine sensibility examining itself, 'is the delineation of the deeper and more secret workings of human emotion', and it follows that 'the incidents of a dramatic poem may be scanty and ineffective, though the delineation of passion and character may be of the highest order; as in Goethe's admirable "Torquato Tasso".'

That play is of special significance for this whole debate. Goethe's central concern is to contrast the neurotic self-preoccupation of the poet with the social world of order and action. Tasso's artistic sensibility separates him painfully from the court life which celebrates daring, heroic deeds and mature manly action. He is 'der tatenlose Jüngling' (the young man without achievements)[4] set in contrast to Antonio Montecatino, the successful diplomatist and consummate manager of international affairs. To cite the masterpiece which acted as the great exemplar for this strain in modern European drama, Montecatino is Fortinbras to Tasso's Hamlet. The firm reluctance to write plays with broad Aristotelian action came from the conviction that poetry's most important subject is introspection. The man of action may at times almost be envied the childlike simplicity of his mind − Schiller used the word *naive* to cover the case[5] − but the conviction in the end is that in this most grown-up of ages the representative hero is the self-examining artist, lost in the pale cast of thought. Two lines from Goethe's closet play might serve as an epigraph for a study of this modern drama where reflection replaces action: 'Es bildet ein Talent sich in der Stille,/ Sich ein Charakter in dem Strom der Welt.' [I. ii. 304] (A talent is developed in quietude,/ A character in the mainstream of the world.)

Mill continues his elaboration of the modernist case by arguing that modern civilized people will feel contempt for any literary work preoccupied with external behaviour, and they will commit their serious attention to art solely concerned with 'the delineation of states of feeling', to art which is the 'natural fruit of solitude and meditation'. Poetry should have the quality of internal soliloquy: it should not seem to address the audience but appear as private contemplation accidentally overheard. 'The actor knows that there is an audience present; but if he act as though he knew it, he acts ill.' Language consciously addressed to an audience is vulgarized into stage eloquence, and the central important truth is that, 'Lyric poetry . . . is . . . more eminently and peculiarly poetry than any other'. The most sensitive poetic sensibilities, and their critical champions, were convinced that the subject of literature must be the inside of the poet's head and that it should be absorbed as directly as possible into the responsive imagination of the auditor or reader.

These critical exchanges were of intellectual and academic interest to the writers of the articles and to their general readers. For Dickens and his professional colleagues, academic interest was pale beside the intensity of the practical relevance for their creative work as artists and critics. Of Dickens's contemporaries, Macready, Browning, Forster, and Lewes are of special importance. The five men were in agreement about the great objective of making the English playhouse fit for a modern drama that would be a worthy descendant of the work of Shakespeare. Their interrelationships were based on deep personal affection, with no embarrassment in making open declarations of love, and with the highest professional admiration of one another's achievements. There were also elements of misunderstanding, mistrust and disaffection, which led on occasion to long periods of sullen non-communication, and in one instance to violent rage on the edge of murder.[6]

Of the whole intricate history there is one chapter which is paradigmatic: it defined and explored the question that is still of first importance after a century and a half. The chapter involved Macready's productions of Browning's plays, and the issue was how in theatrical practice the elements of action, character, and language should be related. Macready, restricted – however reluctantly – by contemporary theatrical conditions, was traditional in his conviction that plot must be the spine of any actable play, that character must be revealed through broad stage action, and expressed in what Newman and Mill disparagingly called the language of eloquence – bold words that Macready could effectively shout at the 3000 members of a difficult and potentially unruly audience: 'the good mouthing passages' eagerly demanded by 'Lacey', 'magnilo-quence, and ear-splitting heroicals'.

Macready was obliged to work in the main theatres and to confront the very mixed audience that filled the pit (800 seats in Drury Lane), the boxes (1230), the slips (130), the lower gallery (550), and the upper gallery (350): a good many in the cheapest seats could see only part of the stage and grasp only the simplest of lines shouted with greatest volume and clarity of diction. Looking back to the conditions in most London theatres in the 1840s, Dickens described them with exuberant disgust. This was Sadler's Wells:

> Without, the Theatre, by night, was like the worst part of the worst kind of Fair in the worst kind of town. Within, it was a bear-garden. . . .
>   The play was MACBETH. It was performed amidst the usual hideous medley of fights, foul language, catcalls, shrieks, yells, oaths, blas-phemy, obscenity, apples, oranges, nuts, biscuits, ginger-beer, porter, and pipes – not that there was any particular objection to the Play, but that the audience were, on the whole, in a condition of mind, generally requiring such utterance. Pipes of all lengths were at work in the

gallery, several were displayed in the pit. Cans of beer, each with a pint measure to drink from (for the convenience of gentlemen who had neglected the precaution of bringing their own pots in their bundles), were carried through the dense crowd at all stages of the tragedy. Sickly children in arms were squeezed out of shape, in all parts of the house. Fish was fried at entrance doors. Barricades of oyster-shells encumbered the pavement. Expectant half-price visitors to the gallery howled defiant impatience up the stairs, and danced a sort of carmagnole all round the building.[7]

Under Macready's reign, Drury Lane was not such a depressing shambles, but nor were its galleries filled with poets and scholars. Among the most heart-breaking passages of nineteenth-century prose are those in which Macready expresses his loathing of the theatrical conditions that plagued his artistic life. This is the recurring theme:

Thought upon the state of the public mind in regard to theatres – the *aversion* from the English theatre. My heart and my spirits *sank down* within me. I have borne up long, but now I begin to lose hope and heart. I often, in my secret heart wish that I was at my long rest; there seems no good for me here. I toil, and hope on, but my good genius – oh God! Have done very little to-day. Had no heart to do anything – not even to bear the company of my blessed, blessed children. God help me![8]

Macready, like Dickens, Forster, and Lewes, saw in the young Browning a man who might create a modern English drama of great poetic and theatrical power. The following excerpts from Macready's diaries sketch the desperate optimism and the blood-coagulating despair:

February 16*th* [1836] – Forster and Browning called, and talked over the plot of a tragedy which Browning had begun to think of: the subject, Narses. He said that I had *bit* him by my performance of Othello, and I told him I hoped I should make the blood come. It would indeed be some recompense for the miseries, the humiliations, the heart-sickening disgusts which I have endured in my profession if, by its exercise, I had awakened a spirit of poetry whose influence would elevate, enoble, and adorn our degraded drama. May it be! . . .

May 30*th* [1836] – Arriving at chambers I found a note from Browning. What can I say upon it? It was a tribute which remunerated me from the annoyance and cares of years: it was one of the very highest, may I not say the highest, honour I have through life received.

August 3rd [1836] – Forster told me that Browning had fixed on Strafford for the subject of a tragedy; he could not have hit upon one that I could have more readily concurred in.

Elstree, November 23rd [1836] – Began *very attentively* [sic] to read over the tragedy of *Strafford*, in which I find more grounds for exception than I had anticipated. I had been too much carried away by the truth of character to observe the meanness of plot and occasional obscurity. . . .

April 14th [1837] – Calling at Forster's, met Browning, who came upstairs and who produced some scraps of paper with hints and unconnected lines – the full amount of his labour upon the alterations agreed on. It was too bad to trifle in this way, but it was useless to complain; he had wasted his time in striving to improve the fourth act scene, which was ejected from his play as impracticable for any good result. We went all over the play *again* (!) very carefully, and he resolved to bring the amendments suggested by eleven o'clock this evening. Met Browning at the gate of my chambers; he came upstairs and, after some subjects of general interest, proceeded to that of his tragedy. He had done nothing to it; had been oppressed and incapable of carrying his intentions into action. He *wished to withdraw it*. I cautioned him against any precipitate step – warned him of the consequences, and at last got him to offer to go and bring Forster, whom I wished to be a party to all this business. He came with Browning, and we turned over all the pros and cons – for acting or not acting the play. They both decided on its performance, Browning to have more time than he had asked for the completion of his alterations. It was fixed to be done. Heaven speed us all! I thank God I felt quite satisfied with my conduct throughout this delicate affair of Browning.

April 20th [1837] – After dinner read over *Strafford*, which I strongly feel *will fail* – it is not good.

April 21st – Miss Faucit said to me that her part in Browning's play was very bad, and she did not know if she should do it. She wanted me to ask her to do it. But I would not, for I wish she would refuse it, that even at this late point of time the play might be withdrawn – it *will do no one good*. . . .

April 22nd – Browning came to breakfast, very pale and apparently suffering from over-excitement. I think it is unfortunate that without due consideration and time for arranging and digesting his thoughts on a work so difficult as a tragedy, he should have committed himself to the production of one. I should be too glad of any accident that would impede its representation, and give me a fair occasion for withdrawing it; but this I cannot now do without incurring the suspicion of selfishness and of injustice to him, and therefore, though I feel convinced that the performance of this play on my Benefit night will cause much dissatisfaction – will in some measure compromise my judgement, and injure my future benefits – yet still, *coute que coute*, Browning shall not have the power of saying that I have acted otherwise than as a true friend to his feelings.

Elstree, April 23rd – The more I consider the play the lower my hopes smile upon it; I expect it will be damned – grievously hissed at the end – from the unintelligibility of the motives, the want of action, and consequently of interest. . . .

Elstree, April 30th – Called on Forster, who gave me a ludicrous account of the silliness of Dow about this play of *Strafford*, which he thinks so *very* fine, and that it is to be so greatly successful. Again I repeat my conviction that it *must fail* – if, by some happy chance, not at once to-morrow, yet still at best it will only stagger out a lingering existence of a few nights and then die out – and for ever. It is dedicated to me most kindly by Browning.

London, May 9th – Called on Forster, who informed me how much he had been hurt by Browning's expression of discontent at his criticism, which I myself think only too indulgent for such a play as *Strafford*. After all that has been done for Browning with the painful apprehension of failure before us . . . . without *great assistance* his tragedy could never have been put in a condition to be proposed for representation – without great assistance it never could have been put upon the stage – nor without great assistance could it ever have been carried through its 'perilous' experiment.

February 10th [1843] – Began the consideration and study of the part of Tresham [in *A Blot in the 'Scutcheon*], which was to occupy my single thoughts till accomplished. About a quarter past one a note came from Willmott, informing me that Mr Phelps would do the part, if he 'died of it', so that my time had been lost. Arrived I applied to business; offered

to give to Browning and Mr Phelps the benefit of my consideration
and study in the cuts, etc. I had made one I thought particularly
valuable, not letting Tresham die, but consigning him to a convent.
Browning, however, in the worst taste, manner, and spirit, declined any
further alterations, expressing himself perfectly satisfied with the
manner in which Mr Phelps executed Lord Tresham. I had no more to
say. I could only think Mr Browning a very disagreeable and
offensively mannered person. *Voila tout!*

February 11*th* – Directed the rehearsal of *Blot in the 'Scutcheon*, and
made many valuable improvements. Browning seemed desirous to
explain or qualify the strange carriage and temper of yesterday, and
laid much blame on Forster for irritating him. Saw the play of *Blot in the
'Scutcheon*, which was badly acted in Phelps's and Mrs Stirling's parts –
pretty well in Anderson's, very well in Helen Faucit's. I was *angry* after
the play about the call being directed without me.

March 18*th* – Went out; met Browning, who was startled into
accosting me, but seeming to remember that he did not intend to do so,
started in great haste. What but contempt, which one ought not to feel,
can we with galled spirit feel for these wretched insects about one? Oh
God! how is it all to end?

It ended with a sundering of the relationship, with bitter recrimination on
both sides. By 'these wretched insects' Macready meant Browning and
the tribe of literati who were so utterly preoccupied with self-regard that
they could ignore the unalterable conditions of the contemporary
playhouse. Browning also generalised his lost faith in Macready: 'The
poorest Man of Letters . . . I ever knew is of far higher talent than the best
actor I ever expect to know.'[9]

If Macready was a physical prisoner of the buildings he was obliged to
act in, Browning was an aesthetic prisoner of the conviction that drama,
like all the other arts, must be primarily concerned not with explicit but
with inner experience – the mind, the soul, subtle moods and feelings –
explored through reflective, introverted, *lyrical* verse: in Newman's
phrases, the very spirit of beauty should breathe through every part of
the *actionless* scene – the paradigmatic hero would be *der tatenlose Jüngling*.
Already in the preface to the first edition of *Paracelsus*, Browning had
formulated the theoretical basis for the modern drama of inaction that
Maeterlinck was to astonish the world with half a century later: 'Instead of
having recourse to an external machinery of incidents to create and

evolve the crisis . . . I have ventured to display somewhat minutely the mood itself . . . and have suffered the agency by which it is . . . determined to be . . . subordinate throughout, if not altogether excluded.'[10]

For the formula repeated endlessly since Aristotle that in drama character is revealed through action, Browning offers the proposition that the most important levels of experience are best revealed through *in*action. It is when Hamlet is solitary and pensive that we apprehend the intricate subtlety of his mind. When he is engaged in physical stage action we find that he duels with swords very much like the next man. A play dominated by theatrical behaviour will be general and superficial, not individuated and deep. But Browning recognized Macready as the only theatrical practitioner who might make the stage receptive to modern literature, and he tried to compromise. The effort was painful, however, and he introduced *A Blot in the 'Scutcheon* with undisguised, contemptuous self-irony:

> December 1840
> My dear Macready,
> . . . I have written a spick and span new Tragedy (a sort of compromise between my own notion and yours – as I understand it at least) and will send it to you if you care to be bothered so far. There is *action* in it, drabbing, stabbing, et autres gentillesses, – who knows but the Gods may make me good even yet?
> Yours ever truly
> Robert Browning[11]

Browning's contempt for the plot element ('drabbing' and 'stabbing' of his tale of star-crossed lovers!) meant that his treatment of the action was less than half-hearted. But George Henry Lewes attacked the play in the *Westminster Review*, damning it from the avant-garde position:

> In the worst sense [*A Blot in the 'Scutcheon*] is *written for the stage*, i.e., the poet has asked himself what *situations* could be made out of his subject, not what would be the natural consequences of the passions. He has succeeded so far. But the whole *dramatic* nature of the piece is false. . . . It failed to touch the audience, because it was *untrue*; it succeeded occasionally in rousing them because it was theatrical.[12]

Lewes, since he did not write for a mass audience, had no sympathy with the attempt to compromise with demands theatrical. Dickens, on the other hand, was unique, as a literary genius who gloried in his ability to hold the attention of the whole nation; and Dickens's critical reaction to *A Blot in the 'Scutcheon* is much more interesting than those from the two opposing camps. He wrote in the following terms to Forster, who never did inform Browning, who never again wrote for the stage:

> Browning's play has thrown me into a perfect passion of sorrow. To say that there is anything in its subject save what is lovely, true, deeply affecting, full of the best emotion, the most earnest feeling, and the most true and tender source of interest, is to say that there is no light in the sun, and no heat in blood. It is full of genius, natural and great thoughts, profound, and yet simple and beautiful in its vigour. I know nothing that is so affecting, nothing in any book I have ever read, as Mildred's recurrence to that 'I was so young – I had no mother'. I know no love like it, no passion like it, no moulding of a splendid thing after its conception, like it. And I swear it is a tragedy that MUST be played; and must be played, moreover, by Macready. There are some things I would have changed if I could. . . . I assuredly would have the old servant *begin his tale upon the scene*; and be taken by the throat, or drawn upon, by his master, in its commencement. But the tragedy I never shall forget, or less vividly remember than I do now. And if you tell Browning that I have seen it, tell him that I believe from my soul there is no man living (and not many dead) who could produce such a work.[13]

On a personal level Dickens was hoping to reconcile two of his friends. In more general terms he was trying to bring together the critical positions represented by Macready and Browning, in the conviction that their shared desire to re-create English drama would fail if attention were fixed predominantly on either action or poetic refinement: the heirs of Shakespeare must emulate his combination of large Aristotelian action with soul-revealing, heart-rendingly delicate language.

Browning relegated the central explosion in the play to off-stage action. Dickens would most assuredly have Gerard, the old servant, '*begin his tale upon the scene*; and be taken by the throat, or drawn upon by his master'. Macready, Forster, most theatre-goers and most reviewers also demanded much more stage action to take them by the throat and shake them. On the other hand, Dickens felt the strength of the avant-garde argument and was entirely won over by that sad refrain of Mildred Tresham: 'I was so young, I loved him so, I had/ No mother, God forgot me, and I fell.' In Browning's original text that refrain, in variations, appeared four times, all of which Macready wanted to expunge.

Browning insisted on keeping the three instances that remain in the published text, and Dickens was overwhelmed by the refrain as sounding the true note of tragic poetry.

In Dickens's ambivalent reaction to Browning's play we have in miniature and in human terms an instructive indication of what thwarted so many attempts in the nineteenth-century London theatre to make the desired connection. The physical conditions and conventional expectations made it impossible for the lyrical sensibility at the heart of contemporary English poetry to flourish in the huge theatrical spaces of the patent theatres. Dickens's judgement was surely right: there could be no drama of the highest rank without language of deep and varied poetic power; and none without effective stage action. The common fare of English prose drama had proved the first, and of the second we are still being offered new evidence in the minimalist writing of those who are today still determined to make modern drama aspire towards the conditions of lyric.

Notes

1. *The London Magazine*, vol. 8 (July to Dec. 1823): 'Action . . . plotting?' p. 85; 'The tragedy . . . plot?' p. 86; 'beautiful . . . else' p. 86; 'Ay, on . . . pieces' p. 135.
2. Unsigned review article under the heading 'The Theatre of the Greeks: or the History, Literature, and Criticism of the Grecian Drama. With an Original Treatise on the Principal Tragic and Comic Metres.' (Cambridge, 1827). In *The London Review*, 2nd edn (Feb. 1829) no. 1, pp. 153–71: 'The Greek . . . are found' p. 155; 'e.g. . . . composition' p. 156; 'Aristotle . . . better tragedy' p. 159; 'As the poet's . . . describing' p. 170; 'is the style . . . exhibition' p. 171.
3. *The Monthly Repository*, vol. 7 (1833): 'What is Poetry?' pp. 60–70, and 'The Two Kinds of Poetry', pp. 714–24. Signed 'Antiquus': 'mere circumstance' p. 61; 'two distinct . . . of mind' p. 61; 'this most . . . age' p. 62; 'the shallowest and emptiest' p. 62; 'take a natural . . . without' p. 62; 'the incidents . . . "Torquato Tasso"' p. 63; 'the delineation . . . of feeling' p. 63; 'natural . . . meditation' p. 65; 'The actor . . . acts ill' p. 65; 'Lyric poetry . . . any other' p. 719.
4. *Torquato Tasso* I. iii. 428. *Goethes Werke*, Hamburger Ausgabe in 14 Bänden, Herausgegeben von Erich Trunz (München: Verlag C. H. Beck, 1981) vol. 5, p. 85.
5. 'Über naive und sentimentalische Dichtung', 1975.
6. Forster once 'narrowly escaped coming to a violent end by the hand of the usually amiable Robert Browning, who, stung beyond endurance by his offensiveness at a friend's house after dinner, seized a heavy cut-glass decanter with murderous intent, and was only prevented . . . by the nimble

intervention of the host.' In William Toynbee (ed.), *The Diaries of William Charles Macready: 1833–1851*, 2 vols (London: Chapman & Hall, 1912) vol. 1, p. 226.

7. 'Shakespeare and Newgate', *Household Words*, 4 Oct. 1851 (with R. H. Horne); Harry Stone (ed.), *The Uncollected Writings of Charles Dickens: Household Words 1850–1859*, 2 vols (London: Penguin, 1969) vol. 1, pp. 344, 346, 347.

8. *The Diaries of William Charles Macready*, 12 Mar. 1843.

9. Letter to Christopher Dawson, Jr., 10 Mar. 1844; Thurman L. Hood (ed.), *Letters of Robert Browning*, collected by Thomas J. Wise (London: John Murray, 1933) p. 10.

10. Ian Jack and Margaret Smith (eds), *The Poetical Works of Robert Browning* (Oxford: Clarendon Press, 1983) vol. 1, p. 523.

11. *Letters of Robert Browning*, p. 5.

12. *The Westminster Review*, Feb.–May 1843, p. 604, signed G.H.L.

13. Madeleine House, Graham Storey and Kathleen Tillotson (eds), *The Letters of Charles Dickens* (Oxford: Clarendon Press, 1974) vol. 3, pp. 381–83.

12

Thackeray and Dickens on the Boards

Robert A. Colby

'I do not know if I have ever told you seriously, but I have often thought that I should have been as successful on the boards as I have between them', Dickens wrote to his friend and future biographer John Forster.[1] Dickens is known to have been involved with the stage as early as his twentieth year. So too did Thackeray write at the age of twenty during his *lehrjahre* in Weimar to Frau von Goethe: 'The theatre is all my rage. . . . I intend to try my hand at farce, tragedy or comedy – which I cannot say, all three perhaps.'[2] It is well known that he enjoyed acting in student theatricals both at Charterhouse and at Cambridge, and before that he produced and acted in playlets for his cousins the Ritchies.[3] As a journalist Thackeray wrote both knowledgeably and with relish on the performing arts – ballet and opera, as well as plays – and his novels are replete with references to popular actors, singers, and dancers. His first published book (which preceded *Pickwick Papers* by a year) was a spoof on classical dancing, a so-called 'Ballet Mythologique' entitled *Flore et Zephyr*, with his own illustrations. In the course of their careers, both Thackeray and Dickens were amateur actors from time to time, and made attempts at plays of their own, but neither achieved the success of another rival, Bulwer-Lytton, 'on the boards'.

As things turned out, undoubtedly to the greater benefit of posterity, both Thackeray and Dickens were compelled to rechannel their thespian impulses through fiction. Dickens's remarkable mimetic gifts are well known (he acted out many of his characters to himself before he wrote them down), but Thackeray too had an ability at mimicry rivalling that of Becky Sharp.[4] With him, however, this talent shows up mainly in the theatrical frameworks and devices of his novels – for example, the 'bloody Grand Tableau' in *Catherine*; the 'Manager of the Performance' who manipulates the 'scenes of all sorts' that make up *Vanity Fair*; the mock Restoration Comedy dialogue with which Pen and Blanche regale

each other in *Pendennis*; the parody of French *drames* of intrigue
interlarded in the episodes of *Henry Esmond* involving the Pretender; the
chapter of *The Newcomes* set out as a play script ('Contains Two Or Three
Acts Of A Little Comedy'); the Christmas pantomime format of *The Rose
and the Ring*.

Following the success of *Vanity Fair* that propelled Thackeray to 'the
top of the tree' with Dickens, as he wrote to his mother,[5] their two names
became more and more coupled in the collective mind of the reading
public as journalists-turned-fiction-writers, as satirists of contemporary
life, and particularly as what David Masson labelled 'Metropolitan
Novelists'. 'Thackeray and Dickens, Dickens and Thackeray – the two
names almost necessarily go together . . . the public has learned to think
of them in indissoluble connexion for the prize of light literature', wrote
Masson in the course of reviewing *David Copperfield* and *Pendennis*,[6]
which had been issued in monthly parts almost in tandem, as had *Dombey
and Son* and *Vanity Fair*. Moreover, during the 1850s both were
conspicuously in the public eye on the platform – Dickens as reader from
his own works (first for charity benefits, then commercially), Thackeray as
lecturer on eighteenth-century literature and history, the research for
which was eventually ploughed into *Henry Esmond* and *The Virginians*.

So Thackeray and Dickens both found satisfactory outlets for the 'ham'
in them, while it was left to others to attempt to realize the drama inherent
in their novels on the living stage. In the theatre, however, their fortunes
markedly diverged. Here, as with his fiction, Dickens achieved both
earlier and wider popularity than did Thackeray. From *Pickwick Papers*
onwards, Dickens was grabbed up by the playsmiths; sometimes indeed
his stories (as with *Oliver Twist* and *Nicholas Nickleby*) were seen on the
stage before they had completed their serialization in print. Throughout
the Victorian period there cannot have been a season that did not see
some version or other of Dickens behind gaslight. Sometimes (as with *The
Old Curiosity Shop* and *Martin Chuzzlewit*) there were two or more
versions running simultaneously.[7] Thackeray, to the contrary, was
virtually ignored by theatre managers during his lifetime. Among his
early 'comicalities and whimsicalities' there is on record only a dramatic
sketch based on *The Diary of C. James de la Pluche*, a 'witless version'
(according to a critic, writing after the occasion) performed at the Princess
Theatre on 13 July 1846 – and apparently never repeated.[8] As for
Thackeray's most popular novel, *Vanity Fair* by an Irish expatriate actor
and playwright John Brougham, who had been associated with Dion
Boucicault, it opened at Burton's Chamber Street Theatre on 25 January
1849 – and lasted for a week.[9] (Brougham had more success earlier with

his adaptation of *Dombey and Son* in which he also played both Captain Bunsby and Major Bagstock, and later with his *David Copperfield*, in which he played Micawber.) Thomas Robertson attempted to dramatize *Vanity Fair*, and gave up the effort, but its influence has been traced in his once popular *Caste*.[10] Late in life, Thackeray himself, not being able to secure a commercial production for his play *The Wolves and the Lamb*, arranged a private showing at his last home Palace Green, and, in a reversal of the normal procedure, then turned it into a novel, *Lovel the Widower*, which is highly dramatic in form. This was the extent of Thackeray's presence 'on the boards' during his lifetime. His stage history in general was not only belated, but posthumous.

After a few minor efforts, the 1890s saw something of an upsurge for Thackeray in the theatre. *The Rose and the Ring* at long last was presented as a live Christmas pantomime, with text by H. Savile Clark and music by Walter Slaughter, at the Prince of Wales Theatre on 20 December 1890 – young William Ritchie's first introduction to his illustrious grandfather's work, according to a letter by his mother Anne Thackeray Ritchie.[11] Several versions of *Henry Esmond* are said to have been made during this decade, including one never completed, by Charles Dickens, Junior. Two on record are a play by T. Edgar Pemberton (author, as it happens, of *Dickens on the Stage*), seen briefly in London and Edinburgh during the season of 1897, followed by a rival version the next year by two Americans, Louis Evans Shipman and Glen McDonough, produced in Rochester, New York, for what seems to have been a unique perform-ance.[12] According to a theatre historian, at about this time 'many a dramatization of *The Newcomes*, *Pendennis*, and *The Virginians* has come rapping at the door, but there is no record of any having been accepted and produced'. This was the record in 1903.[13] Subsequently there surfaced a dramatization of *The Newcomes* by Henry Morton (1906, as *Colonel Newcome*), and of *Pendennis* by Langdon Mitchell (1916, as *Major Pendennis*).[14] However, whereas somebody has made a stab at staging virtually the entire Dickensian canon (including *Edwin Drood*), playwrights interested in Thackeray at all have for the most part gravitated to *Vanity Fair*. Even with this perennially popular novel, it was not until 1899, after several fiascos (including a one-act play by James Barrie based on the concluding episodes) that a version succeeded in holding the stage – *Becky Sharp* by Langdon Mitchell. Other adaptations followed, but Mitchell's is the only one that has had any kind of stage history – intermittently revived for some thirty years after its initial season, thanks to the fame of its star Minnie Maddern Fiske. Eventually it became the basis, though much watered down, for the 1934 RKO film *Becky Sharp* which made cinematic history as the first full-length Technicolor motion picture.[15]

Dickens's omnipresence 'on the boards' as against Thackeray's sparse presence there verifies what we have always known about their relative appeal to the populace, but something more is revealed by the different ways in which they were handled (or manhandled) by their stage 'dressers'.

Dickens's novels in general were exploited for their sensational, lachrymose, or farcical elements, which came to be magnified under the glare of gaslight. Consider, for example, these representative titles of Dickens plays, early and late: *Poor Smike* (variants: *The Fortunes of Smike; The Infant Phenomenon; Crummleses, or A Rehearsal Rehearsed; Do the Boys Hall*); *Christmas Carol, or The Miser's Warning; Quilp, or The Wanderings of Little Nell* (variants: *Grandfather's Little Nell; An Angel on Earth*); *Little Em'ly* (variants: *Born with a Caul; The Ark on the Sands*); *Lady Dedlock's Secret* (variants: *Lady Dedlock and Hortense; Jo, The Waif of the Streets; Only a Waif, or The Dedlock Mystery; Move On; Chesney Wold*); *All for Her; Recalled to Life; The Only Way* (the best-known renderings of *A Tale of Two Cities*). As Jane Stedman has observed in *The Dickensian,* 'in adapting Dickens's novels for the stage, Victorian playwrights often botched up versions hastily for nonce appeal. . . . Dramatists generally reduced Dickens's characters to mere silhouettes . . . in order to preserve plot and sub-plots, or they disproportionately enlarged the comic lead, cutting the story line to its most elementary situations.'[16] In most of the plays hacked out of the Dickens canon, a few outsized figures from his gallery tend to hog centre-stage: Sam Weller from *Pickwick Papers*; Fagin, Bill Sikes, and Nancy from *Oliver Twist*; Sairey Gamp, Tom Pinch, and Pecksniff from *Martin Chuzzlewit*; Captain Cuttle from *Dombey and Son*; Micawber, Uriah Heep, and Daniel Peggotty from *David Copperfield*. It is also significant that the novels most frequently dramatized, and those which seem to have appealed most to theatre-goers, were among those which Dickens himself selected to read from: *Pickwick Papers, Oliver Twist, Nicholas Nickleby, Martin Chuzzlewit*, and *David Copperfield*. Conspicuously missing from this list are the serious late books which have elevated Dickens's prestige in the post-World War II period: *Hard Times, Little Dorrit*, and *Our Mutual Friend*. These were indeed the least dramatized, and the least successful when they were, of Dickens's novels during his lifetime and throughout the nineteenth century. Also absent from this company is the book that many regard as his most artistic and beautifully written – *Great Expectations*. Dickens planned a reading of it, but for some unknown reason never performed it. No less a figure than

W. S. Gilbert attempted a stage version in 1871 (just when he was beginning his collaboration with Sullivan) which failed.[17] Of the 'advanced' Dickens, *Bleak House* alone was popular on the stage but, as we have seen, was pared down either to the sin and expiation of Lady Dedlock (by analogy with Lady Isabel Vane and Lady Audley) or to the piteous plight of Little Jo.

Dramatizations of Thackeray, on the other hand, while few, were confined to his 'big four', so that he was seen on the stage at his very best, if in diluted form. To be sure his wit and irony evaporated in the rapid give-and-take of theatrical dialogue, motivations were simplified, subplots were ignored, and interesting minor figures were jettisoned, as his vast canvasses were squeezed into a series of tableaux vivants. The story of *Henry Esmond*, to those who took it in via the proscenium arch, was primarily the romance of Henry and Beatrix – with a happy ending – and the intrigue around The Pretender. The spotlight in *Vanity Fair* was invariably cast on the more colourful of Thackeray's two non-heroines. The best-known version was pointedly entitled *Becky Sharp*, having been commissioned by Mrs Fiske. (Miss Crawley is given short shrift, and the elder Osbornes and Sedleys, as well as the O'Dowds, are left out altogether.) So too were the dramatizations of *Pendennis* and *The Newcomes* conceived as star vehicles for seasoned character actors, John Drew and Herbert Beerbohm Tree respectively, and as a result the focus shifts from youth to age. Major Pendennis becomes the Dutch uncle-matchmaker who sets all to rights; Colonel Newcome becomes the last vestige of imperial old glory (according to one reviewer, Beerbohm Tree as the Colonel resembled the Emperor Franz Joseph, and another reported that he stretched out the death scene, which in the novel occupies half a paragraph, to forty-five minutes).[18] Yet most of Thackeray's characters were retained in these dramatizations – if huddled together at times. In *Becky Sharp*, for example, Mitchell contrives to get about half of the cast of characters into Miss Crawley's Park Lane drawing room in Act I in order to recapitulate the first thirteen chapters of the novel. In *Major Pendennis*, with something of a strain, he manages to bring three out of four of Pen's lady-loves into Pen's rooms in the Middle Temple.

To Mitchell's credit, somehow the literary quality of Thackeray was approximated. In Act II of *Becky Sharp*, set in the Duchess of Richmond's ball on the eve of the Battle of Waterloo, in which by his own admission Mitchell departed most from Thackeray's text, he gave Becky a speech to Rawdon in defence of her extravagance which is very much in character:

There's only one man, dear, since male and female were created who succeeded in enjoying his honeymoon without those *triste* things – milliners' and dressmakers' bills and after all, Eve was no doubt an engaging creature, but how dull it must have been to have her come down to breakfast every day in the same simple toilette.

And in the first scene of *Major Pendennis* he replicates the Major's typical swagger in this speech of consolation to Pen for the loss of Miss Fotheringay:

Never forget that I had a high ambition for you . . . I'm done; you're coming on . . . I hope to see you go up, sir, up, and carry the family with you. Why not? Our name is an old and honored one. God help me, sir, one of your ancestors John, Baron Pendennis, the founder of the family in 1220 – who built the Castle, well, sir, he may have been a trifle predatory and piratical in his habits and temperament – our times are more regular – Christian, if you like to call it that – but, hang it, pirate or not he did something – he did not merely swill at the trough, and consider that a crown was due him in the next world because he never broke the peace in this! No, sir, your family have been doers of the word, doers – and honored for it – I myself stuck it out at Waterloo – Nothing to boast of – but I am glad I was about, and did my share.

As Warrington remarks, the Major has 'a gouty conscience'. All in all, in Mitchell's Thackeray plays, an image of the master emerged over the footlights of a wit and urbane critic of society, the aspect of Dickens that tended to get lost in transit.

Samplings of Mitchell's style and approach confirm the conclusion of Paul Wilstach in his review of the stage history of both novelists at the turn of the century that Thackeray, because of the longer time-span that ensued between publication of his novels and their dramatic versions, benefited from a 'more advanced technique of playwriting' than fell to Dickens's lot.[19] Wilstach pointed out, moreover, that writers who tackled Thackeray were inspired by a more sincere admiration for his works, as against the 'mercenary expediency' of those who battened on Dickens. It is true that while Dickens was taken up mainly by hacks like Edward Stirling, William Moncrieff, and Andrew Halliday, Langdon Mitchell, Thackeray's best-remembered adapter, was a playwright of some distinction who remains an important figure in the history of American drama for having come the closest in America to achieving a comedy of manners. Mitchell came from a literary background (the son of the novelist-physician Silas Weir Mitchell, whose work he also dramatized), and so was a man of letters as well as of the theatre with a special affinity for English polite comedy, both old (the Restoration Wits and Sheridan) and new (having lived in London during the heyday of Oscar Wilde and Sir Arthur Wing Pinero).[20] Hence Dickens, while he remained more popular, became associated with the Adelphi and Surrey type of theatre, while Thackeray in the course of his traffic across the stage, however infrequent, became associated with stylish theatre.

A collateral effect of Thackeray's belated emergence in the theatre was that he became judged anew alongside Dickens, and critical reactions reveal how the literary reputations of this erstwhile 'Castor and Pollux' of the novel had diverged by then. For example, one of the first reviewers of *Becky Sharp*, while aware of the intransigence of this epic novel to dramatization, commended Mitchell's play as 'sprightly in humor, graphic in illuminative detail, picturesque in action, and true to literary ideals of the highest kind'. The depiction of Becky was judged to be more or less 'a consistent replica of Thackeray's brilliant creation'.[21] According to the *New York Times*, the audience at the première performance at the Fifth Avenue Theatre was a literary one, with Thackeray's novel at their fingertips, and 'Memory stood in place of the author as Chorus'.[22] It was in fact a gala event, attended by luminaries both of the theatre and of high society. Harper and Row paid tribute to the play with a special 'Becky Sharp' edition of *Vanity Fair*, substituting photographs of scenes from this spectacular production for Thackeray's original 'illuminations'. An interesting contrast is offered by the reception of J. Comyns Carr's version of *Oliver Twist*, one of Dickens's most perennially popular novels on the stage, which also opened at a theatre on Fifth Avenue five years after the début of *Becky Sharp*. The *New York Times* reviewer remarked of this play made from Dickens's 'coarse and extravagant novel' that it did not differ much from the crude version by Almar first seen in New York in 1839, and intermittently revived. Noting that actors were frequently attracted to the roles of Fagin, Sikes, and Nancy, this critic went on to lament:

> But for what good reason anybody should wish to see such monsters on the stage . . . presented merely as such, and not being subservient to any intellectual or moral purpose – it is difficult to determine . . . however there are all sorts of people, and all varieties of taste . . . and 'blood and thunder' drama still has an audience.[23]

It is evident too from comments made on plays made from *David Copperfield* and *Pendennis* that these autobiographical novels, reviewed together on their initial publication, were perceived on different wavelengths by the turn of the century. 'If ever an author was especially gifted to cheer the down-hearted, to inspire hope, and to give or restore faith in the Things that Matter, that author is Charles Dickens. And of course everybody knows, these thrice-blessed qualities are nowhere to be found in greater abundance than in "David Copperfield",' reads a contemporaneous review of Louis Napoleon Parker's *The Highway of Life* (1905).[24] This reviewer went on to demur that the play was more a reminder of the novel than an exact reproduction, 'a series of snapshots of a number of comic and serious episodes of the immortal story'.

On the other hand, by the time Langdon Mitchell came to dramatize *Pendennis* in 1916, he was established as a writer of sophisticated comedy with *The New York Idea* (1906), a reputation that was undoubtedly instrumental in persuading the famed actor John Drew to play the Major, and subsequently influenced the reviews of the play. One of the reviewers of *Major Pendennis* objected that any compression of Thackeray 'must fail to suggest the variety and vastness of his vision of the human comedy', and thought Mitchell's play somewhat lacking in theatrical robustness, but conceded that 'the dialogue in all four episodes is written with distinction', and that the author, knowing his Thackeray, was 'more than ordinarily endowed with literary tact'.[25] A more enthusiastic reviewer predicted that *Major Pendennis* would be 'caviar to the mob', inasmuch as it was 'devoid of all cheapness, all the bosh, and all the rank futilities that, grouped in a theatrical entertainment, make for popular success'. So, concluded this critic, the appeal of the affairs of Arthur Pendennis was not to the *hoi polloi*, but 'to the person who knows how to eat an artichoke, to the person whose palate is properly beguiled by the right kind of madeira, to the person who relishes Dunsany . . . for this class rates dramatic finish above dramatic flourish, grace and tone above mere whooping, door-busting, and tub thumping'.[26] This is a passing judgement by a young theatre pundit named George Jean Nathan, who was to go on to co-edit with H. L. Mencken that *épater*-er of the 'booboisie' called *The Smart Set*.

From a culling of the reviews of plays derived from the novels of Thackeray and Dickens, one can easily gather that discerning theatre-goers were close enough to their early reading of both to detect inadequacies in their stage adaptations. Those who came to these authors for the first time in the theatre got ersatz merchandise, but of different sorts. Both were reduced on the stage, but whereas Thackeray was flattened, Dickens was made banal. Perhaps for this reason, critics tended to be in awe of Thackeray, while condescending to Dickens. 'Thackeray has always been a difficult novelist to dramatize, unlike his great rival Dickens whose plots have been a treasure house to melodramatists,' reads a typical comment. 'Homely, robust, pint-a-porter fun', was Brooks Atkinson's reaction to *Pickwick Papers*, as brought to life by Cosmo Hamilton and Frank C. Reilly.[27]

From an eyewitness to the performances of Sir Herbert Beerbohm Tree, the first actor to play Colonel Newcome after winning plaudits for his Fagin in *Oliver Twist*, and for his virtuoso feat of doubling as Micawber and Daniel Peggotty in *David Copperfield*, we get in particular a capsule of the disparate attitudes of the cultivated reader towards the two novelists as they entered into fresh competition. Tree, it appears, was a disappointment in a revival of *Colonel Newcome* that he took to America. One of his admirers, William Leonard Courtney, then editor of the *Fortnightly Review*, wrote in a letter to an American friend in which he tried to account for the failure:

> If Tree had been a reader of books – he emphatically was not – he might have understood Thackeray better. . . . You cannot get at the author of 'Vanity Fair' from the outside, or by any ingenious or *a priori* methods; you have got to live with him in prolonged intimacy; his books must be at your bedside; his curious, elusive spirit, half-preacher half-cynic, must be your constant companion.

On the other hand:

> You can have a very good bowing acquaintance with Dickens and do him little or no injustice. His characters have the melodramatic tinge and strike one easily and forcibly. They are not pure creations of the Comic Spirit like some of the characters of Thackeray and Meredith. Farce, sheer undiluted Farce enters into them so largely that for stage purposes they suit admirably an actor with a frank liking for caricature.[28]

These reviews of Thackeray and Dickens 'on the boards' signal to us how they came to be viewed *vis-à-vis* each other as writers. If in the Victorian period they stood together 'in indissoluble connexion for the prize of light literature', by the Edwardian period the two had become citizens of Two Nations, culturally speaking, the author of *Vanity Fair* elevated into the pantheon of literature for the elite, 'the man who put together Dombey' relegated to popular entertainer. Apart from his association with high-brow theatre, a certain aura became attached to Thackeray by upwardly-mobile actors who clung to his coat-tails. Mrs

Fiske commissioned *Becky Sharp* out of an ambition to follow up her success in a dramatic version of *Tess of the D'Urbervilles* with an equally prestigious literary comedy. For Marie Tempest (later Dame Marie), who starred in a rival version of *Vanity Fair* in England (co-authored by her husband), the role of Becky Sharp marked her graduation from soubrette roles. Edmund Drew found in *Major Pendennis* a rise from the light boulevard comedies that had made his reputation. E. S. Willard, who introduced Colonel Newcome to American audiences, was the self-educated son of a Brighton tradesman eager to enhance his prestige with the role of a dignified gentleman.[29] Thackeray's own latter-day prestige was furthered by a revival of Mitchell's *Becky Sharp* at the august Players' Club (founded by Edwin Booth to enable actors to mingle with gentlemen). This was the only twentieth-century play, and the only play by an American, to be included in the Players' Club repertory of classics.[30] Mitchell himself became the first Professor of Playwriting at the University of Pennsylvania. So circumstances conspired to enshrine Thackeray among the nobs and snobs whom he himself had so incisively satirized.

On hindsight we can conclude that both Thackeray and Dickens were prized for the wrong reasons by a good many of our grandparents. The trivialization of Dickens on the stage may well have delayed his due recognition as a major and serious novelist. At the same time the image of Thackeray perpetuated via the footlights of an elegant cynic and dilettante has not helped his subsequent reputation, his wit having been played up at the expense of his wisdom. Dickens has since been taken up by academia with consequences familar to us all. Thackeray to date has not enjoyed such a wholesale 'rescue'. The following of club-men, cultivated amateurs, and cultural aspirants who gathered around him earlier in the century has largely fallen away, and he has yet to be fully rediscovered by students and scholars. Along with the Dickens 'boom' in the universities since World War II, intelligent film makers and television producers have been mining his riches – in particular his late works like *Great Expectations* and *Our Mutual Friend*. This media renaissance so far has not redounded substantially to the benefit of Thackeray (to judge by the tacky BBC masterpiece *Vanity Fair* and Stanley Kubrick's egregious film transmogrification of *Barry Lyndon*). Generally speaking, though of limited achievement so far, cinema and video seem potentially better equipped for the adaptation of the kaleidoscopic and panoramic fiction of the Victorian Age than the more constricted 'boards'.

Yet there is the recent Royal Shakespeare Company production of *Nicholas Nickleby* to remind us that the stage can be a fluid medium under inventive direction. A subsequent adaptation of *Vanity Fair* displayed at the Donmar Warehouse on the so-called 'London Fringe' with a versatile cast of seven performers 'who both play the major roles and throw the narrative between them like a game of catch', with minimal backdrops evocative of the period, seems to have been trying to go one better than Thackeray as 'Manager of the Performance'. According to a reviewer: 'The seizure of Thackeray's commentary by the very characters about whom it is being made, adds a dimension of radical self-awareness that transforms the exercise beyond mere animated reading, and goes some way to answer those who protest that, however well done, such adaptations do not make a play.'[31] It was also pointed out that this adaptation benefited from techniques worked out in the RSC *Nicholas Nickleby*. The one time Siamese twins of 'light literature' have continued in association, if collaterally. Unfortunately this *Vanity Fair* has not proved exportable like the *Nicholas Nickleby*, so once more Thackeray's rival has had the upper hand.

Notes

1. 30–31 Dec. 1844 and 1 Jan. 1845; in Kathleen Tillotson (ed.), *The Letters of Charles Dickens*, Pilgrim Edition (Oxford: Clarendon Press, 1977) vol. 4, p. 244.

2. 26 Aug. 1831; in Gordon N. Ray (ed.), *The Letters and Private Papers of William Makepeace Thackeray*, 4 vols (Cambridge, Mass.: Harvard University Press, 1945–46) vol. 1, p. 154. Hereafter referred to as *Letters*.

3. *Letters*, vol. 1, p. 16 (to his mother); Gerald Ritchie, *The Ritchies in India* (London: John Murray, 1920) p. 12.

4. For illustrative examples, see Gordon N. Ray, *The Age of Adversity* (New York: McGraw-Hill, 1955) passim; Robert A. Colby, *Thackeray's Canvass of Humanity* (Columbus: Ohio State University Press, 1979) ch. 4. A good summation of Dickens as a performer is found in the introduction to *Charles Dickens: The Public Readings*, Philip Collins (ed.) (Oxford: Clarendon Press, 1975).

5. 7 Jan. 1848; *Letters*, vol. 2, p. 333.

6. 'Arthur Pendennis and David Copperfield', *North British Review*, vol. 15 (May 1851) p. 57.

7. For details see: T. Edgar Pemberton, *Dickens and the Stage* (London: G. Redway, 1888); Paul Wilstach, 'Dramatisations of Dickens', *Bookman*, vol. 14 (Sept. 1901) pp. 52–62; J. B. van Amerongen, *The Actor in Dickens* (New York: D. Appleton, 1927), especially section entitled 'Dickens on the Stage'; Dorothy Pierce, 'Stage Versions of Dickens's Novels', *Bulletin of Bibliography*, Jan.–Apr. and May–Aug. 1937. Playbills of a number of these productions are preserved in the Townsend Walsh Scrapbook, Billy Rose Theatre Collection of the Performing Arts Research Center, New York Public Library at Lincoln Center (hereafter abbreviated as BRTC, LC).

8. Paul Wilstach, 'Dramatisations of Thackeray', *Bookman*, vol. 16 (Jan. 1903) p. 492. One possible reason for this production was the topicality of *The Diary of C. James de la Pluche* since it deals with the Railway Mania.

9. Charles Odell, *Annals of the New York Stage*, 15 vols (New York: Columbia University Press, 1927–1949) vol. 5, p. 440. According to Odell, Miss Chapman was 'one of the most vivacious soubrettes known to our stage', but obviously she could not save the play. A photograph of her is reproduced in *Annals*, vol. 5, p. 434.

10. Wilstach, 'Dramatisations of Thackeray', p. 497.

11. Letter to Mrs Savile Clark, undated, from Kingsley Lodge, Wimbledon. Anne Thackeray Ritchie Correspondence, Fales Collection, Bobst Library, New York University. Unpublished.

12. Wilstach, 'Dramatisations of Thackeray', pp. 494–95.

13. *Ibid.*, p. 496.

14. The scripts of these two plays are in BRTC, LC.

15. For details on these and other adaptations, see Robert A. Colby, '"Scenes of All Sorts . . .": *Vanity Fair* on Stage and Screen', *Dickens Studies Annual*, vol. 9 (1981) pp. 163–94. Lately the film *Becky Sharp* has been restored to its original Technicolor version at UCLA, after having been distributed for many years in inferior prints. For a brief account of this restored version, shown in the autumn of 1984 at the 22nd annual New York Film Festival at Lincoln Center, see Robert A. Colby, 'Becky Rediviva', *Thackeray Newsletter* (Nov. 1984) no. 20, pp. 2–3.

16. 'Boz and Bab', *Dickensian*, Sept. 1962, p. 175.

17. This version, never published, is described on the basis of a surviving script by Stedman in 'Boz and Bab', pp. 175–78. In keeping with Gilbert's first profession, the spotlight is thrown on Jaggers, in whose office the concluding act takes place. Oddly enough, Miss Havisham is omitted.

18. Reviews of *Colonel Newcome* in Toledo *Blade*, 1 July 1906; New York *Herald*, 2 Oct. 1906; Boston *Transcript*, 4 Oct. and 6 Nov. 1906. Robinson Locke Scrapbook, BRTC, LC.

19. Wilstach, 'Dramatisations of Thackeray', p. 492.

20. These details, and others to follow later in this paper, have been gleaned from the Langdon Mitchell Scrapbook, BRTC, LC. The fullest account of his career is in David M. Price, 'Langdon Mitchell and His Plays', Dissertation, Graduate Faculty in Theatre, City University of New York, 1978.

21. Edward Fales Coward, 'An Appreciation', *The Picture Book of Becky Sharp* (Chicago and New York: Edward Stome and Co., 1899).

22. *New York Times*, 13 Sept. 1899.

23. 'Revival of *Oliver Twist*' [Proctor's Fifth Avenue Theatre], *New York Times*, 1 Nov. 1905; Townsend Walsh Scrapbook, BRTC, LC.

24. Review by John Savoy; Townsend Walsh Scrapbook, BRTC, LC.

25. *Vogue*, 15 Oct. 1916; Robinson Locke Scrapbook, BRTC, LC. In 'The Difficulties of Dramatizing a Classic', *New York Times Magazine*, 12 Nov. 1916, Mitchell confided to an interviewer: 'I came an awful cropper. I ran into the time limitation of the theatre. After all, you can't have a young man madly in love with three women in two hours.' Among the other problems he mentioned were making Helen Pendennis palatable ('I really couldn't have my audience laughing the dear lady out of the theatre. As it is, she mentions "sin" a time or two, and I hear them near a titter') and having to make the Major 'mellow' earlier than in the novel. Blanche Amory in particular he found 'a strange type to American audiences. . . . Imagine a girl from Kansas being

"affected".' Nevertheless, as a playwright dramatizing novels, he cited no less a precedent than Shakespeare.

26. Review dated 4 Nov. 1916 from New York (no paper indicated); John Williams Scrapbook, BRTC, LC.

27. Charles Collins, 'Devoirs to Our First Comedian', Chicago *Post*, 13 Jan. 1917; Robinson Locke Scrapbook (John Drew) BRTC, LC; Brooks Atkinson, Boston *Sunday Post*, 6 Mar. 1927; Townsend Walsh Scrapbook, BRTC, LC.

28. 'An Open Letter to an American Friend', *Fortnightly Review*, Aug. 1917; rpt. in *Herbert Beerbohm Tree: Some Memoirs of Him and His Art*, collected by Max Beerbohm (London: Heinemann, [n.d.]) pp. 253–54.

29. Archie Binns, *Mrs Fiske and the American Theatre* (New York: Crown, 1955) pp. 86–88; Hector Bolitho, *Marie Tempest* (London: Cobden-Sanderson, 1936) pp. 105, 113–15; Charles Collins, 'Devoirs to Our First Comedian' [John Drew] Chicago *Post*, 13 Jan. 1917; Note on E. S. Willard in *The Middleman*, Robinson Locke Scrapbook (E. S. Willard) BRTC, LC.

The promotion of some of these productions contributed to this snob appeal; for example, Marie Tempest featured in *Vogue*, 15 Mar. 1911, in one of her costumes as Becky Sharp to demonstrate current styles; John Drew photographed as Major Pendennis against the background of his East Hampton Estate (Robinson Locke Scrapbook, BRTC, LC).

30. For an account of this production, see Colby, '"Scenes of All Sorts . . ."' pp. 175–76, and notes 34, 35 to that article.

31. As reported in *Sunday Observer*, 13 Jan. 1985, p. 49. See also, Donald Hawes, '*Vanity Fair* on the Stage', *Thackeray Newsletter* (May 1985) no. 21, pp. 1–2.

Since this essay was completed, word has been received of a new sixteen-part television adaptation by Alexander Baron on BBC 1, which appears to have been fuller, better produced, and on the whole far more successful than the BBC Masterpiece production of 1967, starring Susan Hampshire. The review of this latest production by David Nokes (*TLS*, Dec. 25–31, 1987, p. 1432) suggests that 'Thackeray's style may adapt better to the small screen than Dickens's'. While television 'always has difficulties with Dickens's eccentricities and exuberance,' he writes, 'Thackeray's style of caricature depends upon the sort of visual detail . . . that works perfectly on screen.' Nokes praises the entire production, particularly the Becky of Eve Matheson and the Jos of James Saxon.

13

The 'Sensation Scene' in Charles Dickens and Dion Boucicault

Judith L. Fisher

By the time Dion Boucicault introduced his 'sensation scene' in the 1857 production of *The Poor of New York*, Charles Dickens had been impressing his audiences for nineteen years with his novelistic version of the sensation scene. Both artists found the scene's vigorous action and spectacular effects ideal for their dramatic styles and thematic concerns. And both Dickens and Boucicault increasingly sophisticated the sensation scene. Dickens eventually used it to create tragic overtones, while Boucicault gave the scene an archetypal comic function. Paradoxically, then, although Dickens and Boucicault used the scene to engage the audience and developed it to crystallize their works' argument, its ultimate dramatic and thematic functions were different for them.

Arguing for direct influence is a dubious proposition without actual records in diaries or letters. But it is tempting to do so in this case because Dickens's and Boucicault's conceptions of the sensation scene are so similar, as is their development of it. Moreover, Boucicault could have learned from *Oliver Twist* (1838), *Barnaby Rudge* (1840–41), *Dombey and Son* (1848), *David Copperfield* (1849–50), *Bleak House* (1853), and *Hard Times* (1854) – all of which have sensation scenes and pre-date Boucicault's *The Poor of New York*. At the least, Boucicault was familiar with Dickens; his acting début in Bristol was as Mantilini in a production of *Nicholas Nickleby* on 26 December 1838.[1] He also wrote a dramatic version of *The Cricket on the Hearth*, titled *Dot*, and dramatized *Nicholas Nickleby* as *Smike*, both in 1859. Richard Fawkes, Boucicault's biographer, has also found a partial manuscript for a Boucicault play based on *Bleak House*.[2] This familiarity suggests a shared dramatic temperament which, perhaps, accounts for the affinities between the Dickensian and Boucicault sensation scene.

The sensation scene itself retains the same formal characteristics no matter what the thematic transformation. It usually falls near the end of the play or novel and is set off from the rest of the text or play by a change in rhetorical and dramatic rhythm. The scene features grandiose mechanical or visual effects and vigorous action which is often life-threatening to one of the characters. The scene culminates an episodic dramatic pattern – a swift juxtaposition of the scenes working towards the climax – which becomes increasingly complex. This pattern anticipates modern cinematic techniques, using cross-cutting and fades-in and fades-out in both stage production and narrative structure. Fades, the standard scene shifts, used either lighting and dimming or scenery shifts to change the physical scene around continuous action. This technique allowed plays to cross-cut between several lines of action in the story. Dickens's narrative shifts in *Bleak House* exemplify such cross-cutting on a larger scale, but his subtle shifts of perspective between the crowd and Bill Sikes in the chase scene in *Oliver Twist* are also analogous to theatrical technique. Since this technique kept the action continuous without breaking to change scenes, it was an effective means of building dramatic tension.

The patterning also exists on a thematic or symbolic level. Boucicault's and Dickens's mature sensation scenes in the Irish plays and novels such as *Dombey and Son* are exceptional because they are integral parts of the plot instead of purely excrescent thrills and chills. By the time of *Great Expectations* or *David Copperfield*, the sensation scene is an inevitable outcome, not a coincidence. In *The Colleen Bawn* (1860) and *Arrah-na-Pogue* (1864), the scenes epitomize the complexities of the moral and political struggle. In these later works, the moral point embedded in the scene is larger than life, not residing in one character or the immediate story. Thus, the grandiosity of the scene and action is necessary to emphasize the universality of the argument.

But early Dickens in *Oliver Twist* and early Boucicault in *The Poor of New York* use the sensation scene primarily for audience engagement and theatrical excitement. These scenes encourage the audience to participate vicariously in the action but are not essential to the plot. The sensation scene in *The Poor of New York* rests purely on coincidence. Badger, the reformed minor villain, is confessing his villainy to Paul and Lucy, lovers separated by Badger's machinations. Just as he is explaining that the documents which would restore Lucy's fortune are hidden in an old tenement, Dan (Paul's sidekick), from his vantage-point by the window, observes a fire – not only in the same area, in the same street, but in the very building Badger is talking about. In this rather awkward approach,

Boucicault introduces two techniques which will become standard. First, Dan describes the fire before the audience sees it, setting the stage for the sensational effect. Moreover, feeble as this rationale might be, we are given a reason to be present at the scene. We must, through Badger, rescue the documents. And, as we arrive on the scene, who do we see but Bloodgood, the major villain, slinking away from the fire which he has set to destroy those very documents he could not find.

The actual scene in *The Poor of New York* is more isolated and controlled than later ones. The action breaks between sighting the fire and arriving on the scene and much of Badger's heroic action takes place off stage. But the fire still introduces the realism characteristic of a Boucicault sensation scene. Although the tenement is a façade and New York is a painted backdrop, a real fire can be seen inside the building. It suddenly breaks through the windows, actually reaching out into the stage. We follow Badger's progress as the shutters of the tenement fall away, revealing him in the garret, looking for the documents. The actual fire, created by burning canvas behind the building façade, was, of course, the great reason for the sensation of the scene. The audience could *see* the flames were real, not painted, so that Badger's mission created a genuine sense of danger. The stage directions read, a 'crash is heard, Badger disappears as if falling with the inside of the building. The shutters of the windows fall away, and the inside of the house is seen, gutted by the fire.'[3] The stage directions also describe the appropriate cries from the crowd, to cue the audience to *its* reaction. The final touch is the tableau which freezes the principal actors in poses appropriate to the moment of tension: Dan and Paul hover over Badger's body, leaving us uncertain whether or not Badger rescued the documents. We can see the turning-point in this suspense; whether the play turns tragic or comic depends upon the discovery of those documents. The tenement fire is the only scene in *The Poor of New York* with exaggerated stage effects and action in what is otherwise a drawing-room play. Therefore, it underscores the importance of the missing documents even as it redeems Badger's character.

Obviously, the tenement fire gives us sensational action and scenery. But just as obviously, the pattern is weak. That there should happen to be a fire in that precise building at that precise time is dramatic expedience. And that Bloodgood should resort to setting alight an entire building for one set of papers also suggests the pure theatricality of the scene. This same sort of contrivance characterizes Dickens's first sensation scene in *Oliver Twist*. In fact, the accidental nature of Bill Sikes's death by hanging is a shrewd piece of irony because accident provides the same death as would the law courts. Sikes's hanging is the most descriptive of Dickens's sensation scenes. The beginning of the scene is signalled by a rhetorical change from dramatic dialogue and action to a more distant descriptive narration, designed to suggest a panoramic crowd scene.[4] Like Boucicault, Dickens used the crowd to give the reader a role. Again and again the crowd 'cries', 'execrates', and 'roars' as it pursues Sikes. Dickens describes the crowd's cries echoing as if 'the whole city had poured its population out to curse him' (vol. 1, ch. 50, p. 506). Their psychic energy pursues the now-terrified bully onto the roof. The visual emphasis, in both dramatizations of *Oliver Twist* and Cruikshank's illustration, is a panorama of London's roofs with Sikes balanced on one roof in the foreground. In both novel and play the anonymous crowd (and through them, the reader or audience) demands retribution and forces Sikes into his life-threatening situation. His actual death is sheer melodrama (without music). Justly, Nancy herself, so to speak, arises to avenge her murder. A supernatural vision of Nancy's eyes causes Sikes to slip:

> 'The eyes again!', he cried in an unearthly screech.
> Staggering as if struck by lightning, he lost his balance and tumbled over the parapet. The noose was on his neck. It ran with his weight, tight as a bowstring, and swift as the arrow it speeds. He fell for five-and-thirty feet. There was a sudden jerk, a terrific convulsion of the limbs; and there he hung, with the open knife clenched in his stiffening hand. (vol. 1, ch. 50, p. 508)

This melodramatic justice is completed by Sikes's dog launching himself at his master's swinging shoulders and missing, dashing his brains on the stones below. Dickens's staccato prose style reads like stage directions, and the active voice describes the bare action as it happens. The scene, like the tenement fire, is visually exciting and engages the audience, but, again like *The Poor of New York*, the actual scene is not necessary for plot or story. Sikes has to die but not necessarily so spectacularly – although it is wonderful theatre. One dramatized version of *Oliver Twist* reveals how easily the Fagin-Sikes story-line was converted into parallel lines of action using fades.

When the novel was produced in 1838 at the Royal Surrey in London, Dickens's rhetorical tension adapted naturally into the theatrical methods for creating dramatic tension. The coherency in this production is only in the continuous action; as yet there is no thought-out poetic justice to motivate the action. In addition, the Surrey production uses only conventional scenery and backdrops. Sikes's death is too individual to demand any great technical effects. To look at this production is to see the

sensation scene without Dickens's sense of cosmic symbolism or
Boucicault's technology, which allowed such scenes to be staged.

The sensation scene of the Surrey *Oliver Twist* was the culmination of
six scenes, which paralleled the capture of Fagin with the death of Sikes.[5]
In scene i, down stage, Fagin overhears Nancy preparing to betray him.
Then the forestage drop is lowered, cutting off Fagin and Nancy, and
leaving Noah Claypole to skulk off-stage after Nancy. This stage business
is suggested by Cruikshank's illustration, which shows Noah already in
the foreground, listening to Nancy talking to Rose and Mr Brownlow. All
the theatre needed was the existing stage equipment to dramatize the
illustration.

Immediately after Noah leaves the stage, the drop rises for scene iii,
revealing Nancy's garret – Sikes murders her in a grotesquely drawn-out
scene. The theatre production exaggerated Dickens's murder scene so as
to increase the audience's desire for revenge. Sikes drags Nancy across the
stage, bleeding and screaming.[6] (Her murder was so popular, some
productions took twenty minutes to do her in.) When she is finally dead,
the forestage drop falls again. Sikes wanders horror-stricken across the
front of the stage. The lights then cut across the stage to reveal Fagin in
gaol, usually in a tableau of Cruikshank's famous engraving. For scene vi
the lighting cuts back across to show Toby Crackitt's garret in a full stage
scene. A stage direction, 'street noise in pursuit', starts Sikes out of the
window and across a façade of roof-tops, backed by a painted panorama.
In the play the audience heard more of the crowd noise than they saw of
Sikes on the roof-tops. His actual hanging preserved the instantaneous
quality of the novel, showing it only in a 'flash scene', a sudden
illumination by igniting limelight.[7] What they did see was the vivified
Cruikshank illustration and an exact enactment of Dickens's description.
The sensation here depends on increasing suspense through non-stop
action and lots of crowd noise to stir up the audience; the only grand
technical effect is the flash scene. None the less, it is a sensation scene
because of the violence of the chase and the dramatic rightness of Sikes's
murder. Both the novel and the play emphasize a kind of 'destiny' which
causes Sikes's death; the crowd is a Chorus of Justice which is validated by
Sikes's own guilty vision. In this moral 'voice', *Oliver Twist* is more
sophisticated than *The Poor of New York*, although Boucicault's coinciden-
tal fire has the Dickensian touch of bringing all the threads together. Both
these tendencies become the *raison d'être* for later sensation scenes.

Productions of Dickens's novels benefited from the technical
achievements of Boucicault's sensation scenes. While *Oliver Twist* relies
on standard theatre techniques and painted drops and façades, later

productions heightened the dramatic tensions in the sensation scenes by using Boucicault's 'actuality'. And Boucicault himself increased the reality of his effects to keep pace with his political commentary. This constant development was unusual as sensation scenes became standard theatrical baggage. Dickens and Boucicault had many imitators who never grew beyond the stage of *Oliver Twist* and *The Poor of New York*. Crazy, murderous Lady Audley shoving her first husband down a well or Mazeppa, doomed to his wild horse ride on a tread-wheel in Astley's hippodrome exemplify this stagnation.[8] But Boucicault's and Dickens's sensation scenes changed with the demands of their art, while always retaining their sensational impact. *The Colleen Bawn*, *Dombey and Son*, and *David Copperfield* manifest the increased importance of dramatic and thematic patterning. The visual effect now echoes the moral complexities of the work. The actual sensation scenes are still pantomime-like, but the crowd as Chorus is gone. The audience is neither asked to participate in any retribution nor given a role, so they are better able to relate the scenes to the whole work instead of being absorbed in only that scene.

The Colleen Bawn introduces the first of Boucicault's 'outsiders' – Irish outlaws, played by Boucicault himself, who combined the joviality of the stage Irishman with a more serious role of moral touchstone.[9] This play focuses on the collision between morality and social ambition. Hardress Cregan, an Irish aristocrat, must marry Anne, an Irish aristocrat, to save his estate – and to save his mother from the attentions of the Irish overseer Corrigan. But Hardress is already married to the Colleen Bawn, Eily O'Connor, an Irish peasant girl. Torn between his love for Eily and his shame for her rough ways, Hardress tacitly gives his servant Danny permission to murder her. Danny, ironically, is also an Irish peasant, but one domesticated by many years of service. And to compound the irony, Hardress has crippled Danny in a fit of violence in their boyhood. The misguided Danny lures Eily to a cave beneath the cliffs of the sea and attempts to drown her. Myles-na-Copaleen, a good-natured Irish bootlegger, is working his still in the cave, hears the struggle, and saves Eily. He hides her and reunites Eily with Hardress (through the priest Father Tom) after Hardress has suffered for his supposed murder. The sensation scene is this 'murder' and rescue. After Eily is thrown into the sea by Danny, Myles has a spectacular leap into the sea to rescue her.[10]

Unlike the tenement fire, Eily's 'murder' is not just extra thrills but is necessary, at least according to Danny, for Hardress can find no other way out of his financial straits than to marry Anne. Danny's blind loyalty is set up early in the play, making him a natural instrument. Hardress is given enough disdain for Eily's peasant ways to make it possible for him to want her out of the way. And we know in advance that Myles's still is in the cave. Dramatically, everything in the play leads towards this scene at the end of Act II, and Act III is the reaction to it – the scene creates the rest of the play.

But more importantly, the scene comments on the social tensions at work. Eily, like Arrah in *Arrah-na-Pogue*, is presented as a type of Ireland itself. Her dark beauty, her brogue, and her values make her a distinct national type. Cregan, then, is forced to kill, or at least disown, that most natural part of himself. Anne, ironically, is sympathetic towards Eily, making the conflict a political one faced by the Irish among themselves although indirectly caused by the English occupation. Corrigan, the local agent and villain, is an Irishman corrupted by English materialism. It is Myles, the outlaw and social misfit, who saves Eily (Ireland) from murder by one of her own, a murder which English domination over Ireland has necessitated, even if unconsciously. Myles is also the agent of moral punishment, withholding Eily from Hardress, until Father Tom finally reconciles them. So, the exaggeration in the sensation scene stresses the depth of the emotions and the depth of the outrage being inflicted on Eily and Ireland. Boucicault suppresses the sheer sensationalism of the scene in favour of his thematic point by omitting the suspense at the end of the scene. We know that Myles has saved Eily; after the rescue, 'Myles and Eily rise up [from the water] – he turns, and seizes rock – Eily across left arm'.[11] The dramatic irony makes us less participants than observers of the rest of the play. Knowing the comic resolution will occur, we become involved in the moral lessons Hardress and his mother must learn.

Dickens also subordinated his sensation scene in *Dombey* and *Copperfield* to his psychological pattern. *Dombey and Son* sacrifices almost all visual effect for the psychological sensation. The horrible death of Carker, falling into the path of the train, is an overpowering impression from Carker's point of view. The change in rhetorical style echoes this change in perception. No longer a straightforward narrative, the crucial paragragh is one long sentence, building to a climax and stressing Carker's reactions:

> *He heard* a shout – another – *saw* the face change from its vindictive passion to a faint sickness and terror – *felt* the earth tremble – *knew* in a moment that the rush was come – *uttered* a shriek – *looked* round – *saw* the red eyes, bleared and dim in the daylight, close upon him – *was beaten down, caught up, and whirled away* upon a jagged mill that spun him round and round, and struck him limb from limb, and licked his stream of life up with its fiery heat, and cast his mutilated fragments in the air. (Italics mine; vol. 9, ch. 55, p. 456)

The moment of Carker's death is precisely when the verb tense changes from active to passive. The sensational visual effects and action are not gone but must be imagined and so become more horrible. Carker's 'punishment' is worse than Sikes's because we experience it with him – we are not allowed the luxury of merely watching the just execution. In each case, however, retribution is motivated by the villains' internal guilt and accomplished by an external agent. And their degree of guilt as well as the immensity of their crime is reflected in their spectacular deaths.

Carker's death is not simply a psychological reality, but it is also a working of Divine Justice. Like Sikes's death it is an appropriate 'accident'. However, the means of Carker's death, the train, has been a superhuman 'character', a destroyer of old evil, throughout the book, as William Axton has pointed out.[12] We can see here the fruition of Sikes's 'accidental' death, accident becoming something determined in the cosmic scheme of right and wrong. Dickens explained his theory of the justified accident in a letter to Forster in 1859:

> Where the accident is inseparable from the action and passion of the character; where it is strictly consistent with the entire design, and arises out of some culminating proceeding on the part of the individual which the whole story has led up to; it seems to me to become, as it were, an act of divine justice.[13]

Dickens created the need for this culminating action in his brilliant chase sequence in chapter 55. And the proper instrument has been present since the opening instalment. Axton has noted the determinism in Carker's death: 'A certain supernal mechanism of fatality invests the episode with a power that seems independent of the author's control, with the results that he and the reader stand apart together as fellow witnesses of a meaningful consummation.'[14] Carker's death turns the traditional sensation scene inside out, but in so doing makes it unplayable in the theatre as it is presented because Dickens's rhetorical impressionism replaces the stage machinery – the overt description of action of *Oliver Twist*. So one could really question whether Carker's death is still a sensation scene.[15]

David Copperfield uses the action of *Oliver Twist* and increases the determinism introduced in *Dombey* to create in the shipwreck a scene that takes the Steerforth/Emily story from domestic melodrama to modern tragedy. As the hero in tragedy should be larger than life, so is Steerforth in David's eyes. As the tragic action suggests more than individual actions so does the shipwreck. *Copperfield* compared to *Oliver Twist* exemplifies Earle Davis's distinction between melodrama which 'grows with coincidence' and tragedy which is a 'destiny'.[16] From the beginning

of the novel Emily is afraid of the sea and its destructive power. And
Steerforth feels the sea is 'hungry' for him the first time he goes to
Yarmouth (vol. 10, pt 1, ch. 21, p. 412). On the night Ham and Emily
announce their engagement, Steerforth tells the story of a dismal
shipwreck (vol. 10, pt 1, ch. 21, p. 419). Ham has the strongest precogni-
tion of the tragedy when, after Emily has run off, he looks out to sea and
sees 'the end of it' out there (vol. 10, pt 2, ch. 32, p. 27). David tells us that
Ham's attitude haunted him (David) until the 'inexorable' end came
(vol. 10, pt 2, ch. 32, p. 27). These are just a few strands in the complex
image of the sea as source of life, source of death, and, finally, the
instrument of Fate.

As in both *Oliver Twist* and *Dombey and Son*, the actual scene of the
wreck and Ham's death is rhetorically set off from the rest of the text.
Dickens's rhetoric emphasizes the inevitability of the action and
reinforces its supra-human stature. Dickens uses Ham's name only twice
in the central scene (vol. 10, pt 2, ch. 55, pp. 475–76), using 'he', and
deliberately beginning five sentences with 'He'. Since he also refers to
Steerforth as 'he', the two men are confused and become emblems instead
of individuals: emblems of mankind and Christ as suggested earlier by
Ham's name (one of the three sons of Noah) and by the pronoun 'he' as
well as the Biblical cadence of Dickens's narration:

> And now he made for the wreck, rising with the hills, falling with the
> valleys, lost beneath the rugged foam, borne in towards the shore,
> borne on towards the ship, striving hard and valiantly. The distance
> was nothing, but the power of the sea and wind made the strife deadly.
> At length he neared the wreck. He was so near, that with one more of
> his vigorous strokes he would be clinging to it, – when a high, green,
> vast hill-side of water, moving on shoreward, from beyond the ship, he
> seemed to leap up into it with a mighty bound, and the ship was gone!
> (vol. 10, pt 2, ch. 55, p. 476)

This sensation scene includes sensational action, visual effects, and is the
culmination of the sub-plot. Dickens's careful patterning makes the
shipwreck a symbolic necessity, not a theatrical device.

The power of this scene was such that it was the climax of Dickens's
public reading of *David Copperfield*. The revisions of the novel for the
stage production also suggest the strength of the Ham/Emily/Steerforth/
shipwreck pattern. If you wanted to stage the sensation scene, you had to
tell their story. So the novel was adapted by George F. Rowe as *Little
Em'ly* in 1869 for the Olympic. The scenes were staged much the same as
Sikes's death, but the realism of the effects put the shipwreck on the

technical level of Boucicault, who had already produced a spectacular ship explosion in 1863 in *The Octoroon*. The action continues while the scenes change, again increasing tension which this time culminates not in a single figure flash-scene, but a larger-than-life shipwreck. And, as in Boucicault's *Poor of New York*, we are prepared for the scenic effects. We begin in Peggotty's Ark and *hear* the storm every time the door opens. The next two scenes, 'Near the Beach' and 'The Sea', continue the preparation with storm noises and a constant rush of characters — once again a crowd, but this one is in chaos. Then as the actors rush across the stage to the rescue, the forestage drop is lifted 'to reveal "*Sea in a Storm*. Ship pitching among breakers. Landing stair and wooden pier R. Steerforth seen on mast of ship. . . . ship sinks."'[17] The sense of destiny in this scene is only possible because the sea is the agent of justice. Unlike a locomotive which is constructed and therefore controllable, the sea is immense and indifferent to the fortunes of humans. Dickens can only make the train a larger symbol by shrinking our point of view to Carker's. Such a perspective was impossible to dramatize until film. Since the sea is an uncontrolled natural force, it automatically lends itself to cosmic symbolism. Boucicault capitalized on the same sense of gigantic nature diminishing human efforts in *Pauvrette; or, Under the Snow* (1858), wherein an enormous avalanche crashes down on a tiny Alpine cabin.

Arrah-na-Pogue also pitted man against nature: Shaun the Post has to climb a seemingly insurmountable cliff. Here, however, Boucicault turns natural forces to comic effect, for Shaun triumphs over nature. That opposition is also an analogy to the political theme of the play.[18] The political opposition in *Arrah* is a triangle — true Irish versus Irish corrupted by English materialism abetted by English law. In the character of Arrah we have Ireland, beloved by Shaun the Post, the Irish outsider. The play's use of the pointedly anti-British ballad, *The Wearing of the Green*, the trial scene wherein Shaun mocks the British legal system, the inept British officers, the Irish hero-rebel named Beamish MacCoul, and Shaun's legal but morally unjustified imprisonment make *Arrah-na-Pogue* Boucicault's most inflammatory play. The sensation scene of Shaun's escape from prison is a microcosm of the political tensions and produces an Irish victory — wishful thinking on the stage. The escape scene is one of Boucicault's most complex, technically and dramatically.

Arrah wanders outside the prison wall, whistling *The Wearing of the Green*. Inspired by her song, Shaun prepares to escape from prison by scaling the wall which is built into a cliff, rising steeply from the sea. As he leaves the cell, the scene dissolves. Shaun actually scales the wall while the backdrop changes to accompany his progress and fresh sections of the prison wall and then the cliffs emerge as Shaun climbs over the flats. The walls slide in from the stage flies and drop into the floor as Shaun ascends; each flat is painted to represent an ever higher section of the wall, the last one showing the summit and the sky. So Shaun actually climbs down stage while he seems to be scaling the wall.

This precarious escape from the English to the tune of an 'up-the-Irish' song is plainly a political symbol. Moreover, the scene takes on additional urgency when, as we have seen Shaun ascending, the scene shifts to Arrah, who is attacked by Feeny, another Irish villain who works for the English. Will Shaun get there in time? He does: 'Shaun's arm is seen over the edge of the battlement; it seizes Feeny's ankle, who utters a cry. As he is dragged to the edge of the precipice, he throws up his arms, and falls over with a cry.'[19] But then the drums of the English are heard. We know that O'Grady is rushing towards us with a pardon. Will it arrive before the soldiers shoot Shaun, who is too exhausted to move? And, again, it does.

In this play, Arrah, the figure of Ireland, is not only the victim but the inspiration for Shaun's superhuman effort. And the three lines of suspense, escape, Arrah's peril, and the pardon, add up to one large victory of Irish over English. It is thematically important that Shaun's escape is successful before he is pardoned, to emphasize his moral justification. The pardon becomes a legal nicety. The implied analogy is clear: just as Shaun could – when he had to – climb the impossible wall to escape and rescue Arrah, so too can the Irish – if *they* try hard enough – defeat the more powerful English and win Home Rule. *Arrah-na-Pogue* anticipates *The Shaugraun*, Boucicault's last Irish drama (1874). This one takes the English/Irish antagonism even further. It is set during the Fenian Insurrection of 1866 and forces a young English officer to choose between duty and his love for an Irish girl. But *The Shaugraun* works its magic without a specific sensation scene, using instead a series of thrilling chase scenes in and out of the fog.[20]

The predominant characteristic of Boucicault's sensation scenes is that the outsider figure, and not the conventional hero, is pivotal in the action. It is as if this character had freer scope of action. Moreover, rebel sentiments come more naturally from an outlaw's mouth.[21] The audience is not asked to agree with Myles or Shaun as they are asked to identify with a hero, but the excitement of the scene temporarily engages the audience on the outlaw's side. Dickens, too, leaves his heroes out of his sensation scenes – until *Great Expectations*. The boat collision in this novel relies on the limited psychological perception of one character – Pip. The first-person narrative has the intensity of Carker's experience but with more visual and psychological clarity. David Copperfield only observed the shipwreck and Ham's heroic effort, while Pip is the helpless victim of the boat collision. Pip has to be in the boat collision because he represents Dickens's larger theme: the futility of an individual's attempt to direct life or control fate. The scene brings together directly or indirectly all the characters who have attempted to control their own or others' lives. Pip has been the main character self-deluded into believing that his fairy-tale perception of his life was his pattern. Magwitch has deluded himself that he could tailor another being to his pattern. Pip and Magwitch are also reminders of Estella's origin and the tragedy of her training. And, of course, Compeyson, who controlled Magwitch and so, to an extent, started the whole process, is finally destroyed. The scene occurs logically; rowing out to meet a ship was an expeditious way to escape England. Dickens's irony is complex in this scene. The escape is thwarted by the instrument of the escape: the steamboat. But Magwitch had been claimed as a prisoner by the intercepting galley the moment before the boats collided, so the collision actually frees Magwitch again – literally, because he is physically free to pursue Compeyson under the water, and metaphorically free because the wound he receives 'frees' him from having to die a criminal's death. Pip is also freed by the accident from his loathing and shame of Magwitch.

Perhaps the most important quality in this sensation scene is the sense of inevitability. Pip can only sit there and wait for the steamboat to bear down on them, his helplessness underscored by his crippled arm. The starkness of his narration, the iambic pentameter rhythm, and the repetition turn the scene into a tragic soliloquy. Pip's fragmentary memories emphasize the scene as the 'moment of Destiny':

I heard them calling to us, and heard the order given to stop the paddles, and heard them stop, but felt her driving down upon us irresistibly. In the same moment, I saw the steersman of the galley lay his hand on his prisoner's shoulder, and saw that both boats were swinging round with the force of the tide, and saw that all hands on board the steamer were running forward quite frantically. Still in the same moment, I saw the prisoner start up, lean across his captor, and pull the cloak from the neck of the shrinking sitter in the galley. Still in the same moment, I saw that the face disclosed was the face of the other convict of long ago. Still in the same moment, I saw the face tilt backward with a white terror on it that I shall never forget, and heard a great cry on board the steamer and a loud splash in the water, and felt the boat sink from under me. (vol. 4, ch. 2, pp. 547–48)

Compared to Bill Sikes's death, this is a masterpiece of visual and psychological sensation. The immensity of the steamboat looming over the two galleys, the paddles flashing death, suggests the enormous futility of Pip's action. And like *Dombey's* narration, Pip preserves the instantaneous and simultaneous quality of the actions. The suddenness of the scene actually jars us into realizing that some such calamity was inevitable. The Pip we know could never have gone to the Continent to live a miserable life with Magwitch. He would never have made his final step into maturity by conquering his aversion to Magwitch and understanding the convict from his, not Pip's, point of view. The scene is predetermined by Pip's entire progress from self-delusion to self-knowledge. And, unlike *Dombey and Son*, we lose nothing of the visual or dramatic impact.

The genuine sense of destiny in *Great Expectations'* boat collision gives the sensation scene tragic overtones. It is an irony of the nineteenth-century stage that in searching for a contemporary tragic form, dramatists settled for nineteenth-century versions of Shakespeare. Plays such as Sheridan Knowles's *Virginius* (1820), Bulwer-Lytton's *Richelieu* (1838), or Tom Taylor's *'Twixt Axe and Crown* (1870) could imitate the language but not the imagination of Shakespeare. But in the sensation scene, which capitalized on the modern world, there was a tool to present everyone's struggle to define themselves against the uncaring structures of modern society. The similarity in the concept of the sensation scene for Dickens and Boucicault is apparent in the way *The Poor of New York, Oliver Twist, The Colleen Bawn, The Octoroon, Arrah-na-Pogue,* and *David Copperfield* shared sensations and could be staged with the same conventional techniques. Dickens's sense of action was schooled by the stage, which was in turn invigorated by the dramatic potential of his sensation scenes. Boucicault developed the technical expertise to realize his and Dickens's visions. Both artists learned that using the scene to crystallize themes only increased the overall effect of the scene, which could then be anticipated by the audience or reader. By combining the grandness of action demanded by classical tragedy with the personal relevance demanded by the nineteenth-century audience, they could externalize the psychological states of an individual in physical action.

But Dickens and Boucicault also made sensational action manifest a universal moral order, because the scenes dispensed a larger justice. We can see Boucicault's political themes use symbolic action to move towards comic victory and reconciliation. He pits an individual such as Shaun or Myles against an institution such as the army or social class and suggests a new order based on love which abolishes these artificial distinctions. Dickens's view is inherently darker. His characters are defeated by forces beyond their control. Sikes is the author of his own accident after imagining Nancy's eyes. Carker and Pip are defeated by the impersonal forces of the modern world. And most archetypically of all, Ham is drawn to his death by and in the sea. The vastness of the scenes is essential to widen the action from an individual to a symbolic scale. The early sign of this tendency is *Dombey and Son*. Although Dickens uses the melodramatic device of guilt and craven fear to start Carker on his flight, the intensity of the prose and the justness of the actual death turns melodramatic retribution into Orestes being pursued by the Furies – the Cosmos punishing one who has tried to assert his own will over universal law.

Boucicault and Dickens suggest an immanent 'Will' by heightening the actions of individuals until they seem larger than life – Ham swimming out to Steerforth, Shaun scaling the prison wall. And both rely on supra-human 'agents' to change radically the course of events. These scenes, especially in *David Copperfield*, *Arrah-na-Pogue*, and *Great Expectations*, reassert the 'proper' order of the world. It takes the violence of the ship collision or Eily's 'murder' to change the known world and establish a just set of moral relations among the characters. Who in the novels could resolve the situations if not these disinterested agents of justice? Ironically, sensation scenes work against the development of a truly psychological novel or drama because they assert the power of an Order not susceptible to the human will. But the suggestion of an Absolute Order that could act even if individuals were powerless provided a comforting aesthetic, understandable in the face of a shifting society.

Notes

1. All biographical information about Dion Boucicault comes from Richard Fawkes, *Dion Boucicault* (New York: Quarter Books, 1979). The edition used for his Irish plays is *The Dolmen Boucicault*, David Krause (intro.) (Chester Springs, PA: Dufour Editions, 1965).

2. Fawkes, *Dion Boucicault*, p. 266.

3. Dion Boucicault, *The Poor of New York* (New York: Samuel French, 1857) p. 61. This version is from the production at Wallack's Theatre, New York, in 1857.

4. Charles Dickens, *Complete Works* (New York: Heart's International Library [New National Edition], 1867) vol. 1, ch. 50, pp. 503–507. All citations from Dickens's works (except his letters) are from this edition, given in volume, part (if applicable), chapter, and page.

5. The following information about the staging of *Oliver Twist* is from A. Nicholas Vardac, *Stage to Screen: Theatrical Method from Garrick to Griffith* (New York: Benjamin Blom, 1968). The stage adaptation and production were by George Almar.

6. See Vardac, *Stage to Screen*, p. 35, for an excerpt from the stage directions for Nancy's death. Here is a sample: 'He catches her by the hair of the head, drags

her forward and swings her round so that she falls head to L. H. He falls on his knees behind her as she reaches the floor. He knocks her head on the floor still holding her by the hair, she screaming and trying to call for help as long as she can.' And this is just the first stage of the murder.

7. Vardac, *Stage to Screen*, p. 36

8. *Lady Audley's Secret*, dramatized in 1863 by C. W. Hazlewood, sensationalized (if that were possible) Mary Elizabeth Braddon's novel of a scheming woman, angelic in appearance, who murders her first husband to keep her bigamy from being discovered. The novel was a wild success, as was the play, and presents one of the first genuine female villains. In fact, Lady Audley was so wicked that Hazlewood's version toned her down. *Mazeppa* was a cross between a melodrama and an extravaganza. Based on the poem by Lord Byron (1819), the 'play' told the story of the cossack Ivan Stepanovich Mazeppa-Koledinsky (1644–1709). The highlight of the evening at Astley's in 1831 was when Mazeppa was tied to the back of a horse as punishment for a romantic intrigue. The horse 'hurtled along a treadmill between a ground row representing the banks of the Dnieper and a moving cloth of the stormy countryside, the whole effect being enhanced by copious thunder and lightning'. Richard Altick, *The Shows of London* (Cambridge, Mass.: Harvard University Press, 1978) p. 201.

9. I am indebted for this approach to James Hurt, 'Dion Boucicault's Comic Myths', forthcoming in *When They Weren't Doing Shakespeare: Essays in Nineteenth-Century British and American Theatre*, Judith L. Fisher and Stephen Walt (eds) (Athens: University of Georgia Press).

10. *The Colleen Bawn* is made more interesting by the fact that Boucicault based the play on Gerald Griffin's *The Collegians: A Tale of Garryowen*, published in 1829. Griffin had based his novel on a genuine murder case in Limerick, where the Eily O'Connor was not so lucky (Krause (intro.), *The Dolmen Boucicault*, p. 27). The play was first produced at Laura Keene's Theatre in 1860 in New York.

11. Krause (intro.), *The Dolmen Boucicault*, p. 85.

12. William F. Axton, *Circle of Fire* (Lexington: University of Kentucky Press, 1966) p. 227.

13. *The Nonesuch Dickens*, Arthur Waugh (ed.) *et al.* (London: Nonesuch Press, 1938) vol. 3, p. 117.

14. Axton, *Circle of Fire*, p. 150.

15. On the other hand, the scene typifies the sensation scene, which relies not just on spectacular effect, but exploits modern technology. Augustin Daly used a train in *Under the Gaslight* (1867), the first hero-tied-on-the-railroad-track scene, which Boucicault stole for *After Dark* in 1867.

16. Earle Davis, *The Flint and the Flame: The Artistry of Charles Dickens* (Columbia, Mo.: University of Missouri Press, 1963) p. 62. For additional information about *David Copperfield* in the Victorian theatre, see Richard Fulkerson, '*David Copperfield* in the Victorian Theatre', *Victorians Institute Journal*, vol. 5 (1976) pp. 29–36.

17. Vardac, *Stage to Screen*, p. 32. *Little Em'ly* preserved the same poetic justice as *David Copperfield* with Ham swimming out to save Steerforth. *Little Em'ly's* shipwreck added spectacular motion to this version of the sensation scene. The ship moved back and forth and eventually sank right before the viewers' eyes.

It is interesting to note just how many sensation scenes centre on water. Besides these specific ship scenes in *Little Em'ly* and *The Octoroon*, Boucicault's

Formosa features a boat race; *After Dark* has a suicide leap into the Thames; and the tragic fight between Bradley Headstone and Rogue Riderhood on the mill weir became the sensation scene in the dramatic version of Dickens's *Our Mutual Friend*.

18. *Arrah-na-Pogue; or the Wicklow Wedding* was first produced at the Old Theatre Royal, Dublin, 1864, and the next year a revised version was produced at the Princess's Theatre, London. The production details in my dicussion are from the DeWitt version which was the 1864–65 production. See Vardac, *Stage to Screen*, pp. 25–31.

19. Krause (intro.), The Dolmen Boucicault, p. 167.

20. *Ibid.*, pp. 220–21.

21. This outsider figure anticipates John Ford's western hero. There is much similarity between Johnny Ringo of *Stagecoach* who can save the 'civilized', law-abiding characters but who cannot live in their society and any of Boucicault's Irish outlaw-heroes.

14

Dickens and the Early Modern Theatre

Michael Goldberg

It was Shaw's regret that the Victorian stage could not 'enlist the genius of Dickens',[1] a failure which seems all the more surprising given Dickens's fascination with the theatre, his taste for melodrama, and the fact that he was 'himself an incorrigible actor'.[2] Shaw blamed the strangling grip of nineteenth-century censorship for killing serious drama, in consequence of which 'dramatists had to express themselves in novels'.[3] Whatever the merits of such an argument, the fact remains that if Dickens could not succeed any more than Mr Wopsle 'in reviving the drama' of his own time, he was able to exert an influence over the theatre of the future. Indeed, as George Ford has observed, his mark 'is more evident in the twentieth century drama' than in 'any of the novels which supposedly reflect his influence'.[4] What follows is a brief consideration of Dickens, in the context not of the Victorian stage, but in his relationship to the early modern theatre of Shaw, Ibsen and Strindberg.

It is perhaps strange to find Dickens among these intellectually revolutionary figures of the modern drama, for broadly speaking, from his death until the 1930s, Dickens had been 'popularly loved . . . and intellectually rather disreputable'[5] — Mr Popular Sentiment's greatest Victorian asset having turned into his principal twentieth-century liability. It is a sharp irony and a quirk of literary history, that after the 1880s, precisely when Dickens was being abandoned by many sophisticated readers who felt they had outgrown his books, he was being read, assimilated and emulated by some of the leading radical writers these same readers admired in his stead. Even Shavians accepted Shaw's enthusiasm for Dickens 'with an air of apology', but Shaw himself read him 'without shame or stint', unmoved by the intellectual fashions which affected many of his admirers.[6]

Like Shaw, Ibsen and Strindberg also found Dickens well 'worth kidnapping',[7] and openly acknowledged a debt to the great Victorian novelist which reflected itself in their own writing. All were confirmed early readers of Dickens. Ibsen devoured his work in Grimstad at the age of sixteen. Shaw had read *Great Expectations* and *A Tale of Two Cities* before tackling, as 'a cynical blasé person of twelve or thirteen . . . *Pickwick, Bleak House,* and the intervening works'.[8] Strindberg as a youth was reading him in Swedish translation in the house of Dr Lamm. Each of them imitated Dickens or tried to. Shaw's self-styled 'jejeune exploit' *The Irrational Knot* (1880) was, by his own admission, written in the style of Dickens. The same is true of the surviving fragment of Ibsen's projected *nouvelle, The Prisoner at Akershus* (1850), as it is of Strindberg's early stories and his novel, *The Red Room* (1879).

Aside from common indebtedness to Dickens, there is a complex, shifting web of influence and interaction among these later writers themselves which produced a wide range of sometimes surprising permutations. The process is not simply an influence descending lineally down a single conduit but also one spreading laterally over the intricate network making up this four-sided relationship. The phenomenon can in part be described by the appropriated legal term 'eminent domain', which in its literary application suggests a multiple series of sometimes violent expropriations and reciprocal encroachments. Authors seize what they need from others, and enhance or despoil what they steal according to the power of their mimetic talents. At the same time, like literary cannibals, they are liable to the effects of what they ingest.

Shaw, for instance, helped himself generously from the Dickensian cornucopia. He readily adapted Dickensian themes and characters to his own plays, discovering in the process, that he could 'startle the world with daring innovations' by 'lifting characters bodily out of the pages' of the Victorian novelist.[9] In 1890 he introduced Ibsen to a Fabian audience and the following year produced that 'brilliantly misleading book which should have been called the Quintessence of Shavianism',[10] a title that would serve equally well for Shaw's critique of Dickens. In his critical commentaries Shaw constantly juxtaposed the two writers, tending to represent Dickens as an author needing to be completed by Ibsen or himself.

Ibsen may have borrowed the central image of *A Doll's House* from Dickens. In a broader and more important sense, Dickens was working in his later fiction towards an art that found an answering response in Ibsen's plays. The symbolism he evolved to convey the extraordinary depth of meaning in these novels anticipates by thirty years Ibsen's dramatic technique in such plays as *The Wild Duck* (1884) and *Pillars of Society* (1877). In *Dombey and Son,* for example, Mr Dombey sends Walter Gay on a journey in the ominously named ship, the Son and Heir. The ship breaks up in a storm. Simultaneously and almost reciprocally, Dombey's son Paul slips towards a mysterious death. The episode has its counterpart in *Pillars of Society* when Karsten Bernick arranges for his brother-in-law to embark on a 'coffin ship', only to discover his son Olaf has stowed away on the floating wreck in his place. In both these episodes a covert criminality of intention towards others turns into a psychological nemesis which rebounds to injure the perpetrators.

Strindberg's dramatic technique also has many affinities with the surrealism of Dickens, and he certainly saw the application of Dickensian characterization to the theatre. He urged actors at the Intimate Theatre to read Dickens to learn about gesture and expression. At other times he castigated Dickens's characters as 'organ grinder's puppets', a perception which played some part in his own development of 'contrapuntal' dialogue. In fact both Strindberg and Shaw were stimulated to new creative efforts by their criticism of Dickens, thus illustrating and authenticating Pound's view that new composition is in itself the most intense form of criticism.[11]

Ibsen and Strindberg read each other's work, Shaw read them both, and all three read Dickens. The attitudes of the three playwrights to each other were as complex and different as their response to Dickens. Shaw became Ibsen's first English interpreter. Strindberg, but for a last-minute financial hitch, would have become his most interesting Swedish translator. In 1880, Ibsen read approvingly Strindberg's new novel *The Red Room*, which contains a scene of a young man awestruck at meeting someone who was permitted to call Ibsen by the familiar form 'Du'. Seven years later, he wrote that disagreement with Strindberg's observations in *The Father* did not prevent him 'from acknowledging, and being gripped by, the violent force of the author in this new work'.[12] Like one of his own tormented characters, Strindberg feared Ibsen, 'the decrepit old troll', as a 'fertilizing spirit' who might take possession of him, an anxiety not lessened by the conviction that Ibsen had used him as the model for the figure of Hjalmar Ekdal in *The Wild Duck*. He also suspected him of plagiarizing *The Secret of the Guild* (1880) in *The Master Builder* (1892), and *The Father* (1887) in *Hedda Gabler* (1887). Despite such suspicions and repudiations, Strindberg read *Brand* (1866) as a young man and immediately wrote *The Freethinker* (1869), which shows evident signs of Ibsen's influence, while Ibsen's *Peer Gynt* (1867) has often been recognized as the 'direct ancestor' of Strindberg's *A Dream Play* (1901).[13] Ibsen may in his turn have been aided by Strindberg to recover in his four last plays something of the poetic style and magic of his earlier works, such as *Peer*

Gynt. Professor Bradbrook finds 'a flavour of Strindberg' in all these later works,[14] and it is worth noting that when Ibsen was writing them he had acquired a portrait of Strindberg, which he installed in his study, finding 'in the diabolical expression of the eyes', and in the contemplation of the'delightfully mad' face an aid to his own compositions. Strindberg was reciprocally fascinated by a portrait of Ibsen, 'the fanatical sceptic . . . so impressive and terrifying, so repellent, so attractive!' which had been painted in the summer of 1877 by Julius Kronborg.[15]

Since as a critic, propagandist and polemicist, Shaw wrote on all three of the other authors, he is perhaps the best guide to the relationship of the Victorian novelist to Ibsen, Strindberg and himself. For his own part, he wrote in 1934, only the 'stupendous illiteracy of modern criticism', could account for his debt to Dickens being overlooked,[16] and he blithely admitted that a concordance of his writings would reveal 'the Dickens allusions as running four to one against any other writer'.[17] In his own plays Shaw continually exploited 'Dickens's demonstration' that it was possible 'to combine a mirrorlike exactness of character drawing with the wildest extravagances of humorous expression and grotesque situation'. Shaw praised the very quality Dickens had called 'fantastic fidelity', describing it as his ability to draw 'a character more accurately than any of the novelists of the nineteenth century', without ceasing to be 'outrageous in his unrestrained fantasy and fertility of imagination'. Shaw cheerfully appropriated characters in Dickens's novels and transferred them with 'complete success' to his plays.[18] Critics have detected many of these borrowings, the Dickensian forms of Sydney Carton, Jaggers and Rouncewell seeming to reappear in the Shavian ectypes of Dick Dudgeon, Bohun, Conolly and Sartorius among other parallels far too numerous to name.

In addition to character-drawing, Dickens's unerring 'instinct for detecting the social canker' served to corroborate many of Shaw's own political and social opinions. Time and again in such works as *Everybody's Political What's What, Ruskin's Politics*, and in his prefaces to Dickens's novels, he approvingly cites the Circumlocution Office of *Little Dorrit*, the forcing academy of Dr Blimber in *Dombey and Son*, and the 'Coodle' Government of *Bleak House*, as authentic evidence of the administrative muddle and political nepotism that characterized Victorian society. These glaring defects remained live issues for Shaw, and his references to Dickens are, in his own words, a kind of literary and political system of 'shorthand', pointing to abuses which had first gained notoriety through Dickens's exposure of them.

A 'supersaturated Dickensite' as he described himself, Shaw shared with Dickens an intense affinity for the stage. The memory of how Dickens's genius was lost to the Victorian theatre probably led him to try to tempt his own contemporaries, Kipling, Wells and Conrad, to leave 'their positions of safety' as novelists and 'struggle with new difficulties and a new technique . . . for the sake of redeeming the British drama from banality.'[19] Certainly it was often as a dramatic author that Shaw responded to Dickens. He saw in him a useful ally in attacking the brittle professionalism of contemporary stage directing. How many readers would Dickens have deserved, Shaw inquired, had he written the powerful murder scene in *Oliver Twist* as follows: 'SYKES [*sic*] lights pipe – calls dog – loads pistol with newspaper, takes bludgeon from R. above fireplace strikes NANCY. NANCY. "Oh Lord, Bill." (Dies: SYKES wipes brow – shudders – takes hat from chair B.P. – sees ghost, not visible to audience – and exit L.U.E.)'[20]

As a critic Shaw analysed Dickens; as a playwright he revised him. Observing him as he rewrote Dickens to Shavian standards, we can perhaps catch a glimpse of the unfulfilled novelist in Shaw reaching out to contact what he felt was the potential dramatist in Dickens. *Great Expectations* is a prime instance of this process. Shaw was fascinated by the novel, which he had first read as a boy, and for many years he had thought about reshaping its ending. In his extended critical commentary on the book, it was to the ending that he principally turned his attention. He objected to the revised and so-called 'happy' ending suggested by Bulwer-Lytton as a manufactured consolation, and vowed that if he ever edited this 'most perfect of Dickens's works' he would restore the original conclusion.[21] But when he got his chance in 1937 with the Limited Editions Club edition, he found the ending was not quite as he remembered it. It was plausible, but somehow did not belong to the tale. Dickens's revised ending, on the other hand, while 'psychologically wrong', was artistically 'more congruous than the original'. The best ending, Shaw decided, would be one of his own making. He would retain the atmosphere of the Dickens/Bulwer-Lytton ending but remove from it the stock 'happy ending' which Romance keeps 'to misfit all stories'. Of course, he could not tamper with Dickens's novel. However, not content with a merely analytical response to *Great Expectations*, Shaw did attempt a creative revision of the ending in *Pygmalion*. In the epilogue, Shaw was able at last to correct creatively Dickens's 'happy ending' by refusing to allow Eliza to marry Higgins. He would not yield to the unbearably romantic assumption that because Eliza had become 'the heroine of a romance . . . she must have married the hero of it'.[22] This 'adjusted' conclusion to his own play coincides with the view he had arrived at in thinking about the endings to *Great Expectations*. Given Shaw's imaginative reconstruction of other elements in *Great Expectations*, there are strong incentives for thinking that Shaw saw the novel much as he had seen *Cymbeline* or *Antony and Cleopatra*, as unfinished business, or perhaps to extend the image, he saw himself as a kind of literary Pygmalion bringing to Dickens's novel the gift of renewed life. There are many parallels between the novel and the play, including the Pygmalion-Galatea myth, which is prominent in both works, though obviously more deliberate and conscious in Shaw's treatment. Pip's Pygmalion is Magwitch, who converts him into a 'gentleman' as Higgins changes Eliza into a 'duchess'. Both works range over the themes of snobbery, unearned wealth, class, the constricting nature of social convention, and the relationship between speech and social status.[23]

One of the odd features of Shaw's critical evaluation of Dickens is the persistent presence in it of Ibsen. The principal reason for this intervention is that Shaw saw Ibsen as a corrective to Dickens. Whenever he talks of Ibsen, Dickens is in the wings waiting – not to come on, but to see himself as he might have been, once divested of his sentimentality and provided with a new intellectual strength. If one returns to Dickens, Shaw wrote, 'now that Ibsen has opened our eyes we will have to admit that . . . between Dick Swiveller and Ulrick Brendel, there is a mighty difference'. After reading Ibsen, it was impossible to view Dickens in the old way. One could not 'go back from the death of Hedwig Ekdal to the death of Little Nell otherwise than as a grown man goes down on all fours and pretends to be a bear for the amusement of his children', a judgement which clearly anticipates Orwell's comment, 'No grown-up person can read Dickens without feeling his limitations'.[24] To read Dickens, as Shaw does, in the bleak, unremitting light of Ibsen, is to realize his glaring narrowness, especially in thought and in the range of his interests, while at the same time it sponsors a preference for the later novels. Though using a new Ibsenite perspective, Shaw was in part raising the old but not exhausted cry of Dickens's philistinism. 'The appalling thing about Dickens', he wrote in 1909, 'is that in his novels there is nothing personal to live for except eating, drinking, and pretending to be happily married. For him the great synthetic ideals do not exist, any more than the great preludes and toccatas of Bach, the paintings of Giotto and Mantegna, Velasquez and Rembrandt.'[25] Shaw says about Dickens himself what Orwell said about Dickens's characters: they have 'no mental life. . . . They never learn, never speculate.'[26] This 'intellectual innocence' on Dickens's part is accompanied by a shortage of political ideas, though no lack of good political instincts. It was hard, Shaw decided, 'to say what

Dickens believed or did not believe metaphysically or metapolitically',
though his opinions of the Lords, the Commons and the Civil Service
were clear enough, and for Shaw damagingly accurate. Though Dickens's
political outlook matured and his novels improved, Shaw regrets that he
'never had time to form a philosophy or define a faith'.[27] Marxism came
too late for him, yet he was an unconscious 'revolutionist'. He 'ought' to
have been a Comtist, but was not. In the end, Shaw had to settle for
Dickens as 'a sort of unphilosophic Radical', who anticipates Orwell's old-
fashioned, not overly intelligent radical, prized for his 'generous anger at
injustice'.[28]

Shaw's objection to Dickens's lack of ideas in no way implies a
condemnation of Dickens's art, any more than the right 'to criticize
Shakespeare involves the power of writing better plays'. It is 'the
philosophy, the outlook on life, that changes', with time and cultural
evolution, 'not the craft of the playwright' or the novelist.[29] With the
advance of time the 'parable of the doll's house' becomes more apt than
'the parable of the prodigal son'.[30] The philosophical power and 'frozen
truth' delivered by Ibsen's plays are the yardstick by which Shaw
measures serious ideas and in comparison with which he consigns so
many Victorian conventions to the purgatory of irrelevance. He
compares, for example, Dickens's depiction of Chuffy in *Martin
Chuzzlewit* with Foldal in *John Gabriel Borkman* (1896), inevitably to
Dickens's disadvantage: 'You may wince at every step in Ibsen's process,
and snivel with . . . satisfaction at every step in Dickens's; but the upshot
is that you are left with a serious belief in and regard for Foldal, whereas
Chuffy is nothing but a silly and rather tiresome toy.' Still, as Shaw
concedes, Dickens learned, and when he became in his later novels a
'serious master of his art, his progress was on the road that leads away
from Chuffy and towards Foldal: that is, from sentimental, cowardly,
sweet-toothed lying to sympathetic, courageous, nutritious truth'.[31] Since
for Shaw, all art aspires to the condition of Ibsen, it comes as no surprise to
discover Shaw finding the same progress within his own early novel *The
Irrational Knot*, the final chapter of which was remote from the influence of
Dickens and 'so close to Ibsen'.[32] For all his sparkle and clarity, one sees
that Shaw distorted both Dickens and Ibsen as he took them into his eager
Spartan embrace and squeezed them out of shape. If he 'butchered' Ibsen
to 'make a Fabian holiday',[33] he rearranged Dickens to make him a Fabian
prophet. To do so, he had first to tug critical judgement into a new
appreciation of the more sombre splendours of Dickens's late fiction.

Perhaps Shaw's greatest critical achievement regarding Dickens was to have drawn the line between Dickens early and late, and to associate that boundary with a change in the intellectual environment of nineteenth-century Europe. There is for Shaw an enormous 'change from nineteenth-century self-satisfaction to twentieth-century self-criticism'.[34] One way to measure that change, he suggested in *The Quintessence of Ibsenism*, and later in *The Intelligent Woman's Guide*, was to read *The Pickwick Papers* (jolly early Dickens) and then to read *Our Mutual Friend* (disillusioned mature Dickens), which is to say that the change in the general intellectual climate occurs equally within the boundaries of Dickens's novels. The 'Dickens of the second half of the nineteenth century (the Ibsen half) is a different man from the Dickens of the first half.' One can laugh, cry and go happily to bed after reading the novels from *The Pickwick Papers* to *Bleak House* but from *Hard Times* to *Our Mutual Friend* 'every one of Dickens's books lays a heavy burden on our conscience without flattering us with any hopes of a happy ending'.[35] If the earlier novels seem by comparison childish amusements, there are 'noble compensations', for abandoning them. After 'Hedwig you may not be able to cry over Little Nell', but the 'increase in strength and intensity is enormous: the power that indicts a nation so terribly is much more impressive than that which ridicules individuals.' For Shaw the main consequence of Dickens's maturity is that 'occasional indignation has spread and deepened into a passionate revolt against the whole industrial order of the modern world'.[36] At this point in Shaw's Dickensian Quintessence, Dickens can safely take his place among the philosopher-rebels of the nineteenth century and declare with them that it is 'not merely Tom All Alone's that must be demolished . . . but our entire social system'. This clearly is not early Dickens, but a Dickens like 'Karl Marx, Carlyle, Ruskin, Morris . . . rising up against civilization itself . . . and declaring that it is not our disorder but our order that is horrible'.[37]

Even this radical Dickens, however, fell short of the Shavian ideal represented by Ibsen and Strindberg. In 1913 Shaw asked himself why 'the works of Ibsen, of Strindberg' and others were 'so different from those of the great fictionists of the first half of the nineteenth century' since 'neither human nature nor the specific talent of the playwright has changed since the days of Charles Dickens.' Ibsen, after all, 'was not Dickens's superior as an observer, nor is Strindberg'. Yet,

a generation which could read all . . . Dickens . . . from end to end without the smallest intellectual or ethical perturbation, was unable to get through a play by Ibsen . . . without having its intellectual and moral complacency upset, its religious faith shattered, and its notions of right and wrong conduct thrown into confusion and sometimes even reversed.[38]

It was, concluded Shaw, as if 'these modern men had a spiritual force that was lacking in even the greatest of their forerunners', and yet there was no evidence in the lives of Wagner, Ibsen or Strindberg that they were better men in any sense than Shakespeare or Dickens.

Shaw found an explanation for this peculiarity in 'a general law of the evolution of ideas', namely that 'all very serious revolutionary propositions begin as huge jokes'. He illustrated the principle by an anecdote of the two travellers who were asked by Spanish shepherds what their religion was. 'Our religion', replied one, 'is that there is no God.' This reckless remark, says Shaw,

> taken seriously, might have provided nineteenth century scepticis[']
> with a martyr. As it was, the countryside rang with laughter for day
> afterwards as the stupendous joke was handed round. But it was just by
> tolerating the blasphemy as a joke that the shepherds began to build it
> into the fabric of their minds. Being now safely lodged there, it will in
> due time develop its earnestness.[39]

This perceived movement in history, in which truth presents itself first as farce and then in full earnest, makes the difference between Dickens and Strindberg intelligible to Shaw, just as it sharpened his distinction between Dickens and Ibsen: 'Strindberg simply refuses to regard the cases of Mrs Raddle and Mrs MacStinger and Mrs Joe Gargery as laughing matters. He insists on taking them seriously as cases of a tyranny which effects more degradation and causes more misery than all the political and sectarian oppressions known to history.' At the same time Shaw noticed the seeming paradox that Strindberg 'even at his fiercest' was not 'harder on women than Dickens':

> No doubt his case against them is far more complete, because he does
> not shirk the specifically sexual factors in it. But this really softens it. If
> Dickens had allowed us, were it but for an instant, to see Joe Gargery
> and Mrs Joe as husband and wife, he would perhaps have been accused
> by fools of immodesty; but we should have at least some more human
> impression than the one left by an unredeemed shrew married to a
> grown-up terrified child.[40]

Ironically, of course, as Shaw recognized, it was the 'general impression that Strindberg's women' were 'the revenge of a furious woman-hater for his domestic failures', while Dickens was 'a genial idealist'. Such a false impression is produced in Shaw's account, solely by Dickens's humour and his belief that women

> must be admitted to the fellowship of the Holy Ghost on a feminine instead of a human basis; whilst Strindberg takes womanliness with deadly seriousness. . . . The nurse in . . . [*The Father*] who wheedles her old nursling and then slips a strait waistcoat on him revolts us; but she is really ten times more lovable and sympathetic than Sairey Gamp, an abominable creature whose very soul is putrid, and who is yet true to life.[41]

The more modern spirit may be unaccommodating, but for Shaw, its truthfulness is a form of compassion. It is, therefore, an understandable irony that 'none of the modern writers who take life as seriously as Ibsen have ever been able to bring themselves to depict depraved people so pitilessly as Dickens'. Ibsen, Shaw claimed,

> was grim enough. . . . no man has said more terrible things both privately and publicly; and yet there is not one of Ibsen's characters who is not, in the old phrase, the temple of the Holy Ghost, and who does not move you at moments by the sense of that mystery. The Dickens-Thackeray spirit is, in comparison, that of a Punch and Judy showman, who is never restrained from whacking his little figures unmercifully. . . . To Ibsen, from beginning to end, every human being is a sacrifice, whilst to Dickens he is a farce. . . . No character drawn by Dickens is more ridiculous than Hjalmar Ekdal in *The Wild Duck*, or more eccentric than old Ekdal, whose toy game-preserve in the garret is more fantastic than the house of Miss Havisham; and yet these Ekdals wring the heart whilst Micawber and Chivery . . . only shake the sides.[42]

In a lecture given in March 1928 to mark the centenary of Ibsen's birth, Shaw said that Ibsen 'told stories that changed the mind of the world'.[43] Again he invoked Dickens's name by way of contrast: 'One read Dickens and Scott with great delight, but they did not change one's mind. When one had done with them, one's religion, social views, and prejudices remained the same as before. But when Ibsen came he knocked all that into a cocked hat.' In destroying 'respectability' Ibsen stripped the 'moral whitewash' from the genteel suburban hearth. In this, he was 'almost alone among the storytellers of the nineteenth century; the only other man who did the same thing was Karl Marx.'[44]

To leave Shaw's critical juggling with Dickens and Ibsen for a still wider example of group interaction, we must focus on *A Doll's House* (1879). In this case the interaction includes direct borrowing in several directions – Ibsen from Dickens and possibly Shaw; Shaw from Ibsen and possibly Dickens; qualified critical approval by Shaw; critical rejection by Strindberg; an influential commentary by Shaw which shaped public conceptions of Ibsen's play, and a creative rejection or revision by Strindberg in the form of a separate play.

Dickens may have provided Ibsen with the original germ of the idea for *A Doll's House* with Bella Rokesmith's comment in *Our Mutual Friend*, 'I want to be something so much worthier than the doll in the doll's house.' G. M. Young remarks that in 'the profusion of Dickens, the phrase might pass unnoticed', but 'Ibsen remembered it' and fifteen years later made it the watchword of a revolution.[45] Shaw himself claimed to have anticipated the doll metaphor in his early novel *The Irrational Knot* (1880).[46] Looking back in 1905, Shaw felt his novel should be considered 'as an early attempt on the part of the Life Force to write *A Doll's House* in English by the instrumentality of a very immature writer aged 24'. In 1891 he went on to popularize Ibsen's play so well that it still suffers the misfortune of being remembered for the wrong reasons, as a play primarily about women's rights, by people who tend to consult Shaw rather than Ibsen as to its meaning.[47]

In *The Quintessence of Ibsenism* (1891), Shaw entitled one chapter 'The Womanly Woman'. In it he makes a furious assault on the genteel 'ideal of womanliness' as a Victorian abomination hardly worse than the Indian practise of suttee. Nora Helmer, of course, is the play's representative of the 'womanly woman' living 'the happy family life of the idealist's dream', until she is brought to see her family life as a fiction, and her home as a 'mere doll's house in which they have been playing at ideal husband and father, wife and mother'.[48] In his chapter on women in the essay collection *The Swedish People* (1882), Strindberg wrote that it was 'the despotic and debauched eighteenth century that had transformed woman into – a doll'. By estranging her from reality, man estranged her from himself. This situation had deteriorated to the point where men avoided marriage 'for fear of the doll tyranny that awaited them'.[49] At this stage Strindberg concurred with Ibsen in believing men responsible for treating women as dolls, a position he was later furiously to repudiate. Indeed, when Shaw wrote his 1913 preface to the *Quintessence*, he noted that 'the terrible play with which Strindberg wreaked the revenge of the male for *A Doll's House*' had 'just been performed for the first time in London under the title of *Creditors*'.[50] Neither Shaw's anticipation of the doll metaphor nor his interpretation of *A Doll's House* prevented him from borrowing from the play in *Candida*, which by his own admission was to demonstrate that in modern society it was the husband rather than the wife who was treated as a doll.

Like Shaw, Strindberg first hailed Ibsen's play for its beneficial social effects. In dealing a death-blow to Victorian morality, the play would have done enough work in the world, for, said Shaw, 'the highest genius . . . is always intensely utilitarian'.[51] Such approval, however, did not stop Shaw from later seeing the play's technical limitations or viewing it as 'prentice work'. By 1892 he had lost interest in it as a 'stale' play, and in 1903 he was advising the actress Janet Achurch to concentrate on *Little Eyolf* (1894) and *Rosmersholm* (1886) instead. Strindberg, despite qualms about its depiction of relationships and fears that *A Doll's House* would encourage just the kind of woman he most dreaded, reluctantly conceded the play had to be thanked for revealing that marriage could be a nightmare. After it, he wrote, people stopped regarding marriage 'as an automatic provider of absolute bliss, and divorce between incompatible parties came at last to be accepted as conceivably justifiable'.[52]

Shaw's enthusiasm for Ibsen and his frequent yoking together of Ibsen and Dickens may have deflected attention from an important and largely ignored connection between Strindberg and Dickens. Strindberg was early apprenticed to Dickens. He frankly acknowledged Dickens as an inspiration for his first novel *The Red Room*, in which he attacked a state of society with which he could never come to terms. Though this early venture lacks the concentrated power of Dickensian satire at its best, Strindberg's 'Salary Commission for Civil Servants' owes a great deal to Dickens's Circumlocution Office in *Little Dorrit*, a comparison noted by Strindberg's contemporaries. Strindberg once had a notion of forming a Swedish Pickwick Club. He cited Pickwick in his major satire *The New Kingdom* (1882), and one of his sketches is subtitled 'The Dickens Novel'. However, he seems to have shared Shaw's preference for the later novels and listed *Little Dorrit* as one of his favourite books. Strindberg never lost his taste for the Victorian novelist. In 1897, at the age of forty-eight, he rated Dickens as the highest of all English authors, and during the crisis before his final period, the rereading of Dickens restored his serenity and his creative energy.

Even though Strindberg was primarily interested in what he could gain as a playwright from Dickens, he did leave a number of marginal notes which provide a brief critical commentary. In his preface to *Miss Julie* (1888), he condemned Dickens's characters because they derived their individuality not through dramatic utterance but through some external characteristic. An individual who had become

> fixed in his natural disposition, or had adapted himself to some definite role in life – who, in fact, had ceased to grow – was called a 'character'. On the stage such a figure signified someone 'fixed and finished'. Nothing was required for his characterisation but some bodily defect – a club-foot, a wooden leg, a red nose; or the character in question was made to repeat some such phrase as 'That's capital', 'Barkis is willin'' or the like.[53]

It was to avoid falling into the same Dickensian trap that Strindberg deliberately made the figures in *Miss Julie* 'rather colourless'.

On the other hand, Strindberg responded to the special relationship of literary to literal truth which Dickens himself had characterized as 'fantastic fidelity'.[54] What Strindberg appreciated was the way 'Dickens blew life into inanimate objects and made them play a role, harmonizing the setting with the character and the situation'. There is, says Lamm, no 'aspect of Dickens's technique that Strindberg assimilated more completely than this ability to . . . give inanimate objects a fantastic fairytale lustre'.[55] Sometimes these dissociated objects acquire mystical lives of their own, becoming portents and symbols or metaphors for the condition of life.

This surrealistic discovery represents a major extension of Dickensian liveliness into the theatre. One can detect traces of it in the character fragmentations of *Til Damaskas* (1898), which share something of Dickens's depiction of Miss Havisham's inner life through the image of the decaying wedding-cake, the stopped clock, the teeth of the gnawing mice behind the skirting-boards, and the room which embodies the arrested development of her psyche. In the Dickens universe 'objects actually usurp human essences; beginning as fetishes, they tend to – and sometimes quite literally do – devour . . . the powers of the fetish-worshiper',[56] like Strindberg's vampirish cook in the *Ghost Sonata* (1907), who drains the nourishment out of those she serves with food. Strindberg was constantly aware of Dickens's perception of the 'thinged' life of objects and, on the obverse side of this reciprocating metaphor, the dehumanizing of people.

Strindberg knew his own writing, like that of Dickens, magnified and distorted the reality that was its starting-point. Only a visionary could render reality in this way. After reading *David Copperfield*, he wrote of Dickens: 'Using only small, crooked black type, he evokes the same illusion the theatre does with its huge apparatus. Or to be more precise, reading him provides one with hallucinations of actual events.'[57] Both Shaw and Strindberg tried to come to terms with this element in Dickens, that is, an intense sense of reality made even more intense in the transforming fires of surrealism. In his *Open Letters to the Intimate Theatre*, Strindberg told the actors,

> I think Dickens would be a good teacher, because his depiction of human beings is more thorough than the dramatist has time for and because he motivates action endlessly. But he has something else the actor can use: he supplements every character's actions with a wealth of gestures and play of expressions that are incomparably fine. I have recently re-read *David Copperfield*, and my admiration for the teacher of my youth goes beyond words. With only a few sparse words he calls forth the same illusion one gets at the theater with its large apparatus; more correctly stated, he gives me the illusion of actual experiences.[58]

From the very beginning Dickens's art was understood to be theatrical in character; he was perceived, sometimes approvingly, at others slightingly, to be a writer who spoke 'in a circle of stage fire'.[59] 'Charley,' said Thomas Carlyle, after witnessing one of Dickens's dramatic readings, 'you carry a whole company under your own hat.'[60] If the members of that troupe could not find work in the Victorian theatre, in various disguises they crept onto the modern stage under the new management of Ibsen, Strindberg and Shaw.

Notes

1. *Prefaces by George Bernard Shaw* (London: Constable, 1934) p. 196. A correspondent in the *Yorkshire Weekly Post*, 25 Jan. 1908, suggested that if Dickens, like Ibsen, had started as a stage-manager, we should have had important Dickensian plays.
2. *Prefaces*, p. 748.
3. G. B. Shaw, *Pen Portraits and Reviews* (New York: Wm. H. Wise, 1932) p. 275. For other suggestions, see J. B. van Amerongen, *The Actor in Dickens* (New York: D. Appleton, 1927) pp. 150–51.

4. George H. Ford, *Dickens and His Readers* (New York: W. W. Norton, 1965) p. 236.
5. John Gross and Gabriel Pearson (eds), *Dickens and the Twentieth Century* (University of Toronto Press, 1962) p. xviii.
6. Blanche Patch, *Thirty Years with G.B.S.* (London: Victor Gollancz, 1951) p. 157; and *Prefaces*, p. 162.
7. Gross and Pearson (eds), *Dickens and the Twentieth Century*, p. xv.
8. Hesketh Pearson, *Bernard Shaw* (London: Collins, 1950) p. 35.
9. *The Bookman*, vol. 89 (1934) p. 209.
10. Michael Meyer, *Ibsen: A Biography* (New York: Doubleday, 1971) p. 457. For the view that *The Quintessence of Ibsenism* is more about Shaw than Ibsen, see also Ronald Gray, *Ibsen — A Dissenting View* (Cambridge University Press, 1977) p. 205, and Michael Egan (ed.), *Ibsen: The Critical Heritage* (London: Routledge & Kegan Paul, 1972) p. 21.
11. Ezra Pound, *Make It New* (London: Faber & Faber, 1934) p. 4.
12. Evert Sprinchorn (ed.), *Ibsen: Letters and Speeches* (New York: Hill & Wang, 1964) p. 269.
13. Meyer, *Henrik Ibsen: The Farewell to Poetry 1864–1882* (London: Rupert Hart-Davis, 1971) p. 74.
14. M. C. Bradbrook, *Ibsen the Norwegian* (London: Chatto & Windus, 1946) p. 147.
15. Meyer, *Ibsen: A Biography*, p. 775, and *Henrik Ibsen: The Farewell to Poetry 1864–1882*, p. 237.
16. *The Bookman*, vol. 89, p. 209.
17. J. Hennessey and B. Kaufman (eds), *The Letters of Alexander Woollcott* (Toronto: Macmillan, 1944) p. 89; and Patch, *Thirty Years with G.B.S.*, p. 157.
18. *The Bookman*, vol. 89, p. 209.
19. *Shaw: Autobiography 1856–1898*, selected from his writings by Stanley Weintraub (New York: Weybright & Talley, 1969) vol. 2, p. 34.
20. A. Henderson, *George Bernard Shaw: His Life and Works* (Cincinnati: Stewart & Kidd, 1911) p. 416.
21. Stanley Weintraub (ed.), *Bernard Shaw's Non-Dramatic Literary Criticism* (Lincoln: University of Nebraska Press, 1972) p. 63.
22. G. B. Shaw, *Pygmalion* (Harmondsworth: Penguin, 1976) p. 140.
23. See M. K. Goldberg, 'Shaw's *Pygmalion*: The Reworking of *Great Expectations*', *Shaw Review*, vol. 22 (1979) pp. 114–22.
24. G. B. Shaw, *The Quintessence of Ibsenism* (London: Constable, 1891; 1932) pp. 132 and 134; George Orwell, 'Charles Dickens' (1940), rpt. in George Ford and Lauriat Lane (eds), *The Dickens Critics* (Ithaca: Cornell University Press, 1961) p. 169.
25. G. B. Shaw, *The Nation* (1909); rpt. in *Pen Portraits and Reviews*, p. 233.
26. George Orwell, 'Charles Dickens'; rpt. in Ford and Lane (eds), *The Dickens Critics*, p. 167.
27. G. B. Shaw, Introduction to *Great Expectations*; rpt. *Bernard Shaw's Nondramatic Literary Criticism*, pp. 57 and 65.
28. *Ibid.*, p. 57, and in Gross and Pearson (eds), *Dickens and the Twentieth Century*, p. x.
29. *Prefaces*, p. 718.
30. *The Quintessence of Ibsenism*, p. 148.

31. G. B. Shaw in *The Academy* (1897); rpt. in *Pen Portraits and Reviews*, p. 153.
32. *Prefaces*, p. 657.
33. Huntly Carter, *The New Spirit in Drama and Art* (London: F. Palmer, 1912) pp. 36–37.
34. G. B. Shaw, *The Intelligent Woman's Guide to Socialism and Capitalism* (London: Constable, 1928) p. 469.
35. *The Quintessence of Ibsenism*, p. 133.
36. Weintraub (ed.), *Bernard Shaw's Nondramatic Literary Criticism*, p. 43.
37. *Ibid.*, p. 42.
38. *The Quintessence of Ibsenism*, pp. 126 and 129.
39. *Ibid.*, pp. 126–27.
40. *Ibid.*, pp. 129–30.
41. *Ibid.*, p. 131.
42. *Ibid.*
43. Shaw's lecture in London, 19 Mar. 1928; reported in the *Manchester Guardian*, 20 Mar. 1928.
44. From Shaw's lecture of 19 Mar. 1928. This account is taken from J. L. Wisenthal, *Shaw and Ibsen* (University of Toronto Press, 1979) p. 254.
45. G. M. Young, *Victorian England: Portrait of an Age* (New York: Oxford University Press, 1964) p. 91.
46. See Stanley Weintraub, 'Ibsen's "Doll's House" Metaphor Foreshadowed in Victorian Fiction', *Nineteenth-Century Fiction*, vol. 13 (1958) p. 68.
47. See Meyer, *Henrik Ibsen: The Farewell to Poetry 1864–1882*, p. 266; and Brian Downs, *A Study of Six Plays by Ibsen* (New York: Octagon Books, 1972) pp. 138–41.
48. *The Quintessence of Ibsenism*, p. 66.
49. Martin Lamm, *August Strindberg* (New York: Benjamin Blom, 1971) p. 100.
50. *The Quintessence of Ibsenism*, p. 8.
51. E. J. West (ed.), *Shaw on Theatre* (New York: Hill & Wang, 1958) p. 63.
52. Meyer, *Ibsen: A Biography*, pp. 454–55.
53. Cited by Raymond Williams in *Drama from Ibsen to Eliot* (London: Chatto & Windus, 1952) p. 105.
54. John Forster, *Life of Dickens* (London: J. M. Dent, 1927) vol. 2, p. 278.
55. Lamm, *August Strindberg*, p. 73.
56. Dorothy Van Ghent, *The English Novel: Form and Function* (New York: Harper & Row, 1961) pp. 130–31.
57. *Samlade Skrifter*, John Landquist (ed.) (Stockholm: A. Bonnier, 1912–19) vol. 50, pp. 130–31.
58. *Open Letters to the Intimate Theater*, Walter Johnson (trs.) (Seattle: University of Washington Press, [n.d.]) p. 134.
59. John Ruskin, *Unto this Last*, in *Works*, T. C. Cook and Alexander Wedderburn (eds) (London: G. Allen; New York: Longmans Green, 1862) p. 37, 31*n*.
60. Amy Woolner, *Thomas Woolner R. A.* (New York: Dutton, 1917) pp. 232–33.

15

Postscript: Theatricality and Dickens's End Strategies[1]

Mary Margaret Magee

Several of the essays in this collection focus on the figure of the orchestrator, impresario, or stage manager as variously enacted by Dickens himself or by his characters. Nina Auerbach extends a theatrical metaphor to encompass all of Dickens's 'one-man performances' in his novels, an achievement that allowed the novelist finally to become 'a theatre in himself'. Coral Lansbury and James R. Kincaid attribute the same kind of authority to Pecksniff in *Martin Chuzzlewit*. As 'lord of language and master of persuasion', Lansbury's Pecksniff remains the archetypal clown, protean, duplicitous, unreadable. Kincaid pushes this combination to include explicit speculation about the nature of the self and adds to it figures like Micawber from *David Copperfield* who write 'anti-plots'. Characters in this category defy linearity and theories about the discrete self and assume identity only because it can be determined by improvisation. Kincaid argues ultimately that such characters exist in a necessary and subversive territory that undermines the high earnestness and deliberation of the lead characters' plot lines. Dickens's achievement with the Micawbers and Pecksniffs is a revel in timelessness, a delight in the immediacy of performance uninterrupted by considerations of what comes next.

In this context, Jean Ferguson Carr's essay is a sensitive discussion of the uses of metaphors of theatricality for self-presentation, simply, or more interestingly, for self-delusion. Reading *David Copperfield*, the novel which seemed to many of this volume's contributors a particularly apt text for explorations of theatricality, Carr discovers that the theatre functions as a privileged metaphor for the recovery of the past. David's stage-managing role 'creates an impression of willing observance of past scenes and avoids the narrative responsibility to comment on those scenes'. The strategy is thus, according to Carr, both self-effacing and self-aggrandizing because of the power the narrator arrogates to tell his story.

My interest too is in the power implicit in the narrator's directorial role in relation to his subject – even when that subject is himself. And along with many other readers, I find that *David Copperfield* presents itself as an exemplary text. While explicit references to the drama are rare, there is no question that the structure and very nature of David's autobiographical narration is richly susceptible to theatrical interpretation. In order to bring this collection of essays on the Dickens theatre to an end, my contribution is a reading of the concluding chapter of *David Copperfield* (with forays back to the beginning of that novel and into *Great Expectations*) and its resolution of the novel's most prominent theatrical image, the tableau vivant. All of the terms I use, including the language of the theatre and of identity formation, and the sites in which I apply them (beginnings and endings), are designed to highlight David the narrator's inclination to dissociation, in both his narrative strategies and in his self-conception.

In his chapter 'Endings' in *Excess and Restraint in the Novels of Charles Dickens*, John Kucich defines the 'crucial' ending as that which 'features action that breaks out of a limit' – 'crucial endings always satisfy a deep desire to escape the pressure of our fundamental imprisonment in human life and to expend vital energy freely, without constraint.' Although the crucial ending is consituted by expenditure, or total release of energy, the expenditure is at the same time modified by the human need for 'some relation to necessary or inevitable order'.[2] This formulation appears to account perfectly for the quality of the ending of *David Copperfield*: the conservationist impulse is satisfied in the stasis of the last moments while release is achieved in the marriage to Agnes, a reunion for which David has yearned throughout his life. What is left unsaid here is the investment David himself has in concluding his autobiography in this way, a critical problem, surely, in a first-person narrative. I discover a partial solution of the problem in the title of the last chapter, 'A Last Retrospect', which, in turn, recalls the other three retrospect chapters. What follows is an examination of the heuristic available in that group of chapters.

The purpose of the retrospect chapters is to summarize and accelerate the passage of time. David steps out of the story, objectifies the sequences he narrates (in fact, objectifies himself in them), and recalls the past by conjuring or staging salient images or moments. Immediacy is suggested in his use of the present tense; the past is now because David can make the characters act again as if they were present. The narrator's perspective is removed, elevated.

In the first retrospect chapter (18) David recovers his school-days: 'Let me think, as I look back upon that flowing water, now a dry channel overgrown with leaves, whether there are any marks along its course, by which I can remember how it ran.' One way to accommodate this piece of dry river is to perceive it as a frozen moment, a bit of the past lifted out of time and made to live again. But the way in which the conventional metaphor is arrested is disturbing – the buried life is denied. Rather than perceive his self-development as continuous (which it is his concern to demonstrate elsewhere), in this instance David blocks the line and strangely dissociates his adult self from his youthful self. As a metaphor for narrative, the passage is also alarming since it implies that narration, like memory, can be shut off – it is a way of saying that the first part of the story does not exist; it has run dry. Moreover, the 'marks' or signs (or writing) that he recovers of his youth are a series of present tense tableaux, each designed to evoke his youth. These, too, in their emblematic stasis, are dead, in the same way as David would like to believe that part of his past is. Once called up, they are consigned to their fate as leaves in the blocked channel, pages which are merely memorial. The disingenuity of the metaphor is plain whenever David's youth surfaces unpleasantly in his present, both in the form of characters (for example, Jane Murdstone turns up as Dora Spenlow's 'confidential friend') and in the form of memories which will not die. It is clearly the task of the reader to fill the gap between David's desire to manage time and what his metaphors actually perform.[3]

In chapter 43, the second retrospect, the linear figure, as a metaphor of succession, is restored: 'Let me stand aside, to see the phantoms of those days go by me, accompanying the shadow of myself, in dim procession.' The terms of the act of memory are the same, but this time the dream quality is intensified, appropriately, since the subject is the fairy-tale marriage of David and Dora. The anomaly of this period is reinforced in the closing words of the chapter: 'I have stood aside to see the phantoms of those days go by me. They are gone, and I resume the journey of my story.' While the story-as-journey motif informs these passages, they are just as much determined by David's desire to contain, to limit – in fact, to objectify.

The penultimate retrospect chapter (53) reverts also to the linear metaphor: 'there is a figure in the moving crowd before my memory'. This chapter describes Dora's death in the same dreamy mode that David used to describe his marriage to her. The tone of this chapter prepares the reader for the effects of chapter 64, 'A Last Retrospect', which is structured around repetitions of the injunction 'I see'.[4] Once again, David resorts to the traditional metaphor – 'I see myself, with Agnes at my side, journeying along the road of life' – and then asks, 'What faces are the most distinct to me in the fleeting crowd? Lo, these; all turning to me as I ask my thoughts the question!'

These quotations clarify the nature of David's relationship to his material; his thoughts or memory of his friends bring them to life. If not explictly, the implicit scenario here is of a director with a spotlight, choosing which figure or group to light, and by his choice animating the group with life itself. The tableau vivant, or living canvas, is the most useful designation of the procedure because of the effect it gives of timelessness. David recovers his past by staging it in discontinuous scenes, by lighting or by shading it as he chooses. Before I come to the disturbing aspects of this objectification, it is only fair to observe that the *form* of the final retrospect chapter constitutes a very appropriate end strategy. What options does a first-person narrator have at the end of his text? Since David's purposes have been teleological throughout, the goal of his history the marriage with Agnes, once that is achieved there is nothing more to tell. The stasis at the end is a secular version of mystical union, Agnes herself the iconic Beloved whose attribute, the hand pointing upward, has presaged this resolution all along. From this point of view, David has succeeded in doing the impossible: depicting his own death, certainly the equivalent to the transcendence of the novel's end.[5] Moreover, a curious detail in the last chapter confirms this reading. In the passage devoted to Rosa Dartle and Mrs Steerforth, the latter mistakenly assumes that David is in mourning: 'I am sorry to observe you are in mourning. I hope Time will be good to you.' Rosa scolds her and corrects the impression. The point is, of course, that he *is* in mourning – for his past, for himself, and for his story which is almost over. And Time has been good to him because he has been good to Time: he has controlled it, has orchestrated its movements, has arrested its depredations by fixing his friends in their characteristic postures, and ultimately by determining their fates.

What the finality of the conclusion does not engage is the very nature of the speaking subject, always necessarily split between conscious and unconscious motivations.[6] David performs the myth of the transcendental ego in the last chapter, indeed throughout his narration, something his role in the manipulation of the tableaux vivants confirms. In his performance as a unified or homogeneous subject, David denies the complexities of his own motivations, not to mention the heterogeneity of language itself. The point is that David assumes that when he speaks (or narrates his own story), his control of himself and his material is monolithic, whereas, as we have seen, that control has everything to do with David's need to perceive himself as straightforward (consider the metaphor).[7] The richness of Dickens's characterization of David is far more accessible if we are constantly alert to the many-voiced qualities of David's ostensible univocality. This formulation is even more compelling when we compare the novel's end with its beginning. If David parades himself as a unified consciousness, and in effect stages his own death in the final chapter, we might legitimately ask how this first-person novel manages that other critical moment, its hero's birth. This question is important because the subject-object split implicitly problematic in the conclusion is explicitly made problematic in the first chapter.

The two beginnings in the first chapter draw attention to the difficulties of initiating an autobiographical narrative. Moreover, the two beginnings indicate the arbitrariness of any opening strategy, especially in the telling of a life, a project whose nature it is to claim an infinite number of moments of origin. In this case, we practically see David emerge from the womb, and then we encounter several paragraphs of what looks like extremely portentous information; this is followed by the second beginning, which stresses place and family relationships. The combination of the two beginnings and the first one on its own accomplish twin purposes: the first is the one I have already mentioned, to make problematic the very notion of beginning; the second is to provide thematic entry to the novel. Neither purpose outweighs the other, however. They work in tension with each other, resisting comfortable assimilation.

The first start is both peculiarly overdetermined (and therefore unreadable) and at the same time full of thematic signals. While the information ultimately defies systematic interpretation, it does point forward into the text and adumbrates issues with which both readers and narrator will struggle. The opening sentence, 'Whether I shall turn out to be the hero of my own life, or whether that station will be held by anybody else, these pages must show', is not coy. At stake is David's role: is he participant or narrator, subject or object? The distinction provides terms for understanding the novel's first start in which a dialectical, and troubled, relationship is developed between the two points. David's difficulty in saying who he is and in identifying what belongs to him establishes his persona on a precarious footing, a precariousness inaugurated at the moment of his birth, surrounded as it is with inauspicious predictions.

The curious thing about the predictions is that David neither claims nor rejects them. He leaves it to us to decide whether his life is unlucky or not and remarks that perhaps someone else is enjoying the other part of his destiny, the ability to see ghosts and spirits, because *he* is not aware that he has come into it. These disavowals of objects (and I use the word deliberately) that without a doubt belong to him are disingenuous. David's refusal to take a position is evasive in both instances; furthermore, in refusing to accept the ability to see ghosts and spirits, David is ultimately denying the reconstructive work of memory, so crucial to his enterprise. As we have already seen, the retrospect chapters consist in an explicit calling-up or animation of phantoms.

The other object with which David has a vexed relationship is his caul. The most appropriate terms for a reading of the caul are available in Dickens's prefaces to the novel. The sadness 'an Author feels as if he were dismissing some portion of himself into the shadowy world' – the sadness of releasing a book for publication – is analogous to the disposition of the caul in the market-place. The association is made more poignant because the caul is literally a part of David's body. He speaks with remarkable nonchalance about the caul's fate as a commodity: an initial attempt to sell it fails, a rather precise ten years elapse, it suddenly surfaces as the dubious prize in a raffle, and it is won by an old woman who is not exactly elated with her prize. A very odd detail in the story is the fact that David witnesses the final transaction. He admits, 'I remember to have felt quite uncomfortable and confused, at a part of myself being disposed of in that way.' He manages to objectify himself pretty well, however, in order to tell the story. I should think he *would* feel uncomfortable and confused; he is performing an impossible balancing-act in these opening passages. Who is going to be the hero of this book, me or somebody else? Who has my ability to see ghosts, me or somebody else? Who has my caul? Not me, somebody else. The subtext of anxiety that I am reading here is best expressed in part of the novel's title, 'Which he never meant to be published on any account'. The safety of privacy is left behind at the cost of a unified self.

Introducing the subject-object split as a problem is an appropriate way of opening an autobiographical novel, since the narrator-participant is always implicated in the distinction. But Dickens decides to choose and starts the book over with an 'I' who does not mind saying 'I'. Once he does that, however, the status of the first start is thrown into question: what is it and why is it there? It is proleptic in its prefiguring of important relationships and events, but it also ends abruptly and its 'meandering' style is never recovered. The first start begins to look like an excrescence when compared to the second; it does not fit. It is a piece of text that sticks out and hints at a range of undeveloped narrative possibilities. Among these I include the folk-tale style, the attorney who nearly buys the caul, the old woman who does get it, and the information that David was there to witness the raffle. The first opening, with these incomplete mini-narratives, looks forward to a modern novel like Beckett's *Watt*, whose first scene involves characters who never appear again. Beckett deliberately foregrounds problems of opening and narrative sequence; Dickens's purposes are not much different. The first start is not irrelevant but it is formally unassimilable. Whatever its thematic implications, its privileged position at the opening of the book vexes the issue of origins. And continuing, as it does, the metaphor employed in the preface, the first opening functions as another preface, this time a self-consciously fictive one which provides further commentary on the difficulties confronting a first-person narrator.

The novel's first beginning suggests yet another interpretative possibility, however, one in balance with the comments I have already made about theatricality in the retrospect chapters and which recalls Kincaid's remarks about characters who write anti-plots. I have said that at the end of the text, David as a subject represses the Other in the interests of claiming a triumphant unified consciousness, of asserting absolute ego boundaries. I propose now that the first beginning represents a kind of clownish experiment with roles, a performance that delights in itself. Unlike in the later tableaux vivants, David at the beginning is not in control: the tone of his narrative is anything but monolithic — since he tries on several voices, the relationship between himself and all of the others in the first start is extremely unclear, and finally narrative time is subverted; instead of the metaphor of the line in those first four paragraphs, we have the meander. This beginning is like one of Pecksniff's dramas. One thing suggests another, generated perhaps, or perhaps not, by some obscure motif, and the performance is sustained by its own energies. This revel ends because the fundamentally bourgeois hero re-collects himself and starts again in a more suitable manner. The contrast between the two personae is essential to the particular identity David chooses, for his narrative persona as director allows him to channel and even determine both his own plot and those of the other characters, while denying (and controlling) subversive energies.

My object in examining the opening of *David Copperfield* has been to contrast its narrative permeability with the univocality, to mix metaphors, of the conclusion. If there can be a 'crucial' beginning, to use Kucich's formulation, then this is surely it. It enacts the very ideas of potential and expenditure (spending, in fact, very freely), and at the same time foregrounds the subject-object relation critical to our reading of the novel. The stasis of the ending, the way it arrests energy, could not constitute a higher contrast. The extraordinary polysemy of the origin is reduced to one story. David has undoubtedly claimed what is his, but, to resort again to Kristeva, the claiming has entailed a repression of the Other in order to support the myth that his subjectivity was intact. In this light, the method of the retrospect chapters is insidious.

While it may be argued that novels must end somewhere, even if only with the fiction of closure, I will counter with a few remarks about the beginning and ending of *Great Expectations* to show another strategy available to the first-person narrator. In a sense, Dickens inverts his procedure in *David Copperfield*: in *Great Expectations*, the beginning is resolute while the ending 'meanders'.

The moment that Pip can call himself by name is the moment the subject-object split is resolved for him. It is also, not incidentally, the moment that generates the novel's first paragraph. Pip has no antecedents, no pre-narrative birth; he is spontaneously generated in the first words of the text – he gains consciousness when he names himself. This strategy effectively moots the problem of origins: Pip has none. His parents are conveniently dead but they are also formally inconsequential. Although this beginning strikes us as revolutionary in its assumptions, there are, of course, thematic reasons for Pip's isolation. He is an orphan because Dickens is concerned to trace the career of a self-made man and ultimately to critique the Victorian ideal of meliorative progress.

Pip's 'birth' in a graveyard points to the other end of the novel – its conclusion or Pip's textual death. Rather than pretend that absolute closure is possible as he did in *David Copperfield*, Dickens defies death in *Great Expectations* by intimating that narrative is irrepressible. An awareness of ends is presented on the first page of the novel; while narrative moves inexorably forward, in this novel it also moves backward. Although Pip does not literally return to the graveyard at the end, he does return to another site of loss and disappointed expectation, Satis House. The important thing, however, is that the novel's conclusion provides the open-endedness narrative demands. If we allow that the novel has two endings, the last sentence of the suppressed one ('I was very glad afterwards to have had the interview') refers to time beyond the end of the novel – perhaps to a time when Pip is an autobiographer.[8] And even if we don't admit the suppressed ending, the official conclusion is ambiguous enough. First of all, there is no certainty about the nature of the relationship Pip and Estella are forming. Moreover, the presence of the new little Pip, whom the old Pip explicitly identifies as a new version of himself, also undercuts closure.

The critical difference between the endings of the two novels is in the relative position of the heroes. At the end of *David Copperfield*, the narrator continues to hold centre stage and to orient other characters in relation to himself – his is the only voice we hear. In *Great Expectations*, on the other hand, the hero is de-centred – in a self-effacing sort of way, Pip walks out of his story. Moreover, in contrast to David's exalted role as paterfamilias, we read that not only has Pip moved away from England, but that he keeps house with Herbert Pocket and his wife. The longing for father and home, present from the first, is still unfulfilled since Pip remains an orphan, now in terms of national identity, and lives in somebody else's house.

To return now to our original moment in the figure of the impresario – and to redeem David Copperfield from the role in which I have cast him. My discussion has frozen David in the attitude he assumes in the last sentence of the novel and has maintained that the closure he achieves is unnatural, and anti-narrative. A few sentences before the last, David, 'subduing my desire to linger yet', implies that he is aware of narrative's compulsion to produce more narrative. He is not, like Mrs Steerforth, circling eternally around the same loss – nor will he be the 'lunatic gentleman' (ch. 22) who has taken his place at the bedroom window of Blunderstone Rookery. For David has become a writer, composing stories for life just as he did as a youthful Scheherezade, and the text records his coming into that vocation. In this light, David's stage-managing persona is accessible in two ways. He is, first, the director who imperiously controls stage entrances and exits, metes out prominence or obscurity, assigns moral authority and disgrace. He is also, however, the writer who, at least in the terms of this novel, can transform experience into art – a potentially infinite project, intrinsically unsusceptible to finality.

Notes

1. A version of this essay entitled 'Beginnings and Endings: Problems in *David Copperfield* and *Great Expectations*' was presented at the Dickens Project Winter Conference, University of California, San Diego, 28 Jan. 1984. References to Dickens are to the Penguin editions of *David Copperfield*, Trevor Blount (ed.) (Harmondsworth: 1966), and *Great Expectations*, Angus Calder (ed.) (Harmondsworth: 1965).

2. John Kucich, *Excess and Restraint in the Novels of Charles Dickens* (Athens: University of Georgia Press, 1981) pp. 140 and 143.

3. In his article, 'Remembrances of Death Past and Future: A Reading of *David Copperfield*', Robert E. Lougy notices another function of these passages concerning David's youth: 'In lingering among these spots and reviving memories

of the young boy who once walked within them, David attempts to impose his own need for continuity and identity upon the flux and mutability of the natural world' (*Dickens Studies Annual*, vol. 6 [1977] p. 79). Although I focus less on time as one of David's demons, Lougy's observation confirms my emphasis on the tactics of management that determine these portions of the text.

4. Dickens used the incantatory 'I see' again in the closing words of *A Tale of Two Cities*. In a series of four paragraphs delivered in the prophetic mode, Dickens imagines what Sydney Carton's final words would have been had he been given the chance to utter them. Since the theme of the passage is the immortality assured for Carton by his self-sacrifice, and since Carton himself did not in fact speak the words, Dickens is momentarily enjoying the attributes of a hero by impersonating him. Without at all derogating the impact of these words, we might say that Dickens has assumed the novel's most prominent role.

5. In this connection, see Alexander Welsh, *The City of Dickens* (Oxford: Clarendon Press, 1971), ch. 11, 'Two Angels of Death'. The stasis at the end of the novel is narratively possible, so to speak, because Agnes is there – Agnes, who has been characterized throughout the novel in terms of serenity, rest, and death.

6. My discussion at this point is informed entirely by what I learned from Sandy Shattuck, Ana Sisnett, and Ingeborg O'Sickey in our discussions of Julia Kristeva's ideas about the speaking subject in *Revolution in Poetic Language*, Margaret Waller (trs.) (New York: Columbia University Press, 1984). I am adopting Kristeva's terms because they carry the political (in the sense of 'power relations') implications I want to foreground in David's narration.

7. An example, on a very local level, is available in chapter 3 of *David Copperfield*, 'I Have a Change'. Describing his first meal with the Peggottys, David comments that dinner consisted of 'boiled dabs, melted butter, and potatoes, with a chop for me'. Despite the egalitarian *bonhomie* of his sojourn with the family, this kind of detail instantly evokes the class difference that informs all of David's dealings with the Peggottys. The fact of the chop is, of course, unremarked.

8. D. A. Miller has also read the ambiguities of the conclusion of *Great Expectations* and he remarks, in regard to the 'afterwards', that 'the end of narrative proves only its rebeginning, as the life concludes in a desire for the life story'. Miller's understanding of conclusions is based on his premise that 'closure is an act of "make-believe", a postulation that closure is possible'. See *Narrative and Its Discontents: Problems of Closure in the Traditional Novel* (Princeton University Press, 1981) pp. 276 and 267.

Selected Bibliography

Axton, William F. *Circle of Fire: Dickens' Vision and Style and the Popular Victorian Theatre*. Lexington: University of Kentucky Press, 1966.

Bakhtin, Mikhail M. *The Dialogic Imagination: Four Essays*. Michael Holquist (ed.) and Caryl Emerson and Michael Holquist (trs). Austin and London: University of Texas Press, 1981.

Bolton, Philip H. '*Bleak House* and the Playhouse'. *Dickens Studies Annual*, vol. 12 (1983) pp. 81–116.

Bolton, Philip H. *Dickens Dramatized*. London: Mansell, 1987.

Brannan, Robert Louis (ed.). *Under the Management of Mr Charles Dickens: His Production of 'The Frozen Deep'*. Ithaca: Cornell University Press, 1966.

Brooks, Peter. *The Melodramatic Imagination: Balzac, Henry James, Melodrama, and the Mode of Excess*. New Haven, Conn.: Yale University Press, 1976.

Carlton, William J. 'Charles Dickens, Drama Critic'. *Dickensian*, vol. 56 (1960) pp. 11–27.

Churchill, R. C. 'Dickens, Drama and Tradition'. *Scrutiny*, vol. 10 (1941/1942) pp. 358–75.

Collins, Philip (ed.). *Charles Dickens: The Public Readings*. Oxford: Clarendon Press, 1975.

Coolidge, Archibald C. 'Dickens and the Heart as the Hope for Heaven: A Study of the Philosophic Basis of Sensational Literary Technique'. *Victorian Newsletter* (1961), no. 20, pp. 6–13.

Cross, A. E. Brookes. 'The Influence of Dickens on the Contemporary Stage'. *Dickensian*, vol. 34 (1937/1938) pp. 55–62.

Davis, Earle. *The Flint and the Flame: The Artistry of Charles Dickens*. Columbia, Mo.: University of Missouri Press, 1963.

Dexter, Walter. 'For One Night Only: Dickens's Appearances as an Amateur Actor'. *Dickensian*, vol. 35 (1939) pp. 231–42. [Continued in subsequent issues, along with other studies of Dickens's readings and plays.]

Dickens, Charles. *Complete Plays and Selected Poems*. London: Vision Press, 1970.

Dolby, George. *Charles Dickens as I Knew Him*. London: T. Fisher Unwin, 1885.

Dunn, Richard J. 'A Tale for Two Dramatists'. *Dickens Studies Annual*, vol. 12 (1983) pp. 117–24.

Eisenstein, Sergei. 'Dickens, Griffith, and the Film Today', in Jay Leyda (ed. and trs.), *Film Form: Essays in Film Theory*, (New York: Harcourt, Brace, & World, 1957) pp. 195–255.

Fawcett, F. Dubrez. *Dickens the Dramatist: On Stage, Screen and Radio*. London: W. H. Allen, 1952; rpt. Philadelphia: R. West, 1976.

Field, Kate. *Pen Photographs of Charles Dickens's Readings*. Boston: James R. Osgood, 1871.

Fielding, K. J. (ed.). *The Speeches of Charles Dickens*. Oxford: Clarendon Press, 1960.

Fitzgerald, S. J. Adair. *Dickens and the Drama*. London: Chapman & Hall, 1910; rpt. Philadelphia: R. West, 1973.

Fitzsimons, Raymund. *Garish Lights: The Public Reading Tours of Charles Dickens*. Philadelphia: J. B. Lippincott, 1970.

Fleissner, Robert F. 'Dickens and Shakespeare: A Study in Histrionic Contrasts'. *Studies in Comparative Literature* (1965) no. 35; rpt. Brooklyn: Haskell, 1969.

Garis, Robert. *The Dickens Theatre*. Oxford: Clarendon Press, 1965.

Gordan, John D. *Reading for Profit: The Other Career of Charles Dickens. An Exhibition from the Berg Collection*. New York: New York Public Library, 1958.

Johnson, Eleanor and Edgar (eds). *The Dickens Theatrical Reader*. Boston, Mass.: Little, Brown, 1964.

Kent, Charles. *Charles Dickens as a Reader*. London: Chapman & Hall, 1872.

Kucich, John. *Excess and Restraint in the Novels of Charles Dickens*. Athens: University of Georgia Press, 1981.

Lewes, G. H. *On Actors and the Art of Acting*. London: Smith, Elder, 1875; rpt. New York: Grove Press, 1957.

Meisel, Martin. *Realizations: Narrative, Pictorial, and Theatrical Arts of the Nineteenth Century*. Princeton: Princeton University Press, 1984.

Paroissien, David. 'Dickens and the Cinema'. *Dickens Studies Annual*, vol. 7 (1978) pp. 68–80.

Pemberton, T. Edgar. *Dickens and the Stage*. London: G. Redway, 1888.

Perry, John Oliver. 'The Popular Tradition of Melodrama in Dickens'. *Carleton Miscellany*, vol. 3 (1962) pp. 105–10.

Robinson, Kenneth. *Wilkie Collins: A Biography*. New York: Macmillan, 1952.

Rosenberg, Marvin. 'The Dramatist in Dickens'. *Journal of English and German Philology*, vol. 59 (1960) pp. 1–12.

Schlicke, Paul. *Dickens and Popular Entertainment*. London: George Allen & Unwin, 1985.

Taylor, John Russell. *The Rise and Fall of the Well-Made Play*. New York: Hill & Wang, 1967.

Van Amerongen, J. B. *The Actor in Dickens: A Study of the Histrionic and Dramatic Elements in the Novelist's Life and Works*. New York: D. Appleton, 1927.

Vardac, A. Nicholas. *Stage to Screen: Theatrical Method from Garrick to Griffith*. Cambridge: Harvard University Press, 1949.

Woolcott, Alexander. *Mr Dickens Goes to the Play*. New York: G. P. Putnam's Sons, 1922.

Worth, George. *Dickensian Melodrama: A Reading of the Novels*. Lawrence: University of Kansas Press, 1978.

Worthen, William. *The Idea of the Actor*. Princeton: Princeton University Press, 1984.

Zambrano, Ana Laura. *Dickens and Film*. Bowling Green: Gordon Press, 1976.

Index